CROSS-CULTURAL ANXIETY

THE SERIES IN CLINICAL AND COMMUNITY PSYCHOLOGY

CONSULTING EDITORS:

CHARLES D. SPIELBERGER and IRWIN G. SARASON

Averill	• Patterns of Psychological Thought: Readings in Historical and Contemporary Texts
Becker	• Depression: Theory and Research
Brehm	• The Application of Social Psychology to Clinical Practice
Endler and Magnusson	• Interactional Psychology and Personality
Friedman and Katz	• The Psychology of Depression: Contemporary Theory and Research
Kissen	• From Group Dynamics to Group Psychoanalysis: Therapeutic Applications of Group Dynamic Understanding
Klopfer and Reed	• Problems in Psychotherapy: An Eclectic Approach
Reitan and Davison	• Clinical Neuropsychology: Current Status and Applications
Spielberger and Diaz-Guerrero	• Cross-Cultural Anxiety
Spielberger and Sarason	• Stress and Anxiety, volume 1
Sarason and Spielberger	• Stress and Anxiety, volume 2
Sarason and Spielberger	• Stress and Anxiety, volume 3
Ulmer	• On the Development of a Token Economy Mental Hospital Treatment Program

IN PREPARATION

Bermant, Kelman, and Warwick	• The Ethics of Social Intervention
Cattell and Dreger	• Handbook of Modern Personality Theory
Cohen and Mirsky	• Biology and Psychopathology
Iscoe, Bloom, and Spielberger	• Community Psychology in Transition
Janisse	• A Psychological Survey of Pupillometry
London	• Strategies of Personality Research
Manschreck and Kleinman	• Feet of Clay: Quests and Inquiries in Critical Rationality in the Fields of Psychiatry
Olweus	• Aggression in the Schools
Spielberger and Sarason	• Stress and Anxiety, volume 4

CROSS-CULTURAL ANXIETY

EDITED BY

CHARLES D. SPIELBERGER
University of South Florida

ROGELIO DIAZ–GUERRERO
National University of Mexico

HEMISPHERE PUBLISHING CORPORATION

Washington   London

A HALSTED PRESS BOOK

JOHN WILEY & SONS

New York   London   Sydney   Toronto

Hemisphere Publishing Corporation
1025 Vermont Ave., N.W., Washington, D.C. 20005

Distributed solely by Halsted Press, a Division of John Wiley & Sons, Inc.,
New York.

1 2 3 4 5 6 7 8 9 0   D O D O   7 8 3 2 1 0 9 8 7 6

Library of Congress Catologing in Publication Data

Main entry under title:

Cross-cultural anxiety.

    (The series in clinical and community psychology)
    Includes indexes.
    "Based on a symposium at the XVth Interamerican
Congress of Psychology, Bogota, Colombia, in
December, 1974."
    1. Anxiety—Congresses. 2. Ethnopsychology—
Congresses. I. Spielberger, Charles Donald, 1927–
II. Diaz-Guerrero, Rogelio. III. Interamerican
Congress of Psychology, 15th, Bogota, 1974.
IV. Title.
BF575.A6C76   157'.3   76–28389
ISBN 0–470–98940–8

Printed in the United States of America

Contents

Contributors　ix
Preface　xi

I INTRODUCTION

1　The Nature and Measurement of Anxiety, *Charles D. Spielberger*　　3

Stress, Threat, and Anxiety　4
Anxiety: State-Trait-Process　5
The Measurement of State and Trait Anxiety　7
The State-Trait Anxiety Inventory　8
Summary　10
References　10

2　Cross-Cultural Measurement of Anxiety, *Charles D. Spielberger
and Sagar Sharma*　　13

Strategies for Developing Translations of Anxiety Measures　14
Spanish and Hindi Forms of the STAI　19
Summary　24
References　25

II THE MEASUREMENT OF ANXIETY IN
DIFFERENT CULTURES

3　The Development and Validation of an Experimental Portuguese
Form of the State-Trait Anxiety Inventory, *Angela M. B. Biaggio,
Luiz Natalicio, and Charles D. Spielberger*　　29

Translation of the STAI into Portuguese   **30**
Test Construction Procedures   **30**
Psychometric Properties of the Portuguese STAI   **32**
Summary and Conclusions   **39**
References   **40**

**4 The Development and Validation of a French Form of the
State-Trait Anxiety Inventory,** *Jacques Bergeron, Michel Landry,
and David Bélanger*   **41**

Method   **43**
Results   **43**
References   **49**

**5 Development of the Turkish Edition of the State-Trait
Anxiety Inventory,** *William A. LeCompte and Necia Oner*   **51**

Theory and Measurement of Anxiety   **52**
Development of the Turkish State-Trait Anxiety Inventory   **54**
Characteristics of the Turkish STAI   **57**
Discussion   **64**
Summary   **66**
References   **66**

**6 Development and Validation of the Spanish Form of the
State-Trait Anxiety Inventory for Children (IDAREN),**
*José J. Bauermeister, Blanca Villamil Forastieri, and
Charles D. Spielberger*   **69**

Development and Validation of the IDAREN   **71**
Psychometric Characteristics of the IDAREN   **74**
Construct Validity of the IDAREN in Behavior Modification
      Research   **77**
Summary and Conclusions   **82**
References   **84**

III RESEARCH ON ANXIETY IN DIFFERENT CULTURES

7 The Anxiety-Arousing Effect of Taboo Words in Bilinguals,
Fernando Gonzalez-Reigosa   **89**

Language-Mediated Emotional Responses in Bilinguals   **91**
The Anxiety-Arousing Effect of Taboo Words in Bilinguals   **93**
Results   **97**

Discussion   **102**
References   **104**

8 **A Study of Anxiety in Greek Psychiatric Patients,** *Aris Liakos,*
   John Papacostas, and Costas Stefanis   **107**

   Kelly's Personal Construct Theory and Methods of Application   **108**
   Obtaining the Elements of the Anxiety Grid   **111**
   Obtaining the Construct of the Anxiety Grid   **114**
   Summary and Conclusions   **119**
   References   **120**

9 **State and Trait Anxiety in Italian Cardiac and Dermatological**
   Patients: Clinical and Cross-Cultural Considerations, *P. Pancheri,*
   A. Bernabei, M. Bellaterra, and S. Tartaglione   **123**

   State-Trait Anxiety Assessment   **124**
   Anxiety as Process: Defense Mechanisms and Psychosomatic
      Disorders   **124**
   Measurement of Anxiety in Cardiac and Dermatology Patients   **125**
   Discussion of Results   **130**
   References   **132**

IV CROSS-CULTURAL RESEARCH ON ANXIETY

10 **Test Anxiety and General Anxiety in Mexican and American**
    School Children, *R. Diaz-Guerrero*   **135**

    Methodology   **136**
    Results   **137**
    Discussion   **139**
    References   **142**

11 **Multidimensional Aspects of State and Trait Anxiety: A**
    Cross-Cultural Study of Canadian and Swedish College
    Students, *Norman S. Endler and David Magnusson*   **143**

    Method   **146**
    Results   **149**
    Discussion   **161**
    Conclusions   **168**
    Summary   **169**
    References   **170**

V EPILOGUE: A CRITICAL REVIEW OF CONTRIBUTIONS
TO THIS VOLUME

12 **Critique of Research on Anxiety Across Cultures,**
   Wayne H. Holtzman   175

   References   187

   Author Index   189
   Subject Index   193

Contributors

José J. Bauermeister, University of Puerto Rico, Rio Piedras, Puerto Rico

David Bélanger, Universite de Montreal, Montreal, Canada

Marilla Bellaterra, University Degli Studi di Roma, Rome, Italy

Jacques Bergeron, Universite de Montreal, Montreal, Canada

A. Bernabei, University Degli Studi di Roma, Rome, Italy

Angela M. B. Biaggio, Pontificia Universidade Catolica do Rio de Janeiro, Rio de Janeiro, Brazil

Rogelio Diaz-Guerrero, Col. Napoles, Mexico, D.F., Mexico

Norman S. Endler, York University, Toronto, Ontario, Canada

Blanca Villamil Forastieri, College of the Sacred Heart, San Juan, Puerto Rico

Fernando Gonzalez-Reigosa, Florida International University, Miami, Florida, United States

Wayne Holtzman, The Hogg Foundation, University of Texas, Austin, Texas, United States

Michel Landry, Universite de Montreal, Montreal, Canada

William A. LeCompte, Hacettepe University, Baytepe, Ankara, Turkey

Aris Liakos, Athens University Medical School, Eginition Hospital, Athens, Greece

David Magnusson, University of Stockholm, Stockholm, Sweden

Luis Natalicio, University of Texas at El Paso, El Paso, Texas, United States

Necla Oner, Hacettepe University, Baytepe, Ankara, Turkey

Paolo Pancheri, University Degli Studi di Roma, Rome, Italy

John Papacostas, Athens University Medical School, Eginition Hospital, Athens, Greece

Sagar Sharma, Hazeldene H. P. University, Simla, India

Charles D. Spielberger, University of South Florida, Tampa, Florida, United States

Costas Stefanis, Athens University Medical School, Eginition Hospital, Athens, Greece

S. Tartaglione, University Degli Study di Roma, Rome, Italy

Preface

Anxiety is generally regarded as a basic or fundamental human emotion. Although case studies of anxiety and reports of clinical investigations have appeared with increasing regularity in the psychological and psychiatric literature since the 1890s, prior to 1950 there was relatively little experimental research on human anxiety. Over the past quarter century, however, experimental work on human anxiety has proliferated and there have been corresponding advances in theory.

The experimental investigation of anxiety phenomena has been stimulated by the development of objective and reliable procedures for the measurement of anxiety as a transitory state and as a relatively stable personality trait. An encouraging recent development has been the construction of scales for the measurement of anxiety in different national cultural groups. Given the unique qualities of anxiety as an emotional state and the fact that everyone experiences this emotion from time to time, cross-cultural research on anxiety would seem to provide an excellent approach for establishing general laws about human experience and behavior.

Progress in cross-cultural measurement of anxiety now makes it possible for investigators from many different countries to compare their findings with greater confidence. Moreover, cross-cultural research on state and trait anxiety has begun to establish important similarities and differences with regard to personality patterns in different national groups. The goals of this volume are to report recent contributions to cross-cultural research on the measurement of anxiety, to examine general research issues that are encountered in cross-cultural research on stress and anxiety, and to report the results of recent empirical studies of anxiety in a number of different cultures.

The present volume grows out of a Symposium on Cross-Cultural Research on State and Trait Anxiety that was held in Bogota, Colombia, in December 1974, at the XVth Interamerican Congress of Psychology.

Participants in this symposium reported research on anxiety in Brazil, Canada, Mexico, Puerto Rico, Sweden, and the United States for subjects whose native language was English, French, Portuguese, Spanish, or Swedish. Several participants reported cross-cultural studies in which samples from two or more of these cultures were compared. Following the symposium, the papers were revised for this volume and additional contributions were invited from psychologists and psychiatrists who were currently investigating manifestations of anxiety in Greece, Italy and Turkey.

The contents of this book should be of interest to behavioral and medical scientists concerned with human personality and abnormal behavior, especially, those who are interested in cross-cultural research. Useful information is also provided for psychologists and psychiatrists in clinical practice, and for educators who are concerned with the effects of anxiety on human performance.

For their invaluable technical and clerical assistance in processing the manuscripts for this volume, we are greatly indebted to Benjamin Algaze, Florence Frain, Hector Gonzalez, Ruth Hinkle, and Diane Ludington.

C. D. Spielberger
R. Diaz-Guerrero

I

INTRODUCTION

1

The Nature and Measurement of Anxiety

Charles D. Spielberger
University of South Florida, Tampa

The 20th century has been called "the age of anxiety," but concern with anxiety phenomena is as old as the history of humanity. Anxiety is currently a central explanatory concept in most theories of personality and psychopathology, and it is also widely regarded as a principal cause of such diverse behavior as insomnia, debilitating psychological and psychosomatic symptoms, immoral and sinful acts, and even instances of creative self-expression.

Fear or anxiety is widely regarded as a fundamental human emotion that has evolved over countless generations as an adaptive mechanism for coping with danger. In his book, *Expression of the Emotions in Man and Animals*, first published in 1872, Charles Darwin reasoned that the nature of fear reactions was shaped through a process of natural selection, and he vividly described typical manifestations of fear such as rapid palpitation of the heart, muscular tension, trembling, increased perspiration, erection of the hair, dryness of the mouth, changes in voice quality, and dilation of the pupils (see Darwin, 1872/1965). Darwin also noted that fear reactions varied in intensity, from mere attention or surprise, to an extreme degree of panic or terror.

Freud (1933) also conceptualized fear and anxiety as a universally experienced, unpleasant emotional (affective) state. Anxiety was distinguishable from other emotions such as anger or depression by a unique combination of phenomenological and physiological qualities that gave it a special "character of unpleasure" (Freud, 1939, p. 69). In attempting to explicate the meaning of anxiety within the context of psychological theory, Freud was especially concerned with identifying the sources of stressful stimulation that evoked anxiety reactions, and with clarifying the effects of anxiety on symptom formation and behavior.

While Freud's brilliant clinical and conceptual contributions have provided the foundation for a deep understanding of anxiety phenomena, Raymond B. Cattell, one of Freud's most vocal critics, has pointed out that knowledge about anxiety cannot advance beyond a prescientific level until operational procedures are developed for the exploration and assessment of anxiety (Cattell & Scheier, 1961). Fortunately, in recent years, advances have been made in the measurement of anxiety, and one of the most encouraging events with regard to research on anxiety phenomena has been the development and use of scales for the measurement of anxiety in different cultures. Cross-cultural research on anxiety is now beginning to establish important similarities and differences in personality patterns among different national groups.

One important source of ambiguity and confusion in theory and research on anxiety stems from the fact that the terms *stress* and *anxiety* are used interchangeably by many researchers (Spielberger, 1971). Another problem in anxiety research is the failure to distinguish between transitory anxiety states, anxiety as a complex psychobiological process, and individual differences in anxiety proneness as a personality trait (Spielberger, 1972b, 1972c). The failure to distinguish between the concepts of stress and anxiety confounds the objective stimulus characteristics of stressful situations with the subjective emotional reactions that are experienced in these situations. A comprehensive theory of anxiety must differentiate between the situations that evoke anxiety reactions, the properties of anxiety states, the complex psychobiological processes that mediate between stressful stimuli and emotional responses, and the nature of anxiety as a personality trait.

A major goal in this introductory chapter is to clarify the terminology that is used in anxiety research, and to distinguish between the concepts of stress, threat, and anxiety. A second goal is to define and clarify the concepts of state and trait anxiety, and to relate these concepts to anxiety as a psychobiological process. In addition, the measurement of state and trait anxiety will be briefly discussed, and the development of the State-Trait Anxiety Inventory (Spielberger, Gorsuch, & Lushene, 1970) will be described. In the following chapter, Spielberger and Sharma discuss the measurement of anxiety in cross-cultural research.

STRESS, THREAT, AND ANXIETY

The term *stress* has been used to refer to both the dangerous stimulus conditions (stressors) that produce anxiety reactions, and the cognitive, affective, behavioral, and physiological changes (stress reactions) that are produced by stressful stimuli (Lazarus, 1966). Consistent with recent theoretical developments and research findings, it has been proposed that the terms *stress* and *threat* be used to denote different aspects of a temporal sequence of events that results in the evocation of an anxiety reaction (Spielberger, 1972a). According to this view, stress refers to the objective, consensually validated stimulus properties of a situation that is characterized by some degree of physical or psychological danger.

Where *stress* denotes the objective stimulus properties of a situation, *threat* refers to an individual's *perception* of a situation as more or less dangerous or personally threatening to him or her. Situations that are objectively stressful are likely to be perceived as threatening by most people, but whether or not a particular person will interpret a specific danger situation as threatening will depend upon that individual's subjective (idiosyncratic) appraisal of the situation. Thus, a stressful situation may not be perceived as threatening by an individual who either does not recognize the inherent danger, or has the necessary skills and experience to cope with it.

The concept of threat also implies that objectively nonstressful situations may be subjectively appraised as dangerous by persons who, for some reason, perceive them as personally threatening. In general, the appraisal of a particular situation as threatening will be determined by the objective stimulus characteristics of the situation, the individual's past experience with similar situations, and the memories or thoughts that are redintegrated or evoked by the situation.

If a situation or thought is perceived as threatening, irrespective of the presence of real or objective danger (stress), the person who perceives the situation as threatening will experience an increase in state anxiety (A-State). Thus:

$$\text{Stress} \longrightarrow \text{Perception of danger (threat)} \longrightarrow \text{Increase in A-State}$$

An anxiety state may be defined in terms of the intensity of the subjective feelings of tension, apprehension, nervousness, and worry that are experienced by an individual at a particular moment, and by heightened activity of the autonomic nervous system that accompanies these feelings. Anxiety states vary in intensity and duration, and fluctuate over time as a function of the amount of stress that impinges upon an individual and that individual's interpretation of the stressful situation as personally dangerous or threatening.

ANXIETY: STATE-TRAIT-PROCESS

A precise conceptual definition of the pattern of responses that characterizes anxiety as a transitory emotional state (A-State) is a necessary precondition for meaningful research on anxiety phenomena. But the term *anxiety* is also used in the psychological literature to refer to a relatively stable personality disposition or trait, and to a complex process that involves stress, threat, and A-State. Therefore, a comprehensive theory of anxiety will require clarification of the concepts of anxiety as a transitory state, as a personality trait, and as a complex cognitive-emotional process.

The trait-state distinction in anxiety research was initially formulated by Cattell (Cattell, 1966; Cattell & Scheier, 1961), and has been recently emphasized by Spielberger (1966, 1971, 1972a, 1975). Trait anxiety (A-Trait) refers to relatively stable individual differences in anxiety proneness that are manifested in behavior in the frequency with which an individual experiences A-State elevations over time. Persons who are high in A-Trait, for example, psychoneurotic patients, are more strongly disposed to perceive the world as dangerous or threatening than low A-Trait persons. Consequently, high A-Trait individuals are more vulnerable to stress and tend to experience A-State reactions of greater intensity and with greater frequency over time than persons who are low in A-Trait.

The term *anxiety* is also used to refer to a complex psychobiological process (Spielberger, 1972b). In essence, the concept of anxiety as process implies a theory of anxiety that includes stress, threat, and state anxiety as fundamental constructs or variables. Thus, anxiety as process refers to a sequence of cognitive, affective, physiological, and behavioral events. This process may be initiated by a stressful external stimulus that is perceived or interpreted as dangerous or threatening, or by a thought or idea that forecasts threat or that causes the individual to recall an earlier danger situation. Cognitive appraisals of danger are immediately followed by A-State reactions, or by an increment in the level of A-State intensity. It should be noted that while an anxiety state lies at the core of the anxiety process, this process also involves stress, threat, physiological changes, and behavioral reactions.

The concept of anxiety as process is reflected in the traditional distinction between fear and anxiety. *Fear* generally denotes an emotional reaction to the anticipation of injury or harm from some real, objective danger in the external environment. Another defining characteristic of fear is that the intensity of a fear reaction is proportional to the magnitude of the danger that evokes it. In contrast, *anxiety* is traditionally regarded as an "objectless" emotional reaction because either the stimulus conditions that evoke it are unknown or the intensity of the emotional reaction is disproportionately greater than the magnitude of the objective danger. Thus, the traditional distinction between fear and anxiety is based on the assumption that similar emotional reactions result from the operation of different mediating processes.

Research on stress and anxiety obviously requires that attention be given to the process in which stressful stimuli evoke state anxiety reactions, but there are three major problems with process definitions of anxiety. The first stems from the fact that the anxiety process is comprised of a series of component events or variables. Typically, only those process variables of interest to a particular theorist are incorporated in his or her definition of anxiety as process, while other process variables tend to be neglected or ignored. Second, it is difficult to compare and integrate research findings based on process definitions of anxiety because each theorist's definition incorporates different components of the anxiety process. A third difficulty is that standard terminological conventions are not yet established for describing the critical variables such as stress, cognitive appraisal, and threat that contribute to the anxiety process.

In summary, the concept of anxiety as process implies a theory of anxiety that requires specification of the fundamental variables involved in the evocation of an anxiety state. In addition, an adequate theory of stress and anxiety must take into account coping and avoidance behaviors, and the psychological defenses that serve to alleviate anxiety states. The starting point for a comprehensive theory of anxiety is in identifying the variables that are central to the theory, and in specifying precise operations for measuring each critical variable. Only when this is done can the relationships among these variables be empirically verified so that further theoretical development can take place.

THE MEASUREMENT OF STATE AND TRAIT ANXIETY

Since state anxiety is a psychobiological concept, both the phenomenological and the physiological components of A-States should be measured. Various measures of autonomic nervous system activity that have been employed to assess the physiological aspects of transitory anxiety states have been reviewed by Martin (1961). Levitt (1967), McReynolds (1968), and more recently Lader and Marks (1971) also discuss physiological indicants of anxiety. In terms of the volume of research, the galvanic skin response and changes in heart rate appear to be the most popular physiological measures of A-State, but blood pressure, muscle action potential, palmar sweating, and respiration have also been given considerable attention.

Efforts to measure the subjective feelings of apprehension, tension and worry that define the phenomenological component of anxiety states are reflected in the research of Nowlis (Nowlis, 1961; Nowlis & Green, 1965), Cattell and Scheier (1961), and Zuckerman (Zuckerman, 1960; Zuckerman & Lubin, 1965). Zuckerman's Affect Adjective Check List and the A-State scale of the State-Trait Anxiety Inventory (Spielberger et al., 1970) are currently the most widely used self-report instruments for assessing the phenomenological component of A-State. A new multidimensional instrument for measuring moods, the Profile of Mood States (POMS), also includes a self-report scale for the assessment of A-State (McNair, Lorr, & Droppelman, 1971).

Responses to the Rorschach Test are often used in making clinical inferences about the anxiety level of psychiatric patients. The most widely accepted Rorschach indicants of anxiety involve texture and associated "chiaroscuro" responses to the inkblots (e.g., Beck, 1951; Klopfer, 1937–1938; Piotrowski, 1957). But research on anxiety as assessed by the Rorschach Test reveals very little consistency in the empirical findings (Goldfried, 1966; Neuringer, 1962), and the Holtzman (1958) Inkblot Technique (Holtzman, Thorpe, Swartz, & Herron, 1961) appears to provide a more promising, objective procedure for the assessment of anxiety from responses to unstructured stimuli. On the basis of a review of the Rorschach anxiety literature, Auerbach and Spielberger (1972) concluded that shading responses were most clearly related to A-State whereas movement responses (especially *M*) were most consistently related to A-Trait.

The Taylor (1951, 1953) Manifest Anxiety Scale (MAS) and the Mandler-Sarason (Mandler & Sarason, 1952; Sarason & Mandler, 1952) Test Anxiety Questionnaire (TAQ) were the first of a number of psychometric instruments developed to assess individual differences in anxiety in adults. Other instruments designed to assess anxiety in adults have been constructed by Cattell (Cattell, 1957; Cattell & Scheier, 1963); Endler, Hunt, and Rosenstein (1962); Freeman (1953); McReynolds (1968); Spielberger et al. (1970); Welsh (1956); and Zuckerman (1960). A number of self-report scales have also been developed for measuring general and test anxiety in children (e.g., Castaneda, McCandless, & Palermo, 1956; Sarason, Davidson, Lighthall, Waite, & Ruebush, 1960; Spielberger, 1973).

Most of the scales developed to assess anxiety appear to measure trait anxiety, that is, individual differences in anxiety proneness. In current research the Taylor MAS, the IPAT Anxiety Scale, and the A-Trait scale of the State-Trait Anxiety Inventory are used most often for the assessment of trait anxiety in adults. These three scales are highly correlated with one another and appear to measure anxiety proneness in social-evaluative situations (Spielberger et al., 1970). The research evidence has consistently indicated that persons with high A-Trait scores are more strongly disposed than low A-Trait individuals to experience A-State elevations in situations that pose threats to self-esteem, and especially in interpersonal relationships in which personal adequacy is evaluated (Spielberger, 1966, 1971, 1972a, 1972b, 1975).

THE STATE-TRAIT ANXIETY INVENTORY

The State-Trait Anxiety Inventory (STAI) was developed to provide relatively brief, homogeneous self-report measures of both state (A-State) and trait (A-Trait) anxiety (Spielberger, 1966, 1972a, 1975). Item characteristics that were sought in the development of the STAI scales were high internal consistency, as measured by item-remainder correlations and alpha coefficients, and ease and brevity of administration. The item selection and validation procedures that were employed in the construction of the STAI are described in detail by Spielberger and Gorsuch (1966) and by Spielberger et al. (1970).

The STAI A-Trait scale consists of 20 statements that ask people to describe how they generally feel (e.g., "I feel that difficulties are piling up so that I cannot overcome them"; "I take disappointments so keenly that I can't put them out of my mind"). Subjects respond to each item by rating themselves on the following four-point scale: (1) Almost never; (2) Sometimes; (3) Often; (4) Almost always. Individual items were selected for the STAI A-Trait scale on the basis of the concurrent validity of each item as determined from correlations with two widely accepted A-Trait measures, the Taylor MAS and the IPAT Anxiety Scale. Each A-Trait item was also determined to be impervious to situational stress and relatively stable over time.

The STAI A-State scale consists of 20 statements (e.g., "I am tense"; "I feel nervous") that ask people to describe how they feel at a particular moment by rating themselves on the following four-point scale: (1) Not at all; (2) Somewhat; (3) Moderately so; (4) Very much so. *Construct* validity was the major criterion for including each individual A-State item in this scale. The items selected for the A-State scale had higher mean scores in a priori stressful situations (taking an exam, giving a speech) than in a neutral situation, and lower mean A-State scores in a relaxed situation.

In constructing the STAI A-State scale, the essential qualities that were measured were tension, apprehension, and nervousness as these feeling (phenomenological) states varied along a continuum of increasing levels of intensity. Low scores were expected to reflect states of calmness and serenity, intermediate scores were designed to indicate moderate levels of tension and apprehensiveness, and high scores were to correspond with intense states of fright and apprehension, approaching panic.

The STAI has proven to be useful in both clinical work and research. The A-Trait scale provides a means for screening patient and normal populations for people who are troubled by neurotic anxiety problems, and this scale has been used as a research tool for selecting subjects who differ in anxiety proneness. The STAI A-State scale is a sensitive indicator for the transitory anxiety that is experienced by patients and clients in counseling, psychotherapy and behavior therapy, and this scale has been used to measure changes in A-State intensity in experimental research on stress, anxiety, and learning. In the measurement of changes in transitory anxiety over time, the A-State scale may be given on each occasion for which a measure of state anxiety is needed, with instructions for subjects to respond according to how they felt during a particular time period (Spielberger, 1972a, 1975; Spielberger et al., 1970).

SUMMARY

In this chapter, the nature of fear and anxiety were considered in historical perspective, sources of ambiguity and confusion in anxiety theory were identified, and terminological conventions for the definition of critical concepts that are encountered in anxiety research were proposed. It was suggested that the term *stress* be used to refer to the objective, consensually validated stimulus properties of situations that are characterized by some degree of physical or psychological danger; that *threat* be used to denote the perception of a situation as more or less dangerous or personally threatening; and that *state anxiety* refer to the subjective feelings of tension and apprehension, and the heightened activity of the autonomic nervous system that are experienced in situations perceived as threatening. The distinction between anxiety as a transitory emotional state, as a complex psychobiological process, and as a relatively stable personality trait was also proposed. Finally, the measurement of state and trait anxiety were briefly discussed, and the development of the State-Trait Anxiety Inventory was described.

REFERENCES

Auerbach, S. M., & Spielberger, C. D. The assessment of state and trait anxiety with the Rorschach test. *Journal of Personality Assessment*, 1972, *36*, 314–335.

Beck, S. J. The Rorschach test: A multidimensional test of personality. In H. H. Anderson and G. L. Anderson (Eds.), *An introduction to projective techniques.* New York: Prentice-Hall, 1951.

Castaneda, A., McCandless, B. R., & Palermo, D. S. The children's form of the manifest anxiety scale. *Child Development*, 1956, *27*, 317–326.

Cattell, R. B. *Personality and motivation structure and measurement.* New York: Harcourt, 1957.

Cattell, R. B. Anxiety and motivation: Theory and crucial experiments. In C. D. Spielberger (Ed.), *Anxiety and behavior.* New York: Academic Press, 1966, 23–62.

Cattell, R. B., & Scheier, I. H. *The meaning and measurement of neuroticism and anxiety.* New York: Ronald Press, 1961.

Cattell, R. B., & Scheier, I. H. *Handbook for the IPAT Anxiety Scale* (2nd ed.). Champaign, Ill.: Institute for Personality and Ability Testing, 1963.

Darwin, C. *Expression of the emotions in man and animals.* Chicago: University of Chicago Press, 1965. (Originally published, 1872.)

Endler, N. S., Hunt, J. M., & Rosenstein, A. J. An S-R inventory of anxiousness. *Psychological Monographs*, 1962, *76*(17, Whole No. 536).

Freeman, M. J. The development of a test for the measurement of anxiety: A study of its reliability and validity. *Psychological Monographs*, 1953, *67*(3, Whole No. 353).

Freud, S. *New introductory lectures in psychoanalysis.* New York: Norton, 1933.

Freud, S. *The problem of anxiety.* New York: Norton, 1936.

Goldfried, M. R. The assessment of anxiety by means of the Rorschach. *Journal of Projective Techniques*, 1966, *30*, 364–380.

Holtzman, W. H. *Holtzman Inkblot Technique: Administration and scoring guide.* New York: Psychological Corporation, 1958.

Holtzman, W. H., Thorpe, J. S., Swartz, J. D., and Herron, E. W. *Inkblot perception and personality: Holtzman Inkblot Technique.* Austin: University of Texas Press, 1961.

Klopfer, B. The shading response. *Rorschach Research Exchange*, 1937–1938, *2*, 76–79.

Lader, M., and Marks, I. *Clinical Anxiety.* London: Wm. Heinemann Medical Books, Ltd., 1971.

Lazarus, R. S. *Psychological stress and the coping process.* New York: McGraw-Hill, 1966.

Levitt, E. E. *The psychology of anxiety.* Indianapolis: Bobbs-Merrill, 1967.

Mandler, B., & Sarason, S. B. A study of anxiety and learning. *Journal of Abnormal and Social Psychology*, 1952, *47*, 1166–1173.

Martin, B. The assessment of anxiety by physiological behavioral measures. *Psychological Bulletin*, 1961, *58*, 234–255.

McNair, D. M., Lorr, M., & Droppelman, L. F. *Test manual for the Profile of Mood States (POMS).* San Diego: Educational and Industrial Testing Service, 1971.

McReynolds, P. The assessment of anxiety: A survey of available techniques. In P. McReynolds (Ed.), *Advances in psychological assessment.* Palo Alto, Calif.: Science and Behavior Books, 1968.

Neuringer, C. Manifestations of anxiety on the Rorschach test. *Journal of Projective Techniques*, 1962, *26*, 318–326.

Nowlis, V. Methods for studying mood changes produced by drugs. *Revue de Psychologie Appliqué*, 1961, *11*, 373–386.

Nowlis, V., & Green, R. F. *Factor analytic studies of the Mood Adjective Check List.* Tech. Rep. 11, NR 171-342, ONR Contract 68 (12), 1965.

Piotrowski, Z. A. *Perceptanalysis*, New York: Macmillan, 1957.

Sarason, S. B., Davidson, K. S., Lighthall, F. F., Waite, R. R., & Ruebush, B. K. *Anxiety in elementary school children.* New York: Wiley, 1960.

Sarason, S. B., & Mandler, G. Some correlates of test anxiety. *Journal of Abnormal and Social Psychology*, 1952, *47*, 810–817.

Spielberger, C. D. Theory and research on anxiety. In C. D. Spielberger (Ed.), *Anxiety and behavior.* New York: Academic Press, 1966.

Spielberger, C. D. Trait-state anxiety and motor behavior. *Journal of Motor Behavior*, 1971, *3*, 265–279.

Spielberger, C. D. Anxiety as an emotional state. In C. D. Spielberger (Ed.), *Anxiety: Current trends in theory and research* (Vol. 1). New York: Academic Press, 1972. (a)

Spielberger, C. D. Conceptual and methodological issues in anxiety research. In C. D. Spielberger (Ed.), *Anxiety: Current trends in theory and research* (Vol. 2). New York: Academic Press, 1972. (b)

Spielberger, C. D. Current trends in theory and research on anxiety. In C. D. Spielberger (Ed.), *Anxiety: Current trends in theory and research* (Vol. 1). New York: Academic Press, 1972. (c)

Spielberger, C. D. *Manual for the State-Trait Anxiety Inventory for Children.* Palo Alto, Calif.: Consulting Psychologist Press, 1973.

Spielberger, C. D. The measurement of state and trait anxiety: Conceptual and methodological issues. In L. Levi (Ed.), *Emotions—their parameters and measurement.* New York: Raven Press, 1975.

Spielberger, C. D., & Gorsuch, R. L. The development of the state-trait anxiety inventory. In C. D. Spielberger and R. L. Gorsuch, *Mediating processes in verbal conditioning.* Final report to the National Institutes of Health, U.S. Public Health Service on Grants MH 7229, MH 7446, and HD 947, 1966.

Spielberger, C. D., Gorsuch, R. L., & Lushene, R. E. *Manual for the State-Trait Anxiety Inventory.* Palo Alto, Calif.: Consulting Psychologist Press, 1970.

Taylor, J. A. The relationship of anxiety to the conditioned eyelid response. *Journal of Experimental Psychology*, 1951, *41*, 81–92.

Taylor, J. A. A personality scale of manifest anxiety. *Journal of Abnormal and Social Psychology*, 1953, *48*, 285–290.

Welsh, G. S. Factor dimensions A and R. In G. S. Welsh, & W. G. Dahlstrom (Eds.), *Basic readings on the MMPI in psychology and medicine*. Minneapolis: University of Minnesota Press, 1956.

Zuckerman, M. The development of an Affect Adjective Check List for the measurement of anxiety. *Journal of Consulting Psychology*, 1960, *24*, 457–462.

Zuckerman, M., & Lubin, B. *Manual for the Multiple Affect Adjective Check List*. San Diego: Educational and Industrial Testing Service, 1965.

2

Cross-Cultural Measurement of Anxiety

Charles D. Spielberger
University of South Florida, Tampa

Sagar Sharma
Himachal Pradesh University, Simla, India

Cross-cultural research requires a careful calibration of psychological scales in different language systems, a task that turns out to be more difficult than most people realize. The translation of a psychological inventory from the original language inevitably raises many complex theoretical and methodological problems. In order to facilitate the integration of theory and research across cultures, test translators must understand the conceptual framework that has guided the construction of a particular psychological scale, and must be able to adapt and extend this framework where necessary to incorporate relevant aspects of the new culture. Only then will the translation of a scale into another language permit meaningful cross-cultural comparisons and make normative data comparable from a cross-cultural standpoint.

The goals of this chapter are to consider a number of general issues that are encountered in the cross-cultural measurement of anxiety, and to discuss specific strategies that have proven useful in developing translations of the State-Trait Anxiety Inventory (STAI) (Spielberger, Gorsuch, & Lushene, 1970). The construction and development of the Spanish and Hindi forms of

This chapter was prepared while Professor Sharma was visiting associate professor in the College of Social and Behavioral Sciences of the University of South Florida, Tampa.

the STAI will also be briefly described, and information with regard to the reliability and validity of these forms and their equivalence with the English STAI will be presented.

The STAI has been used extensively for research in the United States over the past ten years, as well as for counseling and clinical purposes with adolescents and adults. The State-Trait Anxiety Inventory for Children (STAIC) was developed to measure anxiety in elementary school children (Spielberger, 1973), and this scale has been adapted for use with younger children who lack reading skills.[1]

The STAI has also been translated into a number of different languages. The Spanish form (Diaz-Guerrero & Spielberger, 1975; Spielberger, Gonzalez-Reigosa, Martinez-Urrutia, L. F. Natalicio, & D. C. Natalicio, 1971) and the Hindi form (Spielberger, Sharma, & Singh, 1973) have been carefully validated, and extensive work has been done in constructing a French form (see Bergeron, Landry, & Belanger, Chap. 4, this volume), an Italian form (see Pancheri, Bernabei, Bellaterra, & Tartaglione, Chap. 9, this volume), a Swedish form (see Endler & Magnusson, Chap. 11, this volume), and a Turkish form (see LeCompte & Oner, Chap. 5, this volume) of the scale. In addition, a Spanish version of the STAIC has been recently developed (see Bauermeister, Forastieri, & Spielberger, Chap. 6, this volume), and preliminary translations of the STAI are available in Danish, German, Greek, Hebrew, Hungarian, Japanese, Malay, Norwegian, Polish, Rumanian, Russian, Slavic, Vietnamese, Lugandan and Swahili.

In translating the STAI into different languages, and in establishing the equivalence of the translations of the scales with the original STAI, a set of strategies has emerged that we have observed to be quite effective. Based on these experiences, especially in the construction of the Spanish and Hindi forms of the STAI, it is now possible to propose an approach for the development of translations of anxiety measures that will facilitate cross-cultural research.

STRATEGIES FOR DEVELOPING TRANSLATIONS OF ANXIETY MEASURES

The translation of a scale into another language generally involves four stages: (1) preparation of a *preliminary translation* in the second language; (2) evaluation of the preliminary translation by subject matter and language experts and selection of a set of items for an *experimental form* of the scale; (3) establishment of the cross-language equivalence of the original scale and

---

[1] Papay reported the psychometric characteristics of the STAIC for 2,470 kindergarten through fourth-grade children in the Dallas, Texas, public schools in a paper presented at the Annual Meeting of the American Psychological Association in New Orleans, September, 1974.

the experimental form of the translated scale; and (4) establishment of the reliability and validity of the new scale.

Preparation of a Preliminary Translation

The initial translation of a psychological scale should be carried out by psychologists and/or psychiatrists with the help of language experts. Ideally, the translators should have academic grounding in psychometrics and test theory, and extensive experience in the substantive fields in which the translated scale will be used. In the development of the Spanish version of the STAI, for example, the services of psychologists, psychiatrists, Spanish professors of English, and a professional Spanish interpreter were used (Spielberger et al., 1971). Similarly, the preliminary translation of the Hindi STAI was jointly carried out by professors of English and Hindi, and several psychology professors (Spielberger et al., 1973).

It is essential for scale translators to understand the measurement goals of the authors of the original scale. In constructing the STAI A-State scale, for example, Spielberger et al. (1970) attempted to measure the intensity dimension of state anxiety. At low levels of A-State intensity, they assumed that people feel calm and secure, and that feelings of tension and nervousness are experienced as state anxiety increases, with feelings of extreme fright and panic at the highest levels. Thus, the concept of state anxiety implies an intensity dimension with different qualitative characteristics of anxiety states at different levels of intensity.

In the preliminary translation of a psychological scale, the same format and instructions should be used as in the original version. Special attention should also be given to the psychological content and grammatical form of each item. Even small changes in either content or form may sometimes greatly influence subjects' responses.

In developing translations of the STAI, it has been observed that two or more items in the original scale may have exactly the same translation in another language, while a single item in the original scale may have several different translations that appear to be acceptable. Where literal translations are not possible, the translation should retain the essential meaning of the original item, and it is usually possible to identify a synonym of the key word that reflects the basic underlying meaning.

A serious problem sometimes arises in translating items that are expressed in idiomatic language. In such cases, special care should be taken to translate the *feeling* connotation of the idiom rather than the literal meanings of individual words. When it is possible to identify a comparable idiomatic expression in the language into which a scale is being translated, this corresponding idiom is generally preferable to the literal translation of the original item. Consequently, in translating idioms a clear understanding of the theoretical concepts that are reflected in the dimensions that are being measured is especially important.

For items on which there is disagreement among translators, it may be desirable to develop alternate wordings for such items. It was necessary, for example, in translating the STAI into Spanish to develop alternate wording for 7 of the 40 STAI items. In constructing the Hindi form of the STAI, 2 alternate translations were required for 13 of the 40 items, 3 translations were generated for another set of 13 items, and, for 4 items, there were 4 alternate translations. Biaggio, L. F. Natalicio, and Spielberger (see Chap. 3, this volume) discuss similar problems encountered in the translation of the STAI into Portuguese that required them to generate alternate wordings for a number of items.

Key words in many of the STAI items (especially, for the A-State scale) are clearly synonyms. Such items were deliberately constructed by the test authors (Spielberger et al., 1970) in keeping with the goal of developing a homogeneous scale with high internal consistency. Therefore, items with similar meanings that assessed somewhat different aspects of the experience of anxiety were sought. For example, item 5 "I feel at ease" is highly correlated with item 10 "I feel comfortable." While these items have similar connotations, item 10 implies somewhat more pleasant feelings than item 5, which has the connotation of the absence of tension without the nuance of pleasantness. Similarly, the key words *worry*, *tense*, and *jittery* have overlapping connotations, but *worry* implies cognitive activity associated with an anxiety state whereas *tense* suggests a state of apprehension with associated muscular contraction, and *jittery* has the connotation of motoric involvement in the form of restlessness and trembling.

Studies have shown that some STAI A-State items are better able to discriminate between conditions characterized by different degrees or levels of stress than others (Spielberger et al., 1970). Such findings reflect a new test-theory concept for measuring dimensions that vary in intensity:

> This concept, which we will identify as *item-intensity specificity*, refers to the fact that individual items used to measure the intensity of a personality state are more effective at some levels of the intensity dimension than at others. (Spielberger et al., 1970, p. 11)

The STAI A-State scale includes items at various levels of item-intensity specificity so that it may be used over a wide range of A-State intensities, i.e., the various items in this scale measure the level of intensity of anxiety as an emotional state. Items such as "I feel comfortable" and "I feel at ease" are more effective for measuring low levels of A-State intensity, whereas items with key words such as *tense* and *jittery* have proved more effective in measuring moderate to high levels of A-State intensity.

Whenever possible, the unique psycholinguistic properties of different languages should be utilized in generating item translations. In Spanish, for example, there are two forms of the verb *to be*. *Ser* implies a relatively permanent characteristic of a person, whereas *estar* has the connotation of a transitory state or temporary condition. Similarly, the Hindi verbs *raha hun* and the *rahta hun* correspond, respectively, with the concepts of a transitory state and relatively stable personality trait. Thus, the state-trait distinction is intrinsic to the Spanish and Hindi languages, and the fundamental psychological significance of this distinction would seem to be supported by these psycholinguistic facts.

One final point needs further consideration. The key words in the translation of a psychological scale should be as simple as possible. Therefore, a preliminary translation should be tried out with several samples of different educational background to determine if the items are meaningful in content and not too difficult to be understood by persons with limited education. The establishment of the equivalence of scales in two languages will be facilitated if the tryout samples are comparable to the ones used in the original standardization of the scale in terms of age, sex, socioeconomic status, education, and other demographic and psychosocial variables.

Evaluation of the Preliminary Translation and Selection of Items for an Experimental Form

The second phase in the translation of a psychological scale should involve a careful evaluation of the preliminary translation by experts working in the subject matter area. Knowledge of personality theory and psychopathology are as essential in the translation of an anxiety scale as an adequate background in the original language and in the language of the translation. In seeking evaluations of individual test items, it is essential that the subject matter expert be provided with a copy of the test manual of the original scale, along with the original test form and the preliminary translation.

Expert evaluation of the preliminary translation was a crucial phase in the development of the Spanish and Hindi forms of the STAI. In the development of these scales, the expert evaluators were requested to review each item of the translated scale in terms of content, meaning, form, and clarity of expression, and then to compare the translated items with the original test items. In order to simplify and objectify the evaluation of the translation of individual items, the experts were asked to record a "G" for each item that was considered a "good" translation of the original item, an "S" for items for which the translation was considered "satisfactory," and a "U" for items for which the translations were considered unsatisfactory. For all "U" items, the experts were requested to provide suggestions for improving the translation and making the scale linguistically more acceptable to the people of their country.

Another technique that has been used to evaluate the adequacy of the translation of psychological scales is known as "back translation." This approach was followed by LeCompte and Oner (see Chap. 5, this volume) in constructing the Turkish Form of the STAI. The translations of each STAI item were given to psychologists and English professors who were knowledgeable of both the Turkish and the English languages, with instructions to translate the preliminary Turkish version of the STAI back into the English. The original English form was then compared with the back translation for similarity.

LeCompte and Oner note that idiomatic expressions required frequent consultations with language experts in the back translations. From the standpoint of the literalness or exactness of the translation, they suggest that items may be grouped into the following three categories: (1) items whose translations closely fit the original form; (2) items that create difficulty in finding words that correspond to the original form; and (3) items with a linguistic form that cannot be translated from the original form without changing the grammatical construction. A number of cycles of translation and back translation may be required before an adequate translation can be developed for the latter type of item.

Based on agreement among translators and expert evaluators, a set of items can be selected to comprise the *preliminary form* of a scale that has been translated into a new language. Agreement among expert evaluators may be interpreted as providing evidence of the content validity of the translated scale. When translators and evaluators disagree concerning the translation of a particular item, it is better to include two or more different translations of such items in the preliminary form of the scale. It can then be determined, on the basis of statistical data, which of these alternative items should be included in the *experimental version* of the translated scale. This can be done by computing item-remainder correlations and retaining those items that are most highly correlated with the other items in the scale. Expert opinion as to the similarity of test items in different languages and high item-remainder correlations are important criteria for selecting individual items to be included in the experimental form of a translated scale.

Cross-Language Equivalence of Scales

Empirical demonstration of cross-language equivalence of test items translated into another language is an essential step in the development of a scale that will be useful in cross-cultural research. The cross-language equivalence of a scale can be evaluated by obtaining correlations between the original language version of the scale and its translation. In establishing cross-language equivalence, it is convenient to utilize bilingual subjects. Bilingualism may be defined in terms of reading proficiency in two languages (see Gonzalez-Reigosa, Chap. 7, this volume, for a detailed discussion of bilingualism).

In the development of various translations of the STAI, the original STAI scales and their translations were administered in counterbalanced order to bilingual subjects. In constructing the Hindi Form of the STAI (Spielberger et al., 1973), four different combinations of the English and the experimental Hindi versions of the STAI were presented to bilingual graduate students who were randomly assigned to one of the following presentation sequences:

1. English A-State, Hindi A-State, English A-Trait, Hindi A-Trait
2. Hindi A-State, English A-State, Hindi A-Trait, English A-Trait
3. English A-Trait, Hindi A-Trait, English A-State, Hindi A-State
4. Hindi A-Trait, English A-Trait, Hindi A-State, English A-State

For the combined samples, the coefficient of equivalence for the English and Hindi STAI A-State and A-Trait scales was .85 and .88, respectively. A similar research design was used by Mote, L. F. Natalicio, and Rivas (1971) and by Spielberger et al. (1971) to determine the equivalence of the Spanish and English forms of the STAI. The equivalence correlations for the Spanish and English A-State and A-Trait scales ranged between .83 and .94.

Biaggio et al. (see Chap. 3, this volume) used an even more stringent measure of equivalence, i.e., the correlation between each individual item in the preliminary Portuguese STAI(PX) and the corresponding English items. In general, the high correlations of the Hindi, Spanish, and Portuguese scales with the original English scale provide evidence of the concurrent validity of these scales as well as their psychometric equivalence.

SPANISH AND HINDI FORMS OF THE STAI

In this section we describe briefly the procedures that were employed in the construction and development of the Spanish and Hindi forms of the STAI. Evidence of the reliability and validity of these forms and their equivalence with the English STAI will also be presented.

Spanish STAI: Inventario de Ansiedad: Rasgo y Estado (IDAREN)

The preliminary translation of the STAI into Spanish was carried out by three psychologists—one native of Puerto Rico and two native Cubans who attended college in Puerto Rico. In addition, the English form of the STAI was translated by a professional Spanish-English interpreter. For items expressed by English idioms, care was taken to translate the feeling connotation of the idiom rather than the literal meaning of individual words. For example, "taking things hard" was translated into the Spanish idiom, "muy a pecho" which has a similar (but not identical) connotation of "taking things (to heart) seriously."

Evaluations of the preliminary translation of the Spanish STAI were obtained from 13 eminent psychologists and psychiatrists, representing eight different Latin American countries. These subject-matter experts either were members of the American Psychological Association or held office in the Inter-American Society of Psychology at the time they were contacted. The evaluators were asked to review each item in the Spanish translation, compare it with the corresponding English STAI item, and then give their opinion regarding the adequacy of the translation. A copy of the STAI test manual (Spielberger et al., 1970) was also sent to each evaluator to provide theoretical background and information about the construction of the original scale.

On the basis of the responses of the Latin American subject-matter experts, a final set of 20 A-State and 20 A-Trait items was selected for the Spanish form of the STAI. In order to establish the equivalence, internal consistency and test-retest reliability of the Spanish and English forms of the STAI, two studies were carried out with bilingual subjects, one at the University of Texas at Austin and the other at the Rio Piedras Campus of the University of Puerto Rico. In both studies, the standard English form and the experimental Spanish form of the STAI were administered on two different occasions, with test-retest intervals of 7 to 10 days. While the Texas study was concerned only with determining the equivalence of the English and Spanish forms of the STAI, the subjects in the Puerto Rico study were given an "intelligence" test prior to the administration of the STAI in order to increase the amount of situational stress.

Evidence of the cross-language equivalence of the Spanish and English forms of the STAI was provided by the high correlations obtained between these forms in both studies. For the A-Trait scale, the Spanish-English correlations were .83, .89, .85, and .85. The correlations between the Spanish and English forms for the corresponding administrations of the A-State scale were even higher: .83, .91, .91, and .94. Additional evidence of the equivalence of these scales was reported by Mote et al. (1971), who found correlations between the English and Spanish STAI A-State and A-Trait scales to be .94 and .94, respectively.

Reasonably high item-remainder correlations were also obtained for each individual item in the Spanish A-State and A-Trait scales for the Texas and Puerto Rican samples. Indeed the correlations for the bilingual subjects in these studies were even higher than those reported for the normative samples in the STAI test manual (Spielberger et al., 1970). Furthermore, for the Spanish A-Trait scale, alpha coefficients of .84, .82, .89, and .89 were obtained for the Texas and Puerto Rican samples, and the comparable alpha correlations of the corresponding administrations of the Spanish A-State scale were even higher: .91, .94, .89, and .95. These data provide strong evidence of the homogeneity of the individual items in the Spanish STAI A-Trait and A-State scales, and the high internal consistency of these scales.

The stability of the Spanish STAI A-Trait scale was reflected in test-retest correlations of .84 and .83 obtained over intervals of 10 days for the Texas subjects and one week for the Puerto Rican subjects. For the English form, the test-retest correlations for college students that are reported in the STAI test manual were .80 for a 20-day interval, and .75 for a 104-day interval (Spielberger et al., 1970). Further evidence of the stability of the Spanish A-Trait scale was reflected in the fact that there was relatively little change in the A-Trait means for this scale from the first to the second administration. Thus, the stability of the Spanish A-Trait scale over time compares favorably with the stability of the English A-Trait scale.

Since the STAI A-State scale was designed to be sensitive to the influence of unique situational factors which typically change over time, lack of stability in A-State scores was expected. The test-retest correlations for the Spanish A-State scale were consistently lower than those obtained for the A-Trait scale (.49 to .63), but somewhat higher than those typically reported. Stability coefficients reported in the STAI test manual for the English A-State scale for college students retested after varying time intervals and circumstances ranged from .16 to .54 with a median *r* of .32 (Spielberger et al., 1970). The higher stability coefficients for the Spanish STAI can probably be attributed in part to the fact that the subjects were retested under very similar circumstances.

Evidence of the construct validity of the Spanish STAI A-State scale was provided by the finding that scores on this scale were significantly elevated on the first administration. It may be recalled that the Puerto Rican subjects were first given the STAI after an "intelligence" test. Thus, the finding that A-State scores were elevated is consistent with the assumption that this scale measured transitory changes in A-State that were induced by stress.

There was also a tendency for the Texas subjects to score higher on both forms of the A-State scale the first time it was given, especially the English form. Similar findings were obtained by Mote et al. (1971) for a sample of Mexican Americans in San Antonio. In both studies, the subjects scored slightly higher on the Spanish A-State scale than on the corresponding English form, and A-State scores on the Spanish and English forms were significantly higher on the first administration of these scales than on the second administration. The authors speculate that transitory anxiety (A-State) was higher because responding to tests such as the STAI ("Self-Evaluation Questionnaire") is stressful for subjects who are not accustomed to taking personality tests. The finding that scores on the Spanish A-Trait scale were not influenced by situational stress was consistent with results obtained for the English STAI A-Trait scale (Spielberger et al., 1970).

Further evidence of the construct validity of the Spanish STAI has been reported by Martinez-Urrutia and Spielberger (1973) for a sample of psychiatric patients, and by Rivera-Santiago (1973) for Puerto Rican high school students. The Spanish STAI has also been used in cross-cultural studies to compare the anxiety levels of Mexican and American high school students

(Fogel, 1973); to study the relationship among trait anxiety, sex, general ability, and academic achievement for tenth-grade students in Puerto Rico (Bauermeister & Berlingeri, 1974); and to investigate the anxiety-arousing effects of taboo words for Spanish-English bilingual college students (see Gonzalez-Reigosa, Chap. 7, this volume).

The Hindi STAI

In constructing the Hindi form of the STAI, the general goal was to build an instrument suitable for use in all Hindi-speaking states of India. The general approach to translating the scale was essentially the same as that used in developing the Spanish STAI. The preliminary translation was jointly carried out by three professors of Hindi, two English professors, and four psychologists working at Panjab University, Chandigarh, India.

The preliminary Hindi translation of the STAI was evaluated by 16 psychologists from different regions of India, all of whom were experienced in test construction procedures in the clinical field. The preliminary translation was also submitted for evaluation to five professors of Hindi and five professors of English at Panjab University, all with academic backgrounds in psychology. Based on the ratings and suggestions of these evaluators, a final set of 20 A-State and 20 A-Trait items was selected for the experimental Hindi form of the STAI.

A series of studies was conducted to demonstrate the equivalence of the English and the experimental Hindi forms of the STAI. In the first study, the standard English form and the experimental Hindi form were administered to 160 Hindi-English bilingual graduate students in four different orders. Evidence of cross-language equivalence was reflected in high correlations between the Hindi and English A-State and A-Trait scales of .85 and .88, respectively, and in the comparable mean scores for these scales. These correlations may be interpreted as evidence that the Hindi and English STAIs can be considered as equivalent forms for bilingual college students.

The mean for the English A-State scale was significantly higher than for the Hindi A-State scale, due primarily to higher A-State means for the English scales when they were administered before the corresponding Hindi scales. Thus, the experience of taking the English form first induced greater elevations in A-State for Hindi-English bilinguals than when the Hindi version was given first. Apparently, responding in English was more threatening to these students for whom Hindi was the mother tongue. It may be recalled that similar results were obtained for Spanish-English bilinguals for whom Spanish was the primary language (Spielberger et al., 1971). These findings provide evidence that the STAI A-State scale is sensitive to the relatively mild stress that is introduced when verbal materials are presented in the nonpreferred language to bilingual subjects.

Alpha coefficients for the Hindi STAI A-State and A-Trait scales were .89 and .88, respectively. The corresponding values for the English STAI A-State and A-Trait scales were .87 and .86, respectively. Thus, the items comprising both the Hindi and English editions of the STAI were quite homogeneous for the bilingual Hindi students. Further evidence of the internal consistency of the Hindi form of the STAI was provided by moderate-to-high item-remainder correlations for each Hindi A-State and A-Trait item. It should also be noted that the internal consistency for the individual Hindi A-State items was somewhat better than for the corresponding English items, as might be expected for bilingual Hindi subjects.

In order to determine the test-retest reliability of the Hindi STAI, a sample of 72 graduate students was retested under more or less similar classroom conditions after periods of 30, 50, and 90 days. The Hindi STAI A-Trait scale was stable over time as indicated by high test-retest correlations for this scale, which ranged from .77 to .83 over the 30- to 90-day periods. Thus, the stability of the Hindi A-Trait scale compares quite favorably with the test-retest stability of the English and Spanish STAI A-Trait scales (Spielberger et al., 1971).

Test-retest· correlations for the Hindi STAI A-State scale were consistently lower than those obtained for the A-Trait scale, but this was anticipated because a valid measure of transitory anxiety is expected to be sensitive to the influence of unique situational factors associated with the time of testing. The test-retest correlations for the Hindi A-State scale in this study were comparable to those found for the Spanish form of the scale, and somewhat higher than those reported by Spielberger et al. (1970) for the English A-State scale. This was apparently due to the fact that the subjects in the present study were retested under similar classroom conditions, whereas the subjects in the Spielberger et al. (1970) study were retested in a variety of situations.

The concurrent validity of the Hindi STAI A-Trait scale was evaluated for a sample of 100 Indian graduate students (50 females, 50 males) to whom the scale was administered along with the following anxiety measures: (1) an Indian adaptation of the Taylor (1953) Manifest Anxiety Scale (Krishnan, 1966); (2) the IPAT Anxiety Scale (Cattell & Scheier, 1961); and (3) the Sharma Manifest Anxiety Scale (Sharma, 1970). The Hindi STAI A-Trait scale correlated .80, .71, and .61, respectively, with the Sharma Scale, the IPAT Anxiety Scale, and the Taylor Scale. These moderate-to-high correlations provide evidence of the concurrent validity of the Hindi STAI, and suggest that all four scales measure trait anxiety.

Evidence of the construct validity of the Hindi STAI A-State scale was obtained in a sample of 92 graduate students (46 females, 46 males) who were administered the scale with standard (NORMAL) instructions and with instructions to respond according to how they believed they would feel "just prior to the final examination in an important course" (EXAM condition).

The mean A-State scores in the NORMAL and EXAM conditions were 33.22 and 50.86, respectively ($p < .01$), indicating that A-State scores are higher under more stressful circumstances.

An interesting cross-cultural difference is suggested by comparing the findings for Hindi and American college students under similar experimental conditions. The mean A-State scores for American students in NORMAL and EXAM conditions, such as those described above, were 36.99 and 43.01, respectively, (Spielberger et al., 1970). The substantially greater increase in STAI A-State scores that was found for Hindi students may reflect differences in the examination systems in the two cultures. In general, Hindi students are examined less frequently than American students and it appears that they perceive examinations as more stressful.

Sharma (1973) studied changes in state and trait anxiety as a function of an approaching final examination for a sample of 68 graduate students. These students were administered the Hindi STAI A-State scales on four occasions: 125, 65, 25, and 5 days before final examinations at Panjab University. As the final examination approached, mean A-State scores consistently increased, with the greatest increase occurring between the third and fourth administrations of the scale. In contrast, the A-Trait scores for these students were relatively stable for the same time periods. These findings, and the results of the two preceding studies, provide evidence of the construct validity of the Hindi A-State scale.

In summary, the Spanish and Hindi forms of the STAI appear to be internally consistent, reliable, and valid scales for measuring state and trait anxiety within their respective cultures. Since the Spanish and Hindi forms are essentially equivalent to the English STAI, they provide potentially useful tools for cross-cultural research. Cross-cultural investigations of factors that influence the arousal of anxiety states for persons who differ in trait anxiety would be especially interesting and worthwhile. Research on the relation between state and trait anxiety and learning in different cultures would help to establish the generality of the findings of a large number of studies that have demonstrated the influence of individual differences in anxiety on the learning processes.

SUMMARY

In this chapter, a number of general issues encountered in the cross-cultural measurement of anxiety were examined, and specific strategies that have proven useful in developing translations of the State-Trait Anxiety Inventory were described. It was noted that the translation of a personality scale generally involves four stages: the preparation of a preliminary translation, the selection of items for an experimental form on the basis of evaluations by subject matter and language experts, the establishment of the cross-language equivalence of the translated scale with the original scale, and the establishment of the reliability and validity of the new scale. The four stages in the development of the Spanish and Hindi forms of the STAI were briefly described, and information with regard to the cross-language equivalence, reliability, and validity of these scales was presented.

REFERENCES

Bauermeister, J. J., & Berlingeri, N. C. Rendimiento academico en funcion del nivel de ansieda-rasgo sexo y habilidad general [Academic achievement as a function of level of A-trait, sex, and general ability]. *Revista Interamericana de Psicologia*, 1974, *8*, 53–67.

Cattell, R. B., & Scheier, I. H. *The meaning and measurement of neuroticism and anxiety.* New York: Ronald Press, 1961.

Diaz-Guerrero, R., & Spielberger, C. D. *IDARE: Inventario de Ansiedad: Rasgo-Estado.* Mexico, D.F.: El Manual Moderno, S.A., 1975.

Fogel, F. R. *State and trait anxiety: A cross-cultural investigation.* Unpublished master's thesis, University of Houston, 1973.

Krishnan, B. *Indian adaptation of the Taylor Manifest Anxiety Scale.* Department of Psychology, University of Myosore, India, 1966.

Martinez-Urrutia, A., & Spielberger, C. D. The relationship between state and trait anxiety and intelligence in Puerto Rican psychiatric patients. *Revista Interamericana de Psicologia*, 1973, *11*, 3–4.

Mote, T. A., Natalicio, L. F., & Rivas, F. Comparability of the Spanish and English editions of the Spielberger State-Trait Anxiety Inventory. *Journal of Cross-Cultural Psychology*, 1971, *2*, 205–206.

Rivera-Santiago, J. A. *The effects of psychological and physical threat on A-state for Puerto Rican high school students who differed in A-trait.* Unpublished master's thesis, University of Puerto Rico, 1973.

Sharma, S. Manifest anxiety and school achievement of adolescents. *Journal of Consulting and Clinical Psychology*, 1970, *34*, 403–407.

Sharma, S. Changes in state and trait anxiety scores with the approaching examination. *New Trends in Education*, 1973, *4*, 10–13.

Spielberger, C. D. *Preliminary Manual for the State-Trait Anxiety Inventory for Children ("How I feel Questionnaire").* Palo Alto, Calif.: Consulting Psychologist Press, 1973.

Spielberger, C. D., Gonzalez-Reigosa, F., Martinez-Urrutia, A., Natalicio, L. F., & Natalicio, D. C. Development of the Spanish edition of the State-Trait Anxiety Inventory. *Interamerican Journal of Psychology*, 1971, *5*, 3–4.

Spielberger, C. D., Gorsuch, R. L., & Lushene, R. E. *Manual for the State-Trait Anxiety Inventory.* Palo Alto, Calif.: Consulting Psychologist Press, 1970.

Spielberger, C. D., Sharma, S., & Singh, M. Development of the Hindi edition of the State-Trait Anxiety Inventory. *Indian Journal of Psychology*, 1973, *48*, 11–20.

Taylor, J. A. A personality scale of manifest anxiety. *Journal of Abnormal and Social Psychology*, 1953, *48*, 285–290.

II

THE MEASUREMENT OF ANXIETY IN DIFFERENT CULTURES

3

The Development and Validation of an Experimental Portuguese Form of the State-Trait Anxiety Inventory

Angela M. B. Biaggio
Pontificia Universidade Catolica do Rio de Janeiro

Luiz Natalicio
University of Texas at El Paso

Charles D. Spielberger
University of South Florida, Tampa

The goal of this chapter is to describe the first stages in the construction of an experimental Portuguese language form of the State-Trait Anxiety

The authors wish to express their gratitude to student assistants Sandra Kruel and Lucia Rabelo de Castro for the many hours they spent giving tests, scoring, and coding results; to Sandra Cardoso de Abreu for assistance with the computer analysis of data; and to Benjamin Algaze, Florence Frain, and Georgina Taddia for their contributions to the preparation of the manuscript for publication. For their comments and constructive suggestions with regard to the development of the Portuguese translation of the STAI, we are grateful to Arrigo Angelino, Antonius Benko, Luis I. Biaggio, Aniela Ginsberg, Thereza Lemos Mettell, Maria Helena Novaes, Julio Silveira Nunes, Angela Podkameni, and Aroldo Rodrigues.

Inventory (STAI) (Speilberger, Gorsuch, & Lushene, 1970). The STAI consists of two 20-item scales for the assessment of anxiety as a transitory state (A-State) and as a relatively stable personality trait (A-Trait).

Although published only 5 years ago, the English form of the STAI has been used as a clinical and research instrument in more than 500 studies. The STAI has also been translated into a number of different languages and is rapidly becoming a standard international measure in cross-cultural research on anxiety. The development of the experimental Portuguese form of the STAI has followed procedures similar to those employed in constructing the Spanish form (Spielberger, Gonzalez-Reigosa, Martinez-Urrutia, Natalicio, & Natalicio, 1971).

TRANSLATION OF THE STAI INTO PORTUGUESE

The first step in the construction of the experimental Portuguese form (STAI-PX) was the development of a preliminary Portuguese translation of the STAI by Biaggio and Natalicio based on the concepts of state and trait anxiety as defined by Spielberger (1966, 1972). The translation was sent to a number of Brazilian and Portuguese psychologists and psychiatrists along with the test form for the English STAI. The judges were selected on the basis of their outstanding professional qualifications and bilingual skills. All of the judges were highly proficient in the English language.

The judges were asked to evaluate the adequacy of the preliminary Portuguese translations of individual STAI items by rating each item as either good, satisfactory, or unsatisfactory; six judges responded to this request. All 40 Portuguese item translations were judged as good or satisfactory by four of the six judges. The translations of 19 items were rated good, and 32 items were rated as either good or satisfactory by all six judges.

The 8 items rated as unsatisfactory by two of the judges were rewritten after consultation with two additional experienced bilingual psychologists and a Brazilian-born professor of English who was chairman of the Translator-Interpreter Program at a major Brazilian university. Alternative Portuguese translations were developed for 4 A-State items for which no clear-cut translation could be developed (items 6, 10, 14, and 15), and two alternative item translations were developed for one of the A-Trait items (item 15). These alternative items were added to the 40 original Portuguese A-State and A-Trait item translations to comprise the preliminary form of the Portuguese STAI. Thus, the revised preliminary Portuguese translation consisted of 24 A-State items and 22 A-Trait items.

TEST CONSTRUCTION PROCEDURES

The preliminary form of the Portuguese translation of the STAI that resulted from these procedures was administered to four different samples of

Portuguese-English bilingual subjects in two major Brazilian cities, Rio de Janeiro and Porto Alegre. Sample 1 consisted of four males and eight females who were enrolled in a conversation group at Instituto Cultural Brasileiro Norte-Americano in Porto Alegre, R.S., Brazil. These subjects were either English teachers, advanced students of English, or returning travelers from the United States who were interested in maintaining their English-speaking skills. This sample was heterogenous in age and education level, ranging from high school students and housewives with a high school education to college professors. The mean age was 31 years, with a standard deviation of 12 months.

Sample 2 consisted of 23 university students (1 male, 22 females) enrolled in the Translator-Interpreter Program speciality sponsored by the Letters Department of the Catholic University of Porto Alegre. The mean age for Sample 2 was 26 years, with a standard deviation of 6 months. Sample 3 consisted of 34 advanced students and teachers (13 males, 21 females) associated with the Instituto Brasil Estados Unidos in Rio de Janeiro. The mean age for the subjects in this sample was 26 years, with a standard deviation of 10 months. Sample 4 consisted of 15 senior female students enrolled in the Translator-Interpreter Program in the Letters Department of the Catholic University of Rio de Janeiro. The mean age for these students was 25 years, with a standard deviation of 6 months.

Both the English STAI and the preliminary Portuguese STAI translation were administered to each sample. To control for possible order effects, half of the subjects in each sample was given the English Form first, and the other half was given the preliminary Portuguese Form first. For Samples 1, 3, and 4, the interval between the administration of the two scales was 1 week. For Sample 2, the subjects took both scales on the same day, one immediately following the other.

For the selection of the final set of 20 A-State and 20 A-Trait items for the experimental form of the Portuguese STAI, the data for the four independent samples were combined. Separate item-remainder correlations for males and females were computed for the 24 preliminary Portuguese A-State items and the 22 preliminary A-Trait items. Correlations between scores for each Portuguese item and its corresponding English item were also calculated. The final selection of items for the STAI-PX was based on these item-remainder correlations and the correlations between each preliminary Portuguese STAI-PX item and its corresponding English STAI item.

The three most controversial items, in terms of disagreement among the judges who evaluated the preliminary Portuguese translation, were A-State items 6 and 10 and A-Trait item 15. The two translations for item 6 were "Sinto-me aborrecido." and "Sinto-me perturbado." Since the item-remainder and English-Portuguese item correlations were much higher for "perturbado," this item was chosen for the final form.

A somewhat different problem was encountered with A-State item 10 ("I feel comfortable."). The literal translation of this item ("Sinto-me confortável.") seemed to imply physical rather than psychological comfort. All of the judges considered "Sinto-me a vontade." to be the best translation for this item, but this same translation was also considered to be even more appropriate for A-State item 5 ("I feel at ease."). Therefore, two alternatives for item 10 were included in the preliminary translation. These were: "Sinto-me confortável, à vontade." and "Sinto-me 'em casa.'" (literally, "I feel at home."). Since the latter had much better psychometric properties, it was chosen for the experimental Portuguese Form.

The greatest disagreement among the judges was found for A-Trait item 15: "I feel blue." Three alternative translations of this item were developed for the preliminary Portuguese STAI: "Sinto-me deprimido," "Sinto-me melancólico," and "Sinto-me na fossa." The first alternative ("deprimido") yielded the highest item-remainder coefficient and was selected for inclusion in the final set of items for the experimental Portuguese form.

For A-Trait item 11 ("I am inclined to take things hard."), agreement among judges with regard to the adequacy of the translation of this item was high ("Levo as coisas muito a sério."), but low item-remainder correlations were obtained in Samples 1, 2, and 3. In contrast to the anxiety connotation of the English idiom, the Portuguese translation seemed to imply a strong sense of responsibility and hard work. Therefore, in Sample 4, an alternative translation was added for this item ("Deixo-me afetar muito pelas coisas."). This new item yielded satisfactory item-remainder and English-Portuguese item correlations in Sample 4 and was selected for the final set of items.

A different kind of problem was encountered with A-State item 4 ("I feel regretful."). This item was translated as "Sinto-me arrependido," and there was 100% agreement among the six judges with regard to the adequacy of this translation. However, the item-remainder correlations of .25 for males and .23 for females were lower than for any other single item. Since no other alternative translation was available, the item has been retained in the final form of the STAI-PX in spite of these relatively low item-remainder correlations.

In summary, on the basis of psychometric considerations and the professional judgments of Brazilian and Portuguese psychologists, psychiatrists, and linguists who were proficient in the English language, the final set of 20 A-State and 20 A-Trait items was selected for the experimental Portuguese form of the STAI. The psychometric properties of the resulting Portuguese STAI A-State and A-Trait scales are reported in the next section.

PSYCHOMETRIC PROPERTIES OF THE PORTUGUESE STAI

The psychometric characteristics of the experimental form of the Portuguese State-Trait Anxiety Inventory (STAI-PX) were based on the combined data for the four samples of Portuguese-English bilingual subjects. Means, standard deviations, and alpha coefficients were computed separately for males and females. The alpha coefficients were calculated on the basis of Kuder-Richardson formula 20 as modified by Cronbach (1951).

Means, standard deviations, and alpha coefficients for the STAI-PX A-State and A-Trait scales are reported in Table 1. The A-Trait and A-State means were slightly higher for females than for males, and A-Trait means were higher than A-State means for both sexes. It can also be noted in Table 1, for both males and females, that the variability of the A-Trait scores was greater than the variability of the A-State scores.

The finding that the STAI-PX A-State scores were less variable and also several points lower than the A-Trait scores, for both men and women, suggested that the subjects were relatively relaxed when they responded to these scales. For the English STAI, it has been consistently observed that the mean scores for the A-Trait and A-State scales are approximately the same when the measures are obtained under neutral (nonstressful) conditions. A check of the A-State and A-Trait means for the individual samples revealed that the A-State means were lower in Samples 1, 2, and 3, but not for Sample 4.

The STAI-PX A-Trait means were slightly higher for Brazilian male and female college students than for U.S. students, as was the A-State mean score for Brazilian females (Spielberger et al., 1970). In contrast, the mean A-State score for the Brazilian males was slightly lower than that obtained for U.S. undergraduates in general and substantially lower than the scores for U.S. college freshmen in particular. However, since the number of males in the Brazilian sample was small, little interpretive significance should be given to this finding, except that it suggests that the males who participated in the test construction studies for the Portuguese STAI were quite relaxed.

Internal Consistency of the STAI-PX

The alpha coefficients for the STAI-PX A-State and A-Trait scales were quite high for both males and females. Given the small size of the sample, especially the number of males, these findings were encouraging and would

TABLE 1 Means, standard deviations, and alpha coefficients for the experimental form of the Portuguese STAI

Psychometric property	A-State		A-Trait	
	Males ($N = 18$)	Females ($N = 66$)	Males ($N = 18$)	Females ($N = 66$)
Mean	34.28	38.98	38.78	40.58
Standard deviation	10.95	10.00	14.61	13.27
Alpha	.93	.88	.93	.87

seem to warrant the conclusion that the STAI-PX component scales are satisfactory with regard to their internal consistency. Indeed, the alpha coefficients for the Portuguese STAI are higher than those obtained for male high school and college students in the United States, and the alpha coefficients for females are comparable to those obtained for U.S. female students (see Table 3, Spielberger et al., 1970).

Item-remainder correlations for each STAI-PX A-State item are reported in Table 2 for males, females, and the total sample. The median item-remainder correlation was .59 for males and .62 both for females and for the total sample. Except for item 4, the item-remainder correlations were above .30 for all of the A-State items and .50 or higher for all but three items (4, 5, and 10).

Item-remainder correlations for each of the STAI-PX A-Trait items are reported in Table 3. For both males and females, the A-Trait item-remainder correlations were even higher than those obtained for the A-State scale. With the exception of item 6 for the males, all of the A-Trait item-remainder correlations were .40 or higher, and these correlations ranged from .47 to .83 for the total sample. The median item-remainder correlations for males, females, and the total sample were .75, .595, and .615, respectively. For 70% of the STAI-PX A-Trait items, the item-remainder correlations were .60 or higher.

In summary, the alpha coefficients for the STAI-PX A-State and A-Trait scales and the item-remainder correlations for each individual A-State and A-Trait item provide strong evidence of the internal consistency of the Portuguese STAI. These findings also clearly demonstrate that the STAI-PX meets the test construction goal of developing homogeneous, univariate scales for measuring state and trait anxiety. With respect to internal consistency, the STAI-PX compares favorably with the English (Spielberger et al., 1970) and Spanish (Spielberger et al., 1971) forms of the STAI.

Equivalence of the Portuguese and English Forms of the STAI

The equivalence of the experimental Portuguese STAI and the English STAI was determined by computing correlations between scores for the Portuguese and English A-State and A-Trait scales for each of the four bilingual samples and for the data from all samples combined. The correlations for the Portuguese and English A-State and A-Trait scales are reported in Table 4. With the exception of Sample 3, the equivalence correlations for the A-Trait scales were relatively high. The equivalence correlations were high for the A-State scales in Samples 2 and 4, but only moderate for Samples 1 and 3.

Strictly speaking, the correlations reported in Table 4 are equivalence coefficients *only* for Sample 2, for which both the English and the Portuguese

TABLE 2 Item-remainder correlations for the Portuguese STAI A-State scale

Item	Males (N = 18)	Females (N = 66)	Total (N = 84)
1. I feel calm. *Sinto-me calmo.*	.81	.64	.67
2. I feel secure. *Sinto-me seguro.*	.75	.55	.60
3. I am tense. *Estou tenso.*	.72	.61	.64
4. I am regretful. *Estou arrependido.*	.25	.23	.24
5. I feel at ease. *Sinto-me a vontade.*	.52	.29	.34
6. I feel upset. *Sinto-me perturbado.*	.43	.74	.71
7. I am presently worrying over possible misfortunes. *Estou preocupado c/ possiveis infortunios.*	.58	.65	.61
8. I feel rested. *Sinto-me descansado.*	.60	.51	.51
9. I feel anxious. *Sinto-me ansioso.*	.60	.59	.60
10. I feel comfortable. *Sinto-me "em casa."*	.40	.45	.47
11. I feel self-confident. *Sinto-me confiante.*	.57	.50	.52
12. I feel nervous. *Sinto-me nervoso.*	.45	.77	.74
13. I am jittery. *Sinto-me agitado.*	.66	.59	.61
14. I feel "high strung." *Sinto-me uma pilha de nervos.*	.36	.65	.63
15. I am relaxed. *Estou descontraido.*	.76	.63	.66
16. I feel content. *Sinto-me satisfeito.*	.45	.66	.63
17. I am worried. *Estou preocupado.*	.69	.79	.78
18. I feel overexcited and rattled. *Sinto-me super excitado e confuso.*	.49	.61	.60
19. I feel joyful. *Sinto-me alegre.*	.69	.64	.65
20. I feel pleasant. *Sinto-me bem.*	.73	.66	.68
Median correlations	.59	.62	.62
Range of correlations	.25 to .81	.23 to .79	.24 to .78

TABLE 3 Item-remainder correlations for the Portuguese STAI A-Trait scale

Item	Males $(N = 18)$	Females $(N = 66)$	Total $(N = 84)$
1. I feel pleasant. *Sinto-me bem.*	.92	.62	.68
2. I tire quickly. *Canso-me facilmente.*	.68	.60	.61
3. I feel like crying. *Tenho vontade de chorar.*	.56	.47	.50
4. I wish I could be as happy as others seem to be. *Gostaria de poder ser tao feliz quanto os outros parecem ser.*	.57	.65	.62
5. I am losing out on things because I can't make up my mind soon enough. *Perco oportunidade porque nao consigo tomar decisoes rapidamente.*	.78	.41	.50
6. I feel rested. *Sinto-me descansado.*	.26	.57	.48
7. I am "calm, cool, and collected." *Sou calmo, ponderado, e senhor de mim mesmo.*	.67	.42	.48
8. I feel that difficulties are piling up so that I cannot overcome them. *Sinto que as dificuldades estao se acumulando de tal forma que nao as consigo resolver.*	.75	.63	.66
9. I worry too much over something that really doesn't matter. *Preocupo-me demais com as coisas sem importancia.*	.71	.62	.64
10. I am happy. *Sou feliz.*	.84	.65	.67
11. I am inclined to take things hard. *Deixo-me afetar muito pelas coisas.**	–	.83	.83
12. I lack self-confidence. *Nao tenho muita confianca em mim.*	.81	.46	.53
13. I feel secure. *Sinto-me seguro.*	.78	.64	.67
14. I try to avoid facing a crisis or difficulty. *Evito ter que enfrentar crises ou problemas.*	.63	.42	.47
15. I feel blue. *Estou deprimido.*	.75	.56	.61
16. I am content. *Estou satisfeito.*	.84	.60	.65
17. Some unimportant thought runs through my mind and bothers me. *As vezes, ideias sem importancia me entram na cabeca e ficam me preocupando.*	.77	.56	.61

TABLE 3 (*continued*)   Item-remainder correlations for the Portuguese STAI A-Trait scale

Item	Males (N = 18)	Females (N = 66)	Total (N = 84)
18. I take disappointments so keenly that I can't put them out of my mind. *Levo os desapontamentos tao a serio que nao consigo tira-los da cabeça.*	.85	.57	.63
19. I am a steady person. *Sou uma pessoa estavel.*	.64	.59	.60
20. I become tense and upset when I think about my present concerns. *Fico tenso e perturbado quando penso em meus problemas do momento.*	.71	.64	.65
Median correlations	.75	.595	.615
Range of correlations	.26 to .92	.41 to .83	.47 to .83

*This translation was substituted for the initial Portuguese translation in Sample 4, which consisted of female subjects only.

forms of the STAI were administered during the same testing session. For the other three samples, an interval of 1 week intervened between the administrations of the two scales. It is, therefore, encouraging that the highest equivalence correlations between the Portuguese STAI and the English STAI were obtained for Sample 2. Moreover, it should be noted that correlations between equivalent forms of the A-State scale would not necessarily be expected when this scale was administered with a 1-week interval. Indeed, the low correlations obtained between the Portuguese and English A-State scales in Samples 1 and 3 could reflect the impact of different situational stress factors associated with the two occasions of measurement.

A possible explanation for the lower equivalence correlations in Sample 3 is that the subjects in this sample were somewhat lower in English proficiency

TABLE 4   Correlations between the English STAI and the Portuguese STAI-PX A-State and A-Trait scales in four samples of bilingual subjects

Sample	N	A-State	A-Trait
1	12	.58	.92
2	34	.90	.95
3	23	.50	.59
4	15	.89	.75
Combined	84	.69	.77

than the other three groups. The subjects in Sample 1 were mostly teachers of English and persons who had spent substantial periods of time in the United States, while the subjects in Samples 2 and 4 were university students who were in training to serve as translators and interpreters of English. While the subjects in Sample 3 were knowledgeable about and interested in the United States, they had substantially less experience and proficiency in English.

Construct Validity of the Portuguese STAI

The construct validity of the STAI-PX is currently being evaluated in several different investigations in which the A-State and A-Trait scales were administered under stressful and nonstressful conditions. In one study, the two scales were administered to a group of 17 college students immediately before they took an examination in statistics. The scales were then readministered during a regular class period. The means and standard deviations of the STAI-PX A-State and A-Trait scores obtained on these two occasions are reported in Table 5.

It can be noted in Table 5 that the mean A-State score in the stressful condition was approximately 10 points higher than in the nonstressful condition. The difference between these means was statistically significant ($t = 3.32$, $p < .005$). In contrast, the mean A-Trait scores were essentially the same in both the stressful and nonstressful experimental conditions. These results demonstrated that the STAI-PX A-State scale was sensitive to situational stress, while the A-Trait scale was relatively impervious to situational factors. Similar findings have been reported for the English Form of the STAI in investigations of examination stress (Spielberger et al., 1970).

Further evidence of the construct validity of the Portuguese STAI was demonstrated in a recent study by Kacelnik, Oliveira, and Farias (1975). These investigators tested 30 eighth-grade students in an experimental situation in which cognitive dissonance was induced. The students were required to write arguments in favor of their having to take an unexpected and very difficult exam under low reward conditions. Their scores on the Portuguese STAI A-State and A-Trait scales on this occasion were then compared to their anxiety scores under neutral conditions. The means and

TABLE 5 Mean A-State and A-Trait scores under stressful and
nonstressful conditions

Psychometric property	A-State scores		A-Trait scores	
	Stress	Nonstress	Stress	Nonstress
Mean	45.71	35.35	37.53	37.35
Standard deviation	15.32	9.57	8.13	11.35

TABLE 6 Means and standard deviations for the Portuguese STAI-PX A-State and
A-Trait scales following dissonance induction and under neutral conditions

Psychometric property	A-State scores		A-Trait scores	
	Dissonance	Neutral	Dissonance	Neutral
Mean	64.86	39.63	40.60	41.40
Standard deviation	10.85	13.68	11.88	10.59

standard deviations for the STAI A-State and A-Trait scores obtained in the dissonance and neutral conditions are presented in Table 6. A-State scores were substantially higher after dissonance induction ($t = 6.78$, $p < .001$), whereas A-Trait scores were essentially the same in the dissonance and neutral conditions ($t = .58$).

Taruma, Fernandez, and Paschoal (1975) found significantly higher A-State scores 24 hours before patients underwent minor surgery than when the same patients were discharged from the hospital ($t = 5.89$, $p < .001$). In contrast, the difference in A-Trait scores before and after surgery was not statistically significant. Table 7 presents the means and standard deviations of the A-State and A-Trait scores that were obtained before surgery and upon discharge.

SUMMARY AND CONCLUSIONS

The translation, construction, and preliminary validation of an experimental Portuguese form of the State-Trait Anxiety Inventory has been described in this chapter. The adequacy of the preliminary Portuguese translation was evaluated by Portuguese-English bilingual psychologists, psychiatrists, and linguists, and this preliminary translation was then administered to four samples of bilingual Brazilian students. On the basis of the judgments of experts and the empirically determined psychometric properties of individual items, a final set of 20 A-State and 20 A-Trait items was selected for the experimental form of the Portuguese STAI (STAI-PX).

The psychometric characteristics of the STAI-PX were based on the responses of four samples of Portuguese-English bilingual subjects. Alpha

TABLE 7 Scales for patients 1 day before surgery and upon discharge
from the hospital

	A-State		A-Trait	
	Before surgery	Upon discharge	Before surgery	Upon discharge
Mean	50.83	36.43	44.53	40.63
Standard deviation	13.05	13.72	10.56	9.39

coefficients and item-remainder correlations for individual STAI-PX items were comparable to those reported for the English and Spanish forms of the STAI. Thus, the internal consistency of the STAI-PX A-State and A-Trait scales was considered to be very satisfactory, especially when the difficulty in securing Portuguese-English bilingual subjects was considered.

The equivalence of the Portuguese form and the English STAI was evaluated and found to be acceptable, especially for those samples of bilingual subjects with greater proficiency in English. Further research is planned in which more stringent criteria for bilingualism will be employed. We also plan to test subjects who currently live in Brazil and/or Portugal, but whose native language is English.

The results of several studies of the construct validity of the STAI-PX were also described in this chapter. In these studies, A-State scores were found to be substantially more elevated under stressful conditions than under neutral conditions, whereas A-Trait scores were similar under both conditions. Other studies are currently being conducted to evaluate the construct validity of the Portuguese STAI. Data are presently being collected on large samples of high school and college students in order to provide additional normative information about the psychometric properties of the STAI-PX.

In conclusion, the research findings reported in this chapter provide strong evidence of the usefulness of the experimental Portuguese Form of the STAI as a measure of state and trait anxiety in Portuguese-speaking subjects. It is hoped that the availability of the STAI-PX will stimulate research on stress and anxiety in Brazil and Portugal and that cross-cultural research on these important topics will be facilitated.

REFERENCES

Cronbach, L. J. Coefficient alpha and the internal structure of tests. *Psychometrika*, 1951, *16*, 297–335.

Kacelnik, E., Oliveira, E. S., & Farias, M. E. *Relationships between cognitive dissonance and anxiety*. Unpublished senior research paper. Pontificia Universidade Catolica de Rio de Janeiro, 1975.

Spielberger, C. D. Theory and research on anxiety, In C. D. Spielberger (Ed.), *Anxiety and behavior*. New York: Academic Press, 1966.

Spielberger, C. D. Anxiety as an emotional state. In C. D. Spielberger (Ed.), *Anxiety: Current trends in theory and research* (Vol. 1). New York: Academic Press, 1972.

Spielberger, C. D., Gonzalez-Reigosa, F., Martinez-Urrutia, A., Natalicio, L. F. S., & Natalicio, D. S. Development of the Spanish edition of the State-Trait Anxiety Inventory. *Interamerican Journal of Psychology*, 1971, *5*, 145–157.

Spielberger, C. D., Gorsuch, R. L., & Lushene, R. E. *Manual for the State-Trait Anxiety Inventory*. Palo Alto, Calif.: Consulting Psychologist Press, 1970.

Taruma, H., Fernandez, E., & Paschoal, C. R. *STAI scores of surgical patients, a validation study*. Unpublished senior research paper. Pontificia Universidade Catolica de Rio de Janeiro, 1975.

4

The Development and Validation of a French Form of the State-Trait Anxiety Inventory

Jacques Bergeron
Michel Landry
David Bélanger
Université de Montréal

A series of studies was conducted in developing and validating a French form of the State-Trait Anxiety Inventory (STAI). This work was undertaken at the Université de Montréal with the objective of providing adequate measures of anxiety for use with the French-Canadian cultural group. The STAI was constructed by Spielberger, Gorsuch, and Lushene (1970) to provide reliable, relatively brief, self-report ratings of A-Trait and A-State. Since the usefulness of the STAI has been demonstrated in experimental research on stress and anxiety, it was expected that the development of a French form of this test could provide a suitable instrument for use in our laboratory experiments on stress reactivity and the psychophysiological

Preparation of this paper and related research was supported by the Ministère de l'Education de la Province de Québec (programme FCAC). The authors would like to express their appreciation to Franco Lepore for his assistance in preparing the manuscript.

41

correlates of anxiety. A validated French translation of the STAI with appropriate normative data would also be highly useful for cross-cultural research on bilingualism and for comparisons between the English-speaking and French-speaking populations of Canada.

Through repeated administration of the French form of the STAI A-Trait and A-State scales to several hundred university students, we were able to arrive at more accurate French translations of each scale item, translations that conveyed the appropriate emotional tone. These efforts led to the gradual introduction of slight modifications in individual items to ensure that the meaning of the translated words and idioms was more consistent with the meaning of the English items. Reliability and validity studies were then conducted on additional independent samples of high school students, college freshmen, and other undergraduate college students. Next, normative data were collected from a large sample of college students, taking into consideration sex, socioeconomic level, and the degree of urbanization of the population. The latter two factors had no significant influence on the results.

Another investigation attempted to evaluate the degree of equivalence of the experimental French form and the standard English form of the STAI. Both scales were given on two different occasions, in counterbalanced order, to bilingual subjects enrolled in a graduate course in translation. Finally, in order to evaluate the concurrent validity of the French version of the STAI, correlations were recently obtained between this scale and Cormier's (1962) French edition of Cattell and Scheier's (1961) IPAT Anxiety Scale.

This chapter does not attempt to report in detail the results of each of these studies. Most of the results are in the process of being prepared for publication. Instead, we discuss the findings in a recently conducted experiment in which the results were interesting and intriguing. The findings of this study are presented in the context of a more comprehensive discussion on the meaning and value of the distinction between state and trait anxiety. This experiment will provide an example of the type of results that have been obtained with this French version of the STAI.

This experiment was essentially a study of the reliability and construct validity of our French form of the STAI, using a procedure that, to our knowledge, had no equivalent in the literature at that time. The experimental design, based on two separate testing sessions for each of two different samples of college students, was specifically developed for the purpose of testing the stability of trait anxiety: the A-Trait scale should not be affected by changes in the environment, nor by individual fluctuations in state anxiety, when a neutral situation changes into a stressful one. The experiment was also designed to demonstrate the stability of the state anxiety score over the interval of 2 to 3 weeks for subjects placed in similar emotional conditions. It seemed to us that evaluation of A-Trait stability under conditions of variations in stress and A-State stability over time in the absence of variations in stress conditions would provide an especially meaningful demonstration of the validity of the distinction between anxiety as a transitory emotional state and as a relatively stable personality trait (Cattell & Scheier, 1961; Spielberger, 1966, 1972).

METHOD

The experiment used 267 college students of both sexes from the same school. The subjects were given the French form of the STAI on two occasions with a mean interval of 18 days. At each testing session, the examiner met the subjects in groups of 25 to 30 in their respective classrooms and promised that their answers would remain confidential. The French STAI was then administered with the instructions given in the STAI Test Manual (Spielberger et al., 1970).

The first testing session took place during a regular class; it was identical for all subjects and was defined a priori as a neutral situation. For the second session, the subjects were divided into two groups. Group 1 responded to the questionnaire under a stress condition, the session being held during the 20 minutes immediately preceding an important and stressful examination in physics, a subject about which these students felt particular apprehension. Group 2 consisted of students whose schedule did not carry an exam on that day. For this group, the second session took place under neutral conditions during a regular physics class.

RESULTS

Internal Consistency

In order to study the internal consistency of the French form of the STAI, Kuder-Richardson's Formula 20, as modified by Ferguson (1951) for application to complex scales with multiple-choice items, was used for determining the internal consistency of the responses to the first administration of the scale. With this formula, the proportion of item covariance in relation to the total test variance can be evaluated. The results of this analysis are presented in Table 1 in which it can be noted that the KR-20 coefficient for the A-State scale was .86 for boys and .90 for girls. The

TABLE 1 Internal consistency coefficients (K-R 20) for both scales of the French form of the STAI

	N	A-State	A-Trait
Male	113	.86	.88
Female	154	.90	.89

KR-20 coefficient for the A-Trait scale was .88 and .89, respectively, for boys and girls. These high internal consistency coefficients are very satisfactory and comparable with the alpha coefficients reported in the STAI Test Manual for college students (Spielberger et al., 1970).

For the A-State scale the internal consistency coefficient was .91 for the measures obtained in the neutral situation for both Group 1 and Group 2 in the first administration, and for Group 2 in the second administration. In the stress situation, the coefficient was .95. This may indicate, in accordance with the data of Spielberger et al. (1970), that stress increases the consistency of responses on the A-State scale. The STAI manual reports typically higher alpha reliability coefficients (.92 and .94) when the A-State scale was given under stress conditions than when it was given following a brief period of relaxation training (.89). Also, item-remainder correlation coefficients were higher for individual items when the A-State scale was given under more stressful conditions.

In the present experiment, the internal consistency coefficients for the A-Trait scale could also be compared for the scores obtained in the neutral and stress conditions. It is particularly interesting that these coefficients did not vary between the two conditions, although the internal consistency coefficients for the A-State scale for these same subjects increased in the stress condition.

These results support the conclusion that the French form of the STAI is made up of homogeneous items. Moreover, the items either all measure the same factor or, at least, they measure the same combination of factors in identical proportion. Both the A-Trait and A-State scales are homogeneous, at least functionally, and made up of parallel items since internal consistency is directly proportional to intercorrelations among items. In brief, the scales meet the most basic conditions of reliability.

Test-Retest Reliability

The test-retest reliability of the French form of the STAI was evaluated by means of a Pearson product-moment correlation coefficient. For both the A-State and A-Trait scales, Table 2 gives the correlations found between the neutral and stress sessions for Group 1 and between the two neutral sessions for Group 2. It can be noted that, for both groups, high correlations were obtained for the A-Trait scale, varying from .86 to .89. When compared to stability coefficients for other trait anxiety scales and those reported in the STAI Test Manual, the test-retest correlations for the French form of the STAI are very satisfactory. These results indicate that the A-Trait scale measures the same underlying anxiety factor in spite of the time interval between sessions, and, more significantly, this trait anxiety factor was not influenced by the testing conditions (neutral or stressful situations).

TABLE 2 Test-retest reliability coefficients for
both scales of the French form of the STAI

	N	A-State	A-Trait
Group 1			
Male	79	.43	.87
Female	103	.51	.86
Group 2			
Male	34	.45	.89
Female	51	.66	.88

The lower correlations obtained for the A-State scale (from .43 to .66) were expected and consistent with the definition of a *transitory* emotional state. These correlations between A-State measures were relatively low, even between the two neutral situations (Group 2). Thus, the variation in state anxiety was linked to conditions that influenced the individual student and not to differences between the two experimental situations as such. When compared to the high correlations obtained for the A-Trait scale, the lower correlations for the A-State scale provided evidence of the validity of the distinction that has been made between the concepts of state and trait anxiety. It should be noted that the reliability of the A-State scale may be assessed more appropriately by the internal consistency coefficient, since by definition, its test-retest reliability is likely to be relatively low. Since a high degree of internal consistency of the STAI A-State scale was demonstrated in this study, the French adaptation of the STAI is reliable and comparable to the English form of the STAI and other anxiety measures.

Construct Validity

In evaluating the construct validity of the A-State scale, Group 1 was expected to have higher scores in the stress situation than in the neutral situation, while the A-State scores of Group 2 subjects who were given the A-State scale under two similar neutral conditions were expected to remain unchanged from the first to the second administration. Theoretically, the A-Trait scores of both groups should not vary from one situation to the next.

The A-State data from Group 1 are presented in Table 3. It is quite evident that the introduction of the stressful exam condition caused an important increase in the state anxiety scores. The student *t* test was used to statistically assess significant differences among the mean scores, and the difference between the A-State means for the two sessions was significant at the .001 level for both male and female subjects.

The mean A-State scores for Group 2 subjects who·were given the questionnaire under neutral conditions on two occasions are presented in

TABLE 3 A-State means, standard deviations, and comparisons of means between neutral and stress situations (Group 1)

		Neutral situation		Stress situation		
	N	Mean	SD	Mean	SD	t
Male	79	38.4	8.77	45.2	12.51	5.15*
Female	103	43.3	11.90	49.6	13.44	5.02*

*$p < .001$.

Table 4. The mean for male subjects remained the same, as predicted, but the average A-State scores for females increased on the second administration. Although this increase was not as large as that found for Group 1, it was significant at the .05 level. This result was unexpected and raised questions concerning the validity of the A-State scale that prompted us to replicate the same experiment with other high school, university, and college students of both sexes. In these experiments, we did not find any significant increase in state anxiety in the second neutral administration of the test.

We are led to conclude that the increase of A-State scores of the Group 2 females in the present experiment is due to some factor specific to the experimental conditions. Moreover, the interpretation of the results allows for some interesting, though daring, speculations. The second administration of the test took place, like the first, during a regular physics class, but it occurred just a few days before the quarterly examination on this subject. It is therefore possible that for female subjects, for whom physics is generally a difficult subject, the second testing situation was less neutral than the first. In the context of other results obtained in our laboratory, it would appear that females anticipate sooner and are more sensitive to the stress associated with an examination situation than male subjects. Moreover, it should be pointed out that the increase in state anxiety among the Group 2 females in this study was lower than that noted among the Group 1 female subjects who were given the test immediately before the exam. As a whole, the results seem to indicate

TABLE 4 A-State means, standard deviations, and comparisons of means between two neutral situations (Group 2)

		First situation		Second situation		
	N	Mean	SD	Mean	SD	t
Male	34	42.9	10.75	43.0	10.39	.06
Female	51	42.8	12.16	46.5	13.23	2.51*

*$p < .05$.

TABLE 5 A-Trait means, standard deviations, and comparisons of means between neutral and stress situations (Group 1)

		Neutral situation		Stress situation		
	N	Mean	SD	Mean	SD	*t*
Male	79	41.3	9.52	40.2	9.52	−2.05*
Female	103	43.6	10.77	42.0	10.37	−3.03**

*p < .05.
**p < .01.

that there was a gradual increase in state anxiety among the female population as the moment of examination drew nearer, a phenomenon that was not apparent in the male population. Considered with the fact that the female subjects showed higher correlations than males between the two A-State administrations, as can be seen in Table 2, these results suggest that the so-called emotional instability of women may be only apparent and may be due rather to greater emotional sensitivity that is more readily aroused by the anticipation of an anxiety-laden event.

The A-Trait scale proved to be less stable than predicted, as can be seen from the data presented in Table 5 and Table 6. On the second administration of the tests, the A-Trait scores decreased between 1 and 2 points, but these small decrements were statistically significant in three out of four cases. Other investigators (e.g., Allen, 1970; Edelman, 1970) have reported variations in STAI A-Trait scores, and Taylor (1953) observed a similar phenomenon with the Manifest Anxiety Scale. However, a significant fact in the present experiment is that A-Trait scores declined at the same time that A-State scores increased. Moreover, a detailed analysis of our results (Landry, 1973) showed that the decrease of the A-Trait scores was essentially proportional to the rise of A-State scores. The variations observed by Allen (1970) and Edelman (1970) went in the same direction for both scales.

The observation that the A-Trait and A-State scales varied in opposite directions might be attributed to the subjects' defensive attitude at the time

TABLE 6 A-Trait means, standard deviations, and comparisons of means between two neutral situations (Group 2)

		First situation		Second situation		
	N	Mean	SD	Mean	SD	*t*
Male	34	42.0	10.58	40.8	9.33	−1.38
Female	51	44.1	8.92	42.6	9.41	−2.29*

*p < .05.

they answered the questionnaire. In the stress situation, the subject reacts to the A-State scale first and admits to being very anxious, at that moment, or at least, more anxious than usual. It is therefore normal for him to have a tendency, while responding to the A-Trait scale, to minimize the anxiety he habitually feels. This explanation concurs with Nowlis's (1965) hypothesis that an individual is more likely to be defensive when he reports how he feels *generally* than when he indicates how he feels *here and now*. Defensive attitudes, therefore, do not have the same influence on the A-State and A-Trait scales.

It would be interesting to systematically evaluate how responding to the A-State scale first influences subsequent responses to the A-Trait scale. Spielberger et al. (1970) assume that this influence is negligible, but the results from the present experiment lead us to question the generality of this position. Under stress conditions especially, the order of administration seems to affect A-Trait scores.

The STAI Test Manual reports two experiments by Sachs and Diesenhaus (1969) regarding these problems. These authors found that the order of administration had no effect when the A-State and A-Trait scales were given twice, in counterbalanced order, during two regular class periods. In another experiment, however, they found that mean A-State scores were significantly higher just prior to an exam than during a regular class. Moreover, as reported by Spielberger et al. (1970), they observed "a small but significant decrease in A-Trait scores from the first to the second administration of the scale which the authors interpreted as a general tendency for subjects to obtain lower scores on repeated administrations of personality tests" (p. 15). In the present experiment, we obtained similar decreases in A-Trait scores that appeared to be associated with a rise in A-State scores. These results point to an alternative and/or complementary interpretation of this observed reduction in A-Trait scores in terms of the defensive attitudes that seem to manifest themselves especially in stress conditions.

The presence of such defensive attitudes was well illustrated in a recent experiment by Bucky, Spielberger, and Bale (1972) in which the STAI was administered twice to a large group of Navy flight students. The first testing was done under normal conditions, and then, for the second administration, each student was instructed to respond "as if you had just made your first landing on an aircraft carrier." Unexpectedly, both A-State and A-Trait scores were significantly lower on the second administration of the test. According to Bucky et al. (1972), when the flight students are "confronted with a situation in which they feel particularly vulnerable and where their entire future may be at stake, the defensive tendency to 'look good' increases and anxiety is denied" (p. 276). It is interesting to note that the subjects in this experiment showed a greater decrease in A-Trait than in A-State scores, suggesting that the defensive attitude had a stronger effect on trait anxiety scores.

In a recent review of the literature on anxiety, Zlotowicz (1970) noted that scores on anxiety inventories are affected by the order of administration. When a given test is administered immediately after another one, scores on the second test are generally lower because of an increase in the subjects' defensive attitudes resulting from the administration of the first test. This phenomenon could be present in a test like the STAI when the A-State and A-Trait scales are successively administered since the formal structure and content of these scales may be perceived by subjects as being quite similar. It has been suggested by de Bonis (1973) that the fixed order of administration of the STAI is a weakness. While it seems to us that this conclusion is premature and that more research is needed, nevertheless, our results suggest that precautions must be taken. When the A-Trait scale is administered in a stress situation, people may have a tendency to minimize their trait anxiety, but it remains to be shown whether this tendency depends on the fact that the subject first admitted his anxiety while responding to the A-State scale, or whether this is due to the anxiety-arousing character of the situation itself.

In summary, the analyses of the results in this study provide evidence for the construct validity of the STAI A-State and A-Trait scales. On the one hand, the different meaning, instructions, and format for the A-State and A-Trait scales reduces the possibility of confusing the two scales. On the other hand, the fact that A-State and A-Trait scores moved in opposite directions in the stress situation in this study showed that the subjects distinguished between the two scales and that there were no training or assimilation effects of one upon the other.

The correlations obtained between the A-State and A-Trait scales (varying from .51 to .62) provide further evidence of the validity of the distinction between state and trait anxiety. When considered along with the high internal consistency and differential test-retest stability, these correlations indicate the existence of a moderate relationship between the A-State and A-Trait scales, but not too strong to prevent independent variation in these two forms of anxiety. These findings concur with Spielberger's (1972) theory on this point and, in addition, serve to establish the reliability and construct validity of the French form of the STAI. The results of this experiment also contribute to demonstrating the conceptual value of the distinction between the concepts of state and trait anxiety.

REFERENCES

Allen, G. J. The effect of three conditions of administration on "state" and "trait" measures of anxiety. *Journal of Consulting and Clinical Psychology*, 1970, *34*, 355–359.

Bonis, M. De. Etude de l'anxiété par la méthode des questionnaires. *Revue de Psychologie Appliquée*, 1973, *23*, 15–47.

Bucky, S. F., Spielberger, C. D., & Bale, R. M. Effects of instructions on measures of state and trait anxiety in flight students. *Journal of Applied Psychology*, 1972, *56*, 275–276.

Cattell, R. B., & Scheier, I. H. *The meaning and measurement of neuroticism and anxiety.* New York: Ronald Press, 1961.

Cormier, D. *L'Echelle d'anxiété IPAT.* Montréal: Institut de Recherches Psychologiques, 1962.

Edelman, R. I. Effects of progressive relaxation on autonomic processes. *Journal of Clinical Psychology*, 1970, *26*, 421–425.

Ferguson, G. A. A note on the Kuder-Richardson formula. *Educational and Psychological Measurements*, 1951, *11*, 612–615.

Landry, M. *La fidélité et la validité de l'adaptation française d'un questionnaire d'anxiété.* Unpublished master's thesis, Université de Montréal, 1973.

Nowlis, V. Research with the mood adjective check list. In S. S. Tomkins & C. E. Izard (Eds.), *Affect, cognition and personality.* New York: Springer, 1965.

Sachs, D. A., & Diesenhaus, H. *The effects of stress and order of administration on measures of state and trait anxiety.* Unpublished manuscript, New Mexico State University, 1969.

Spielberger, C. D. Theory and research in anxiety. In C. D. Spielberger (Ed.), *Anxiety and behavior.* New York: Academic Press, 1966.

Spielberger, C. D. Anxiety as an emotional state. In C. D. Spielberger (Ed.), *Anxiety: Current trends in theory and research* (Vol. I). New York: Academic Press, 1972.

Spielberger, C. D., Gorsuch, R. L., & Lushene, R. E. *Manual for the State-Trait Anxiety Inventory.* Palo Alto, Calif.: Consulting Psychologists, 1970.

Taylor, J. A. A personality scale of manifest anxiety. *Journal of Abnormal and Social Psychology*, 1953, *48*, 285–290.

Zlotowicz, M. Origine et perspectives de quelques recherches sur l'anxiété. *Enfance*, 1970, *23*, 113–171.

5

Development of the Turkish Edition of the State-Trait Anxiety Inventory

William A. LeCompte
and
Necla Oner
Hacettepe University, Ankara, Turkey

The pervasiveness of anxiety in modern life is reflected in the multitude of articles and books written on the subject in the past quarter-century (Spielberger, 1972a). If, in fact, anxiety is as important as was first claimed by Freud (1936) and later emphasized in major psychological theories, then a logical question would be to inquire into its universality in human experience. Is anxiety experienced by all people regardless of age, sex, nationality, language, and ability? Or does the experience of anxiety vary from child to adult, from male to female, from the English to the Japanese, and from the bright to the mentally retarded? Answers to these questions can be obtained only after a sound theory of anxiety and appropriate methods of study are achieved.

A systematic evaluation of theoretical issues and empirical findings cannot be obtained as long as there are differences in the conceptual meaning of anxiety and in the methodology used in anxiety research. Although some

The assistance of multilingual members of the Department of Psychology at Hacettepe University with the complexities of translation of the STAI is gratefully acknowledged. The investigators are deeply indebted for their time and efforts.

agreement has been noted in theoretical views and in the methods used to measure anxiety, the fact remains that a meaningful integration of theory and research is still not possible (Spielberger, 1972b). The purpose of the present study was twofold: first, to construct a Turkish anxiety scale to be used in clinical and applied settings, and, second, to facilitate cross-cultural research that will contribute to anxiety theory.

THEORY AND MEASUREMENT OF ANXIETY

An important advance in anxiety theory was an explicit statement of the state-trait distinction by Cattell and Scheier (1961). Later, Spielberger used this distinction in developing his two-factor state-trait theory of anxiety (1966, 1972a, 1972b), and in constructing the State-Trait Anxiety Inventory (STAI) (Spielberger, Gorsuch, & Lushene, 1970). Within the frame of reference provided by Spielberger's theory, earlier research findings indicated that, during the 1950s and early 1960s, anxiety was considered and treated primarily as a personality trait.

The most widely used research instruments for measuring trait anxiety over the past 25 years were the Taylor (1953) Manifest Anxiety Scale (MAS), the Cattell and Scheier (1963) IPAT Anxiety Scale, and the General and Test Anxiety Scales for children and adults developed by Sarason, Davidson, Lighthall, Waite, and Ruebush (1960). More recently, the state-trait distinction has resulted in the construction of scales that measure both state and trait anxiety, such as the Zuckerman (1960) Affect Adjective Check List (AACL) and the Spielberger et al. (1970) State-Trait Anxiety Inventory (STAI).

According to Spielberger's (1966, 1972b) trait-state anxiety theory, state and trait anxiety are conceptually distinguished from one another and from the psychological defenses that serve to protect the individual from anxiety. State anxiety (A-State) is a transitory condition of emotional arousal, a psychobiological affective phenomenon with subjective (phenomenological) and physiological concomitants. This definition of A-State fits Freud's original conception of anxiety as a complex emotional state that can be described by conscious feelings of apprehension and tension, accompanied by activation of the autonomic nervous system. Trait anxiety (A-Trait) is defined as general anxiety proneness, a vulnerability or predisposition to react to different kinds of stressors with elevations in state anxiety. Differences in A-Trait can be inferred from the frequency and the intensity of elevations in state anxiety over time. Individuals high in A-Trait experience elevations in A-State more often, and in a wider variety of situations, than those with low A-Trait. High A-Trait persons tend to perceive relatively neutral situations as threatening and ego-involving.

Research findings generally support the state-trait conceptualization of anxiety and the relationship between A-Trait and A-State. Using Spielberger's STAI and other scales it has been found that individuals high and low in

A-Trait differ in the way they react to psychological stress in evaluative interpersonal situations that pose some threat to self-esteem. However, the two groups do not differ in their reactions to physical dangers. Experimental findings are also consistent with the theoretical expectations that direct or implied ego threats or threats of failure will induce greater elevations in level of A-State for high A-Trait persons than for those who are low in A-Trait. Under failure-feedback conditions, high A-Trait subjects perform less well on learning and concept attainment tasks (Denny, 1966; Spielberger, 1966) and show higher A-State elevations on such tasks (Auerbach, 1974; Hodges, 1968; McAdoo, 1969) than do low A-Trait subjects. Similar results were obtained for performance on intelligence tests (Martinez-Urrutia & Spielberger, 1973), the learning of anagrams (Sarason, 1973) and decimals (Oner, 1972), and for academic achievement (Mandler & Sarason, 1952; Sarason et al., 1960; Spielberger, 1962, 1966).

In experiments where stress was defined by blowing a balloon to bursting (Lamb, 1973) or by a painful but safe electric shock (Hodges, 1968), it was demonstrated that increases in A-State under threat of physical pain or danger was unrelated to level of A-Trait. Hodges and Felling (1970) and Lamb (1973) also failed to find any relationship between A-Trait and A-State under experimental conditions involving physical stress, but in conditions involving psychological stress or threats to self-esteem (such as giving a speech as in Lamb's study), high A-Trait subjects showed greater increases in A-State than subjects who were low in A-Trait.

In two recent studies in which emotional reactions to surgery were measured, elevations in A-State scores were found 1 day before surgery (Spielberger, Auerbach, Wadsworth, Dunn, & Taulbee, 1973), or a day after surgery (Chapman & Cox, 1975) and subsequently declined for all patients 3 to 7 days following surgery. In both studies, high A-Trait patients were consistently higher in A-State than low A-Trait patients, before and after surgery. While Spielberger, Auerbach, Wadsworth, Dunn, & Taulbee (1973) found that threat of surgery seemed to have a similar impact on high and low A-Trait patients, Chapman and Cox (1975) found that changes in A-State elevations 3 days following surgery was a function of A-Trait. Differences between the high and low A-Trait subjects over three testing periods (presurgery, first and third days after surgery) were significant ($p < .001$).

Inconsistencies or differences in research findings suggest caution in generalizing the impact of physical stressors for people who differ in A-Trait. In his book, *Anxiety: Current Trends in Theory and Research* (Volume I), Spielberger stated his concern that

> It is tempting to generalize that persons high in A-Trait do not perceive physical dangers or physical pain to be any more threatening than do individuals who are low in A-Trait, but there is not yet sufficient evidence to justify this conclusion, and there is also some evidence to the contrary. (1972b, p. 42)

A review of research based on the state-trait conception of anxiety is encouraging to researchers in quest of an answer to the question of the universality of anxiety. With an instrument such as the State-Trait Anxiety Inventory (STAI), cross-cultural comparisons are possible. This scale has been used extensively in the United States for research, as well as for counseling and clinical purposes, with adolescents and adults over the past 6 years or so. The reliability of the STAI, its criterion-related and construct validity, the simplicity of the items and ease of administration led the present writers to select the STAI for Turkish adaptation. The STAI has the additional advantage of having already been adapted into Spanish, French, German, Italian, Swedish, Hindi, Hebrew, and several other languages as well.

In the development and standardization of the STAI, more than 6,000 subjects were tested, including high school and college students, young male prisoners, and psychiatric and general medical and surgical patients. The STAI consists of a 20-item A-State scale and a 20-item A-Trait scale. The individual responds to the A-State scale according to how he feels *at the moment.* In responding to the A-Trait scale, the individual is asked to indicate how he *generally* feels. It takes 10 to 15 minutes for college students to complete both scales, and repeated administrations of either scale require less time.

DEVELOPMENT OF THE TURKISH STATE-TRAIT ANXIETY INVENTORY

Four aspects of the development and construction of the Turkish form of the STAI will be reported in this chapter: translation of the English version into Turkish; demonstration of equivalence in meaning between the English and Turkish versions; report of data relevant to the reliability and validity of the Turkish STAI; and the presentation of statistical norms for Turkish students on state and trait anxiety. This chapter is intended as a progress report of on-going research, and the research on the last two aspects is by no means complete. It was felt, however, that there was now sufficient information on the Turkish version of the STAI to make our findings available to professional workers.

Translation Procedures

A number of difficulties were encountered in translating the test items into Turkish. The technique of back-translation was used informally in this research, although no systematic attempt at decentering was made.[1] In this approach to test development, translation of individual items are given to

---

[1] The decentering technique involves altering the original material to correspond to the translated version after each round of translation and back-translation. This technique is of doubtful value in the case of standardized tests with similar items.

another worker who then translates the material back into the original language and the original English version is then compared with the back-translation for similarity. Because of the high number of idioms in the English STAI (e.g., "high-strung," "rattled," "calm, cool and collected") frequent consultation with language experts was necessary.[2] At this phase of the research, extensive pilot testing was also involved, in which bilingual students and language experts were given individual items in both languages and asked to make judgments of similarity.

Demonstration of Transliteral Equivalence of Meaning

The need for an empirical or performance criterion of equivalence in the meaning of test materials that have been translated to another language is now recognized by an increasing number of researchers (e.g., Brislin, 1970). Expert opinion as to the similarity of written material appears to be a necessary step, but this is not sufficient for the demonstration of equivalence. Ideally, some behavioral evidence is required to demonstrate that individuals react in similar ways whether they are exposed to the translated material or to the same item in the original language. In the case of instructions, for example, an investigator can ask subjects to give clearly discriminable responses that demonstrate a similar degree of understanding (e.g., Allport & Pettigrew, 1957).

In the development of the Turkish STAI, bilingual respondents were used, and the criterion of equivalence was defined as obtaining similar scores on the material, whether presented in English or in Turkish. The STAI A-State and A-Trait scales were each divided randomly into two parts, and the test items were then arranged into four separate forms, as follows: Kod A contained all 40 items in English, and Kod B contained all 40 items in Turkish. Kod C had 10 items on both the state and the trait scales rendered into Turkish, and the remaining 10 items of each scale in English. Finally, Kod D contained the converse sequence of English and Turkish items to those that were presented in Kod C.

The respondents for this aspect of the research consisted of samples of 120 girls from Izmir College and 80 boys from Tarsus College. In both samples, the subjects were Turkish adolescents (17 to 19 years old) attending schools in which the language of instruction was English, thus guaranteeing an adequate comprehension of English. In both samples, the testing was done by distributing the forms randomly, with the restriction that equal numbers of respondents received each of the four forms. Approximately 2 weeks after the first administration, respondents who had previously received Kod A were presented with Kod B and vice versa. Similarly, respondents previously receiving

[2] The writers are grateful to Selahattin Erturk, Department of Education, Hacettepe University, for his untiring contributions to the translation of the STAI into Turkish and to the revising of individual items.

TABLE 1 Data collection from bilingual samples

Respondents	Form for pretest	Form for posttest
20 boys 30 girls	Kod A	Kod B
20 boys 30 girls	Kod B	Kod A
20 boys 30 girls	Kod C	Kod D
20 boys 30 girls	Kod D	Kod C

Note. See text for definition of samples of respondents and description of Forms. Small differences between planned sample sizes and those reported in Table 2 reflect attendance differences on the days tests were administered.

Kod C were administered Kod D on retest, and vice versa. The research design, as illustrated in Table 1, provides estimates of cross-language equivalence by allowing the calculation of reliability coefficients in which no item is presented more than once in the same language to the same respondent.

Reliability and Validity of the Turkish STAI

Data on internal consistency and stability of scores on the Turkish scales were obtained with monolingual samples, both for the purpose of evaluating the results of the cross-language study just described and for investigating the stability of anxiety scores over short and long time intervals. A new Turkish form containing changes in four items -that had shown poor results in the data from the bilingual samples was generated and administered to a total of five separate samples at three different universities in Ankara. The following list describes the size and nature of each of these samples and the time interval between pre- and posttests.

1. University students ($N = 59$) from the Psychology Department of Hacettepe University. Both male and female students were tested across a 10-day interval.
2. Students from the War College ($N = 79$). Only males were tested across a 15-day interval.
3. Students from the War College ($N = 81$). Only males were tested across a 30-day interval.
4. Students from the Department of Social Sciences at Middle East Technical University ($N = 18$). Both males and females were tested across a 120-day interval.

5. Students from the Psychology Department of Hacettepe University ($N = 28$). Both males and females were tested across a 365-day interval.

All testing was carried out during the 1974–1975 academic year. For the most part, the tests were administered to intact classroom groups. Although the variety among these 265 respondents was considerable, all of the subjects were students in higher education in late adolescence or early adulthood (i.e., 19- to 22-year-olds).

If the time interval between the first test and the retest is used to order these groups, higher correlations should be obtained for the samples retested with less intervening time. Hence, a monotonic decrease in the size of the test-retest correlations was expected for the A-Trait scores when the samples were ordered from one to five. Since state anxiety is defined as a momentary emotional state that is subject to fluctuation over time, no prediction is possible for test-retest correlations of A-State scores over time. Because of this important difference in the concepts of state and trait anxiety, two interesting predictions relating to the construct validity of the Turkish STAI can be generated: first, with each of the five samples, A-State reliability correlations should be lower than A-Trait correlations; and second, across the five samples there should be more variability in A-State than in A-Trait correlations. Results consistent with these hypotheses have been obtained in other cultures.

Normative Data for Turkish Adolescents

The seven samples described above comprised a total of 450 students in late adolescence and early adulthood. Despite the heterogeneous nature of these samples and the special characteristics of others (e.g., bilingualism), a combined group of more than 400 respondents is probably large enough to make some general statements as to what constitutes high and low anxiety in Turkish adolescents and young adults. In view of the lack of younger respondents in the existing samples, an additional large sample of 15- and 16-year-old adolescents was added to the data base (424 boys, 222 girls). In selecting this sample, an effort was made to collect data from schools located in smaller towns with students who were different in socioeconomic status from the respondents in the Ankara schools. In all, then, the normative data on the anxiety levels of Turkish adolescents and young adults was based on a subject pool of over 950 cases receiving the Turkish STAI on the first administration.

CHARACTERISTICS OF THE TURKISH STAI

Adequacy of Translation

Approximately three cycles of translation and back-translation were required to develop adequate Turkish translations of the 40 STAI items.

Rather than construct Turkish idioms to replace those in the English version that were found to be untranslatable (for example, "I feel blue."), an alternative statement of the appropriate emotional state was often found to be preferable ("I feel sad."). Occasionally, this required footnoting appropriate Turkish words in cases where the respondents in the bilingual samples might be unable to understand an English idiom (for example, footnoting the Turkish word for "tension" as a clarification of the English phrase "high-strung").

Test administrators were instructed to record cases of confusion over words. The fact that there were only a few occurrences of confusion testifies to the adequacy of the translation. More difficulty arose over differences in set that were supposed to be induced by the separate instructions for the A-State and the A-Trait scales. During the early administrations of the scales, the investigators suspected that respondents were not differentiating between these two scales, but rather were treating all 40 items with the A-State set. This problem was avoided by passing out the two scales separately and emphasizing that they constituted different tests. Despite the lack of any widely accepted term in Turkish for those occasions in which an English speaker would describe his subjective state as "feeling anxious," Turkish respondents were not strangers to the specific items in the STAI scales.

Transliteral Equivalence of Meaning

In order to evaluate the degree to which the translated scales functioned as equivalent stimuli for bilingual Turks, means for the samples taking each form of the STAI were calculated and compared. Composite means for the split-language forms (Kods C and D) were computed by combining the 10 items answered in Turkish by one group with the remaining 10 items answered in Turkish by the comparable group receiving the form in which the items were reversed, and doing likewise in the case of the English items. The data in Table 2 show the results of these comparisons.

Inspection of the data in Table 2 indicates that the English and Turkish forms of the STAI were answered quite similarly by the bilingual students. On the state anxiety scale, the English and Turkish means are quite similar. There is an interesting tendency for the students in the bilingual sample to obtain higher scores on the English items of the trait anxiety scale than on the Turkish version of the same items. Critical ratios of the mean differences for females are significant for both one-language and split-language comparisons and are also significant for the one-language forms for males. Thus, there is a systematic tendency for female respondents, especially, to rate themselves as generally more anxious in response to items phrased in English than to the same items phrased in Turkish.

When the data from the second administration 2 weeks later were compared with test scores from the first administration, the similarities of the

TABLE 2 Means for single-language forms and comparable composite means for split-language forms for the Turkish and English editions of the STAI

Nature of sample	A-Trait		A-State	
	Turkish	English	Turkish	English
Females taking split-language forms (*N* = 54)	39.93**	43.12	41.32	40.14
Males taking split-language forms (*N* = 42)	39.29	39.90	40.63	38.98
Females taking one-language forms (*N* = 60)	39.13**	43.76	41.97	41.45
Males taking one-language forms (*N* = 40)	39.76**	41.80	35.33**	40.70
Grand mean	39.32*	42.15	39.81	40.32

Note: ⌐⌐ refers to the set of means being compared.

*p < .05, two-tailed *t*-test for independent samples.

**p < .01, two-tailed *t*-test for independent samples.

means across language of administration became even more striking. These data are presented in Table 3 for each of the eight groups in the design. In these comparisons, where each respondent was his own control in a counterbalanced design, the tendency for the A-Trait means on the English edition to be elevated was again apparent. With no exceptions, the mean for A-Trait on the English edition was higher than its counterpart on the Turkish edition of the test. No such trend was apparent when the English and Turkish editions of the A-State means for each group were compared.

Inspection of the grand means indicates that the mean for the A-Trait scale, English edition, was higher than for any of the other three A-Trait

TABLE 3 Comparisons between means of STAI scores of bilingual respondents over an average of 2-weeks

Sex and experimental condition of sample	A-Trait means		A-State means	
	Turkish	English	Turkish	English
Female, English-Turkish	40.93	43.76	43.00	41.45
Female, Turkish-English	39.13	40.10	41.97	41.50
Female, split-language I	40.35	42.57	42.77	40.84
Female, split-language II	41.76	41.95	39.22	39.07
Male, English-Turkish	40.75	41.80	41.50	40.70
Male, Turkish-English	38.76	41.33	35.33	41.19
Male, split-language I	38.47	39.24	39.37	39.11
Male, split-language II	38.72	39.23	40.31	40.25
Grand means	39.86	41.25	40.43	40.51

means. However, none of these differences were significant in themselves; it was only when the overall trend of the data was considered that the minor elevations in trait means for the English edition of the STAI became relevant. No other trends appeared in the comparisons of means; neither order nor sex effects were present. In fact, the overall impression from these data was that cf a high degree of consistency.

Evidence of the internal consistency of the Turkish STAI was further investigated through the use of alpha coefficients. This measure reflects the degree of reliability of the items in a scale in terms of the amount of overlapping variance. It is thus a generalized form of the Kuder-Richardson Formula 20 for dichotomous items (Cronbach, 1951). Among the bilingual respondents receiving the Turkish STAI on the first administration, alpha coefficients for the state anxiety scale were .96 for females and .94 for males. For the trait anxiety scale, the alpha coefficients were .83 for females and .87 for males. These figures are quite high, indicating that the Turkish test items were quite homogeneous in their contributions of variance to the total scale scores. The corresponding alpha coefficients for the groups receiving the English edition of the STAI A-State scale on the first administration were .88 and .87 for female and male students, respectively, and .85 for both females and males on A-Trait.

In general, respondents were more consistent on the Turkish A-State scale than on any of the other three combinations. For respondents receiving the split-language forms, high alphas on the A-State form were obtained, with values ranging from .87 to .90. The responses were less consistent for the A-Trait form, where the coefficients ranged from .65 to .88. On the second administration, the alpha coefficients were high for every group, ranging from .90 to .96 on A-State and from .81 to .90 on A-Trait. Although the alphas varied over what seems to be a reasonably high range, it should be noted that the respondents were less consistent on the trait scales than on the state scales, regardless of sex, order of presentation, or language of the test.

An item analysis was performed with the data from the 100 respondents in the bilingual sample to whom single-language tests were administered. Item-remainder correlations were also calculated separately for each English and Turkish item. This index measures the degree to which the variance associated with a particular item covaries with total score variance, after the variance for the particular item under consideration has been removed from the total score variance. Item-remainder correlations are a useful measure for identifying items that do not contribute positively (i.e., correlate significantly) to the total score. In the present context, the item-remainder correlations also helped to clarify the hypothesized differences in consistency between A-State and A-Trait alpha coefficients.

Table 4 reports the item-remainder correlations for the 20 A-Trait items. Results for the Turkish form of the STAI can be directly compared with the same item in the English version. Inspection of the data in Table

TABLE 4 Item-remainder correlations for the Turkish and English editions of the STAI

Item number	State item r		Item number	Trait item r	
	Turkish	English		Turkish	English
1	.80	.64	21	.29[a]	.56
2	.73	.57	22	.50	.50
3	.84	.48	23	.56	.58
4	.42	.52	24	.34	.33
5	.78	.56	25	.45	.50
6	.85	.75	26	.61	.47
7	.60	.62	27	.62	.65
8	.65	.55	28	.56	.69
9	.76	.39	29	.49	.58
10	.74	.54	30	.61	.52
11	.55	.52	31	.05[a]	.56
12	.83	.70	32	.64	.50
13	.83	.71	33	.65	.54
14	.83	.65	34	.44	.40
15	.81	.63	35	.59	.68
16	.67	.49	36	.72	.45
17	.84	.65	37	.45	.60
18	.71	.65	38	.53	.63
19	.69	.53	39	.41	.40
20	.44[a]	.53	40	.62	.59

[a]After revision, these three items all gave rise to acceptably high item-remainder correlations in later samples. For example, with 15-year-olds, the data for item 20 (A-State) were .70, and for items 21 and 31 (A-Trait) were .56 and .39, respectively.

4 shows that nearly all of the item-remainder correlations were high and positive. The entire set, with the single exception of Turkish item 31 on the trait scale, were significantly higher than zero beyond the 1 percent level of confidence. For the state scale the item-remainder correlations for 17 out of 20 items were higher in the Turkish form than in the English version, an outcome that would occur by chance less than one time in a thousand if the true item correlations of the two editions were equal. For the A-Trait items, however, 8 items have higher item-remainder correlations in the Turkish form, 11 items have higher correlations in the English version, and 1 item shows no difference, a distribution that would be expected by chance.

Clearly, the Turkish A-State scale items are more homogeneous than those for the A-Trait scale. If these differences were due to language ability alone, they should have appeared on both state and trait scales. Similarly, if they derived from a more adequate translation of the state than of the trait scale items, one would have expected higher correlations for *both* English and Turkish forms of the state scale than for the trait scale. In fact, both scales seem adequately translated, with the exception of items 21 and 31 of the trait scale. Both of these items (plus item 20 of the state scale) were revised, and, in every case, the revised item produced acceptably high item-remainder correlations. The revised form was subsequently used to gather most of the data that are reported in the two following sections in which test-retest reliability and statistical norms for Turkish adolescents are discussed.

Score Stability and Construct Validity of the Turkish STAI

The degree to which scores were stable for individuals was investigated by administering the scales twice to five different groups, allowing, in each case, a different interval of time to pass before the second administration. The amount of time between test and retest ranged from 10 days to a year. It was hoped that this method of evaluating stability would permit greater generalization about test score reliability than is usually possible when data are collected around one or two points in time. In addition, the nature of the hypothesized differences between state and trait anxiety lead to specific predictions that could be investigated more precisely when multiple groups and different time periods between test and retest were employed.

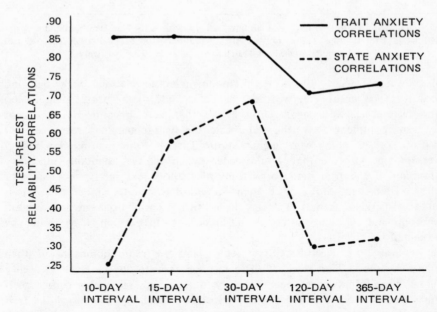

FIGURE 1   Reliability data on the Turkish STAI from five samples arranged according to the time between pre- and posttest.

Test-retest correlations were computed for each group, and these correlations are graphically displayed in Figure 1. It is clear that A-Trait scores were quite stable over time. Test-retest correlations were above .85 during the entire first month after the initial testing. Sometime between 1 month and 4 months, the reliability dropped; for the group that was retested after 4 months, the test-retest reliability remained at .73. In contrast, the test-retest data for A-State were quite different. The individual correlations ranged from a low of .26 to a high of .68, with no discernable pattern of increase or decrease over time.

The test-retest data obtained for the Turkish STAI are quite consistent with differences between the A-State and A-Trait scales as they have been conceptualized for the English STAI. A-Trait scores are designed to tap relatively enduring individual differences in dispositions to experience anxiety, whereas A-State scores measure momentary or transitory feelings of tension, worry, nervousness, and apprehension. The results displayed in Figure 1 provide construct validation for the notion of two types of anxiety. Across the five samples, in no case does the test-retest correlation for A-State equal or exceed that for A-Trait, and the variability for the former is far greater than that for all the A-Trait correlations. The distribution of test-retest correlations in Figure 1 for the A-State scale had a variance of .036 and a range of 5.437, while the corresponding data for A-Trait were .007 and 2.779. Thus, the variance for the A-State correlations was over five times as large as the A-Trait variance, and the range was greater than 2.5 times that of the A-Trait correlations.

Statistical Norms for Turkish Students

In addition to the samples described in the preceding section, an additional group of 15- to 16-year-old students were given the Turkish STAI. This latter group was included to determine whether younger adolescents could understand the scales and to investigate possible changes in STAI scores with age. Table 5 summarizes the data for the 15- to 16-year-old sample and compares it with the descriptive data obtained for the older samples during the first administrations of the STAI.

In Table 5, it may be noted that sex differences were not pronounced. Furthermore, age differences that can be inferred by comparing the 15- to 16-year-old high school students with War College and university students were not strong. Since no difficulties were encountered in administering the scales to the younger age group, the STAI appears to be appropriate for adolescents as well as for young adults. Based on the composite statistics given at the bottom of Table 5, A-Trait scores above 60 and A-State scores above 57 are suggested as cutting points for screening purposes.

TABLE 5 Statistical norms on state and trait anxiety for Turkish adolescents

Description of sample	N	A-Trait		A-State	
		Mean	S.D.	Mean	S.D.
15- to 16-year-old males	424	39.77	9.67	39.74	7.84
15- to 16-year-old females	222	39.81	10.82	41.51	9.54
War College students	160	41.26	11.12	40.89	9.06
University students	143	40.38	11.70	39.41	8.48
Averages	(949)	40.12	10.52	40.30	8.57

Confidence intervals for means at 99 percent

A-Trait

$$40.12 + (2.576)\frac{10.52}{\sqrt{949}}$$

$$39.24 < M < 41.00$$

A-State

$$40.30 + (2.576)\frac{8.57}{\sqrt{949}}$$

$$39.58 < M < 41.02$$

DISCUSSION

The research with bilingual students has provided adequate evidence of equivalence in meaning for the Turkish and the English forms of the STAI, and the reliability and construct validity of this scale has been established with five different samples. The question may now be raised as to how do the overall norms compare with those of other cultures? To date, published normative data are available on American, Spanish, and Hindi samples, although the latter two samples are quite small relative to the American and Turkish samples. For comparative purposes, confidence intervals were constructed around the grand means given in Table 5. The results of this procedure indicated that, at the .995 level of confidence, the general mean for the A-Trait scale falls within a range of 39.24 to 41.00, and for A-State between 39.58 and 41.02. Thus, to the extent that the data from other cultures fall outside these ranges, one may suspect that the samples came from different populations with regard to the anxiety parameter.

Considering first the American data, based on over 1,800 cases described in the STAI Test Manual (Spielberger et al., 1970, p. 8), both the A-Trait and the A-State means fall well below the ranges given for the Turkish data. By this criterion, Turkish adolescents and young adults seem to be somewhat more anxious than the Americans. Turning to the Spanish sample (actually based on 48 Puerto Rican bilingual students), the mean for the A-Trait scale is considerably below the confidence band cited earlier, but that for A-State is within the Turkish range (Spielberger, Gonzalez-Reigosa, & Martinez-Urrutia, 1971, pp. 152–153). The authors of that study attribute the observed elevation in the A-State mean for the Puerto Rican student on the first administration of this scale to the fact that subjects "who are not accustomed to responding to personality tests might be higher in transitory anxiety (A-State) when they are evaluated for the first time than on a subsequent evaluation in a similar experimental situation" (p. 154). This hypothesis can be applied to the Turkish sample as well, but fails to explain either the elevation in A-Trait or the consistently higher means of the Turkish samples when they were retested.

Turning to the Hindi sample (Spielberger, Sharma, & Singh, 1973), inspection of the data indicates that the A-Trait mean is within the range of the Turkish data but that the A-State mean is considerably below the bottom limit of the confidence interval for the Turkish mean. Thus, the order of the A-Trait mean scores for the four countries, from low to high, is Spanish, American, Hindi, and Turkish. The corresponding ranking for A-State means, from low to high, is Hindi, American, with a tie between Turkish and Spanish. Although the A-Trait mean in the Hindi sample is within the range of the Turkish A-Trait mean, and the A-State mean in the Spanish sample is within the range of the Turkish A-State mean, there seems to be no question that the Turkish sample is *consistently* higher than any of the other countries in anxiety. The other countries either fall back to a lower score on retesting, as was the case with the Spanish sample, and/or obtain elevated scores on one scale only, as was the case with the Hindi sample.

The Spanish and Hindi data are remarkably similar in other respects to the Turkish data. Item-remainder correlations for all three of these countries were generally higher than those reported in the STAI Test Manual for American subjects. Alpha coefficients of internal consistency and test-retest correlations with the A-Trait scale scores were acceptably high in all four cultures. The uniformity of these other parameters seems to compensate for the minor differences in mean scores described earlier.

Assuming that the greater anxiety of the Turkish respondents is not artifactual, how is it to be explained? The simplest explanation is to postulate a general main effect of culture in which Turks appear to be more anxiety-ridden. Such an assumption, however, would seem to be of little use in understanding the dynamics of anxiety and might even function to hinder further research.

A more fruitful approach might be to identify various aspects of the testing situation that possibly cause respondents to react with higher anxiety, and then vary them within a given culture. An excellent place to start such a research program would be within the education institutions in which the testing was done. If Turks feel more anxious within the school setting than respondents from other nations do, the elevation of scores on the Turkish STAI scales might be a predictable consequence.

In any case, the present study has demonstrated that the Turkish STAI provides internally consistent and reliable scales for assessing state and trait anxiety in Turkey. It is hoped that the availability of this instrument may stimulate research on anxiety in Turkey.

SUMMARY

This chapter described a set of interrelated studies focusing on the translation, equivalence, reliability, validity, and standardization of the Turkish edition of the State-Trait Anxiety Inventory (STAI). Beginning with a brief summary of the research literature on anxiety, the authors argued that the nature and function of anxiety in Turkey is similar to that observed in Western countries. The Turkish edition of the STAI was introduced and its equivalence with the English STAI was shown in an experimental study using 200 bilingual respondents. Results of this study showed that the Turkish STAI was quite comparable with the English version. Apparently, anxiety exists as an emotional state at a nonverbal level and can be assessed in bilingual respondents using both Turkish and English items.

Following the study of transliteral equivalence, an extensive investigation of test-retest reliability of the Turkish STAI was undertaken using five different samples. Each sample was tested twice, with a different time interval between test administrations, ranging from 10 days to an entire year. Data from this study revealed acceptably high and stable test-retest reliability for the A-Trait scores and a predictably low and fluctuating reliability for the A-State scores over time. The contrast between the results for the two types of anxiety scores with the same respondents was interpreted as providing evidence for the construct validity of the Turkish STAI. A final sample of 646 adolescents was combined with the previous data to generate norms for Turkish adolescents and young adults.

REFERENCES

Allport, G. W., & Pettigrew, T. F. Cultural influence in the perception of movement: The trapezoidal illusion among Zulus. *Journal of Abnormal and Social Psychology*, 1957, *55*, 104–113.

Auerbach, S. M. Anxiety and time estimation: A failure to replicate Felix. *Journal of Genetic Psychology*, 1974, *124*, 187–196.

Brislin, R. W. Back-translation for cross-cultural research. *Journal of Cross-Cultural Psychology*, 1970, *1*, 185–216.

Cattell, R. B., & Scheier, I. H. *The meaning and measurement of neuroticism and anxiety.* New York: Ronald Press, 1961.

Cattell, R. B., & Scheier, I. H. *Handbook for the IPAT Anxiety Scale* (2nd ed.). Champaign, Ill.: Institute for Personality and Ability Testing, 1963.

Chapman, R. C., & Cox, G. B. *Pain, anxiety and depression surrounding elective surgery: A multivariate comparison of abdominal surgery with kidney donors and recipients.* Paper presented at the meeting of the NATO Conference on Dimensions of Anxiety and Stress, Oslo, Norway, 1975.

Cronbach, L. J. Coefficient alpha and the internal structure of tests. *Psychometrika*, 1951, *16*, 297–334.

Denny, J. P. The effects of anxiety and intelligence on concept formation. *Journal of Experimental Psychology*, 1966, *72*, 596–602.

Freud, S. *The problem of anxiety.* New York: Norton, 1936.

Hodges, W. F. Effects of ego threat and threat of pain on state anxiety. *Journal of Personality and Social Psychology*, 1968, *8*, 363–372.

Hodges, W. F., & Felling, J. P. Types of stressful situations and their relation to trait anxiety and sex. *Journal of Consulting and Clinical Psychology*, 1970, *34*, 333–337.

Lamb, D. H. The effects of two stressors on state anxiety for students who differ in trait anxiety. *Journal of Research in Personality*, 1973, *7*, 116–126.

Mandler, G., & Sarason, S. B. A study of anxiety and learning. *Journal of Abnormal and Social Psychology*, 1952, *47*, 166–173.

Martinez-Urrutia, A., & Spielberger, C. D. Trait anxiety and intelligence. *Interamerican Journal of Psychology*, 1973, *7*, 199–213.

McAdoo, W. C. *The effects of success and failure feedback on A-State for subjects who differ in A-trait.* Unpublished doctoral dissertation. Florida State University, 1969.

Oner, N. P. Impact of teacher behavior and teaching technique on learning by anxious children. (Doctoral dissertation, University of Minnesota, 1971). *Dissertation Abstracts International*, 1972, *32*, 6212A.

Sarason, I. G. Test anxiety and social influence. *Journal of Personality*, 1973, *41*, 261–271.

Sarason, S. B., Davidson, K. S., Lighthall, F. F., Waite, R. R., & Ruebush, K. B. *Anxiety in elementary school children: A research report.* New York: John Wiley, 1960.

Scheier, I. H., Cattell, R. B., & Horn, J. L. Objective test for factor U. I. 23: Its measurement and its relation to clinically-judged neuroticism. *Journal of Clinical Psychology*, 1960, *16*, 135–145.

Spielberger, C. D. The effects of manifest anxiety on the academic achievement of college students. *Mental Hygiene*, 1962, *46*, 420–426.

Spielberger, C. D. Theory and research on anxiety. In C. D. Spielberger (Ed.), *Anxiety and behavior.* New York: Academic Press, 1966.

Spielberger, C. D. Anxiety as an emotional state. In C. D. Spielberger (Ed.), *Anxiety: Current trends in theory and research* (Vol. 1). New York: Academic Press, 1972. (a)

Spielberger, C. D. Conceptual and methodological issues in anxiety research. In C. D. Spielberger (Ed.), *Anxiety: Current trends in theory and research* (Vol. 2). New York: Academic Press, 1972. (b)

Spielberger, C. D., Auerbach, S. M., Wadsworth, A. P., Dunn, T. M., & Taulbee, E. S. Emotional reactions to surgery. *Journal of Consulting and Clinical Psychology*, 1973, *40*, 33–38.

Spielberger, C. D., Gonzales-Reigosa, F., & Martinez-Urrutia, A. Development of the Spanish edition of the State-Trait Anxiety Inventory. *Interamerican Journal of Psychology*, 1971, *5*, 145–157.

Spielberger, C. D., Gorsuch, R. L., & Lushene, R. E. *Manual for the State-Trait Anxiety Inventory.* Palo Alto, Calif.: Consulting Psychologist Press, 1970.

Spielberger, C. D., Sharma, S., & Singh, M. Development of the Hindi edition of the State-Trait Anxiety Inventory. *Indian Journal of Psychology*, 1973, *48*, 11–20.

Taylor, J. A. A personality scale of manifest anxiety. *Journal of Abnormal and Social Psychology*, 1953, *48*, 285–290.

Zuckerman, M. The development of an affect adjective check list for the measurement of anxiety. *Journal of Consulting Psychology*, 1960, *24*, 457–462.

6

Development and Validation of the Spanish Form of the State-Trait Anxiety Inventory for Children (IDAREN)

José J. Bauermeister
University of Puerto Rico

Blanca Villamil Forastieri
College of the Sacred Heart

Charles D. Spielberger
University of South Florida

Anxiety is a central explanatory concept in almost all contemporary theories of personality. While empirical research on anxiety has increased

The authors gratefully acknowledge the assistance and cooperation of Ana M. Carrillo, Blanca González, Carmen A. Juliá, and María Ortiz in the data collection and analysis phases of this research. Thanks are also due to Eduardo Forastieri, Arcadio Díaz Quiñones, Marta Traba, Edwin Figueroa, Eduardo Rivera Medina, Carlos Guevara, Myrna Sessman, and Alice Silvey for their recommendations and advice in the translation of the IDAREN. Copies of the IDAREN test form and manual will be available in the near future from El Manual Moderno, S.A., Av. Sonora 206, México 11, D.F. Correspondence concerning this chapter should be sent to José J. Bauermeister, Psychology Department, University of Puerto Rico, Río Piedras, Puerto Rico 00931, or Charles D. Spielberger, Psychology Department, University of South Florida, Tampa, Florida 33620.

dramatically over the past quarter-century, it is generally acknowledged that anxiety research is characterized by contradictory findings. Spielberger (1966, 1972a, 1972b) has argued that ambiguity and semantic confusion arise from the more or less indiscriminate use of the term *anxiety* to refer to two very different types of concepts. Recent research findings suggest that it is meaningful to distinguish between anxiety as a transitory state (A-State) and as a relatively stable personality trait (A-Trait).

Spielberger and his associates have developed the State-Trait Anxiety Inventory (STAI) and the State-Trait Anxiety Inventory for Children (STAIC) to provide reliable, relatively brief, self-report measures of both A-State and A-Trait. The STAI measures state and trait anxiety in adolescents and adults (Spielberger, Gorsuch, & Lushene 1970). The STAIC was constructed to measure anxiety in 9- to 12-year-old elementary school children, but may also be used with younger children with above-average reading ability and with older children who are below average in ability (Spielberger, Edwards, Lushene, Montuori, & Platzek, 1973). Individual STAIC items are similar in content to STAI items, but the format for the STAIC has been simplified to facilitate its use with young children.

The STAIC A-State scale consists of 20 statements (items) that ask children how they feel at a *particular moment in time*. This scale is designed to measure transitory anxiety states, that is, subjective, consciously perceived feelings of tension, apprehension, nervousness, and worry that vary in intensity and fluctuate over time. Elevations in A-State are normally evoked in children who are exposed to stressful situations.

The STAIC A-Trait scale consists of 20 items to which subjects respond by indicating how they *generally* feel. This scale measures relatively stable individual differences in anxiety proneness, that is, differences between children in the tendency to experience anxiety states. High A-Trait children are more prone to perceive socially evaluative situations as more threatening than low A-Trait children and to respond to such situations with higher elevations in A-State intensity.

In general, children who are higher in A-Trait experience A-State elevations more frequently and with greater intensity than low A-Trait children because they perceive a wider range of circumstances as dangerous or threatening. Situations in which failure is experienced, or in which personal adequacy is evaluated, are more likely to be perceived as threatening by a high A-Trait child. But whether or not children who differ in A-Trait show corresponding differences in A-State will depend upon the extent to which a specific situation is perceived as dangerous or threatening by a particular child, and this will be greatly influenced by the child's past experience.

In recent years, there has been a growing interest in cross-cultural research on anxiety and in the measurement of anxiety in different national cultural groups. The STAI, for example, has been translated into Spanish (Spielberger, González, Martínez, Natalicio, & Natalicio, 1971), Portuguese (see Chapter 2), and French (see Chapter 3). Research on anxiety in different cultures and cross-cultural research on anxiety (see, for example, Chapters 7 and 9) has been stimulated and facilitated by the availability of these anxiety measurement instruments (e.g., Azpeitia, 1971; Bauermeister & Colón, 1974; Collado-Herrell, 1971; López-Garriga, 1973; Martínez & Spielberger, 1973; Nazario, 1973; Rivera-Santiago, 1973).

The goals of this chapter are to describe the development and validation of the *Inventario de Ansiedad Rasgo-Estado para Niños* (IDAREN), the Spanish form of the STAIC. The results of a series of studies concerned with establishing the equivalence of the STAIC and IDAREN and the reliability and construct validity of the latter are reported.

DEVELOPMENT AND VALIDATION OF THE IDAREN

The Spanish translation and adaptation of the STAIC was initiated by Villamil (1973). In order to provide a frame of reference for the translation of the STAIC, several members of the Department of Hispanic Studies at the University of Puerto Rico were asked to formulate two lists of words that implied either the presence or the absence of feelings of anxiety. These word lists were then submitted to two bilingual Hispanic Studies professors along with the STAIC A-State and A-Trait scales. The professors were asked to translate the STAIC into Spanish using words from the two lists that were provided.

The resulting Spanish translation of the STAIC was evaluated in terms of content, meaning, format, and clarity of expression by two psychology professors who were experienced in research and clinical practice with Puerto Rican children. Bilingual elementary school teachers were also consulted concerning the appropriateness of the language used in the translated STAIC items for fourth-, fifth-, and sixth-grade children. The selection of items for the preliminary IDAREN A-State and A-Trait scales was based on agreement between translators and evaluators with regard to the equivalence of the Spanish items and the corresponding STAIC items.

The English STAIC and the preliminary Spanish version that resulted from these procedures were administered to bilingual fourth-, fifth-, and sixth-grade children. The Spanish and English A-State scales correlated .60 for males and .75 for females; the Spanish and English A-Trait scales correlated .56 for males and .69 for females. The median item-remainder correlation for the A-State scale was .53 for males and .58 for females. For the A-Trait scale, the median item-remainder correlation was .30 for males and .35 for females. The alpha reliability of the Spanish A-State scale, computed by Kuder-Richardson's Formula 20 as modified by Cronbach (1951), was .86 for males and .90 for females. For the A-Trait scale, the alpha coefficients were .70 for males and .75 for females.

On the basis of these psychometric findings, it was decided that additional work on the adaptation of the Spanish STAIC was required because the item-remainder correlations were too small, especially for several A-Trait items; the correlation between the Spanish and English forms was not high enough to establish the equivalence of these scales; and some children had difficulty understanding the instructions and the key terms in several items.

Construction of the Preliminary Form of the IDAREN

The next step in the development of the Spanish STAIC was to administer the A-State and A-Trait scales to four groups of 18 fourth-, fifth-, and sixth-grade children from different socioeconomic backgrounds. Immediately after the children responded to the scales, they were interviewed to determine their understanding of the instructions and to ascertain their interpretation of each item. On the basis of the reactions of these children, the format and the content of some of the items were revised to ensure clarity of expression. The instructions were also modified to emphasize the characteristics of A-State as a momentary feeling and A-Trait as a more stable, relatively permanent feeling.

In modifying the instructions, advantage was taken of the psycholinguistic distinction between the Spanish verbs, "estoy" and "soy." Although their English translation is the same ("I am"), "estoy" refers to a temporary state or condition, whereas "soy" implies a more permanent characteristic. To emphasize the distinction between A-State and A-Trait, the A-State scale was called *Cuestionario de Como-Estoy-Ahora* ("Questionnaire of How-I-Am-Now"), and the A-Trait scale was entitled *Cuestionario de Como-Soy* ("Questionnaire of How-I-Am"). The format for the A-State scale was modified to include "en este momento" ("at this moment") as part of the stem for each of the 20 items. Several A-Trait items were also modified in terms of content, meaning, and clarity of expression. For example, the item, "I notice my heart beats fast," was rewritten as, "I notice my heart beats fast in the classroom," because the children tended to associate the former statement with physical exercise rather than with psychological stress.

Several alternative items were added to the A-State and A-Trait scales. The three alternative A-State items were: "temor" ("dread, fear"), "triste" ("sad"), "temblando" ("trembling, shivering"). The alternative A-Trait items were "Me pongo nervioso" ("I get nervous."), "Me da verguenza" ("I feel ashamed."), "Me siento tranquilo" ("I feel calm, quiet."), "Tengo miedo pero no se de que" ("I am afraid but do not know of what."), "Me como las uñas" ("I bite my fingernails."), and "Me asusto" ("I get scared."). These alternate items were selected from the earlier translations of the English items and children's common expressions that denote A-State or A-Trait feelings and from the definitions or explanations that were given by the children during individual interviews when they were asked about the original scale items. The

23 A-State and the 26 A-Trait items, with these modifications, constituted the preliminary form of the IDAREN.

Final Selection of Items for the IDAREN

The preliminary form of the IDAREN was investigated in four studies designed to evaluate the equivalence of the STAIC and the IDAREN and the reliability, concurrent validity, and construct validity of the latter. Equivalence was investigated by administering the STAIC and the preliminary form of the IDAREN to 27 bilingual boys and 41 bilingual girls enrolled in the fourth, fifth, and sixth grades in a private, urban, Catholic school. Spanish was the first language for these students, but most courses in this school were taught in English. Bilingualism was defined in terms of reading proficiency in English and Spanish and a semester grade-point average of B or above in these subjects.

Reliability was determined by administering the preliminary form of the IDAREN on two separate occasions to 63 fourth-, fifth-, and sixth-grade students in a different urban public school. The scales were administered 3 weeks apart.

Concurrent validity was determined by administering the preliminary form of the IDAREN and the Spanish STAI (*Inventario de Ansiedad Rasgo-Estado*, IDARE) in a counterbalanced order to a group of 44 male and 44 female tenth-grade students in an urban public school. The IDARE was developed to measure state and trait anxiety in Spanish-speaking adolescents and adults (Spielberger et al., 1971).

To evaluate *construct validity*, the preliminary form of the IDAREN was administered to 101 fourth-, fifth-, and sixth-grade students in an urban public school. The IDAREN A-State and A-Trait scales were first given with standard instructions (norm condition) and then readministered with instructions for subjects to respond according to how they believed they would feel just before the final examination in an important course (test condition).

The selection of the final set of 20 items for the IDAREN A-State scale was based on internal consistency and construct validity. Item-remainder correlations were computed separately for boys and girls on the data obtained from the equivalence, reliability, and construct validity studies (first administration in each case). Point-biserial correlations were also computed for each item for the norm and test conditions. The criteria used to select the final set of 20 items for the A-State scale were item-remainder and point-biserial correlations of .20 or higher for both males and females.

For the A-Trait scale, the criterion used for the selection of the final set of 20 items was based on internal consistency only. The final set of items had item-remainder correlations of .20 or higher for both males and females. For the A-Trait scale, the items "Me preocupa equivocarme" ("I worry about making mistakes.") and "Me sudan las manos" ("My hands get sweaty.") were eliminated. The items "Me pongo nervioso" ("I get nervous") and "Tengo miedo pero no se de que" (literally, "I am afraid, but I do not know of what.") were added in their place.

For the A-State scale, the items "molesto" ("upset") and "descansado" ("rested") were eliminated and replaced by the alternate items "temor" ("dread, fear") and "temblando" ("trembling, shivering, shaking"). The A-State and A-Trait scales that resulted from these procedures comprise what may be regarded as an experimental form of the *Inventario de Ansiedad Rasgo-Estado Para Ninos* (IDAREN).

PSYCHOMETRIC CHARACTERISTICS OF THE IDAREN

The means and standard deviations of the A-State and A-Trait scales of the IDAREN for fourth-, fifth-, and sixth-grade elementary school children are reported in Table 1. It may be noted that there were only minimal differences in the mean A-State and A-Trait scores obtained by boys and girls. The A-Trait means were higher than the A-State means for both male and female students.

Item-remainder correlations computed for each IDAREN A-State and A-Trait item are reported in Table 2. The median item-remainder correlation for the A-State items was .41 for the boys and .49 for the girls. The correlation obtained for item 18 ("siento terror") for the male sample fell below the criterion coefficient of .20, but this item was retained in the final selection of items on the basis of its moderately high item-remainder correlation for girls. For the A-Trait scale, the median item-remainder correlation was .33 for boys and .41 for girls. All of the items, for both males and females, had item-remainder correlations of .20 or higher.

Further evidence of the internal consistency of the IDAREN is provided by the alpha coefficients, computed by Kuder-Richardson's Formula 20 as modified by Cronbach (1951). The alpha coefficient for the A-State scale was

TABLE 1   IDAREN means and standard deviations for elementary school children

	A-State	A-Trait
Boys		
Mean	29.12	33.15
SD	4.97	6.12
N	115	115
Girls		
Mean	29.81	34.34
SD	5.93	6.91
N	117	117

TABLE 2 Item-remainder correlation coefficients for individual IDAREN A-State and A-Trait items for boys ($N = 115$) and girls ($N = 117$)

	A-State		A-Trait	
Item	Boys	Girls	Boys	Girls
1	.50	.48	.46	.44
2	.20	.58	.36	.45
3	.56	.52	.32	.36
4	.54	.53	.33	.37
5	.48	.48	.33	.43
6	.35	.52	.51	.39
7	.27	.49	.24	.54
8	.42	.41	.22	.22
9	.35	.61	.53	.43
10	.45	.40	.33	.46
11	.39	.60	.41	.36
12	.50	.39	.39	.36
13	.48	.33	.31	.42
14	.52	.58	.42	.25
15	.40	.38	.20	.31
16	.27	.56	.41	.46
17	.49	.36	.33	.45
18	.05	.47	.25	.34
19	.31	.42	.37	.46
20	.40	.49	.32	.36

.83 for males and .86 for females. For the A-Trait scale the alpha coefficients were .80 for males and .84 for females.

The test-retest reliability (stability) coefficients for the IDAREN after a 3-week interval are presented in Table 3. Test-retest correlations for the A-Trait scale were moderately high. It may be noted that the stability coefficients for the A-Trait scale were higher than for the A-State scale. Since a valid measure of A-State should reflect the influence of unique situational factors existing at the time of testing, lower test-retest correlations for the A-State scale were anticipated.

TABLE 3 IDAREN test-retest reliability coefficients over a 3-week interval

	N	A-Trait	A-State
Boys	30	.74	.67
Girls	33	.73	.50

Construct and Concurrent Validity of the IDAREN

The A-State and A-Trait scales were administered with standard instructions (norm condition) to one group of subjects and then readministered to these same children with instructions to imagine they were about to take an important test. More specifically, in the second administration of the IDAREN, the children were instructed to respond according to how they believed they would feel before the final examination in an important subject (test condition).

The mean scores in the norm and test conditions for each individual A-State item are reported in Table 4. Point-biserial correlations for each item between A-State scores and the two experimental conditions and *t* tests for the differences between the A-State means for the norm and test conditions are also reported in Table 4. The mean scores for the A-State scale were significantly higher in the test condition (males, 37.65; females, 37.74) than in the norm condition (males, 29.26; females, 28.86) and, with the exception of item 8 for females ("relajado"), statistically significant differences were found between the means for the norm and test conditions for each individual item.

TABLE 4 Mean scores on individual A-State items, point biserial correlations
(*r*) and *t* tests for the norm and test conditions

Item	Males (*N* = 58)				Females (*N* = 43)			
	Norm	Test	*r*	*t**	Norm	Test	*r*	*t**
1	1.96	2.42	.33	4.07	1.80	2.47	.48	6.32
2	1.02	1.39	.41	5.33	1.02	1.38	.30	3.70
3	1.91	2.51	.40	4.88	1.80	2.31	.36	4.72
4	1.23	1.88	.47	6.59	1.36	1.87	.34	4.21
5	1.21	1.67	.37	4.69	1.16	1.78	.42	5.18
6	1.12	1.35	.23	2.75	1.04	1.47	.38	4.10
7	1.07	1.58	.43	5.61	1.07	1.62	.42	4.17
8	2.19	2.51	.23	3.05	1.93	2.18	.14	1.81
9	1.35	1.93	.38	4.46	1.22	1.84	.43	5.58
10	1.79	2.26	.35	4.45	1.80	2.18	.29	3.71
11	1.04	1.47	.42	5.28	1.07	1.62	.40	4.30
12	1.82	2.26	.33	4.25	1.80	2.24	.28	3.25
13	1.81	2.19	.29	4.01	1.64	2.11	.36	4.31
14	1.68	1.98	.22	2.38	1.64	2.13	.34	4.02
15	1.16	1.47	.28	3.61	1.13	1.33	.21	2.15
16	1.18	1.46	.23	3.42	1.24	1.56	.25	2.54
17	1.75	2.23	.30	4.58	1.91	2.27	.24	2.49
18	1.04	1.21	.22	2.32	1.02	1.31	.29	2.79
19	1.14	1.61	.39	5.04	1.20	1.69	.38	4.02
20	1.72	2.26	.40	5.79	1.78	2.36	.41	5.61

*Two-tailed test; $p < .05$ in each case, except item 8 for females.

Furthermore, except for item 8 for females, the point-biserial correlation coefficient was .20 or higher for each individual item. The median point-biserial correlation coefficient was .34 for males and .35 for females.

In contrast to the high point-biserial correlations for the A-State items, the correlations of the A-Trait items with the two experimental conditions were all lower than the criterion value of .20. The median point-biserial correlation coefficients for boys and girls were .06 and .04, respectively, and the difference between the mean A-Trait scores in the norm and test conditions was not statistically significant.

A finding of considerable interest is that the magnitude of the alpha coefficients and item-remainder correlations was higher in the test condition than in the norm condition. The alpha coefficients for males increased from .83 in the norm condition to .93 in the test condition, and from .80 to .95 for females. The item-remainder correlation for item 18, which had a value of .05 for boys in the norm condition, increased to .52 during the test condition.

Evidence for the concurrent validity of the IDAREN is shown by its correlation with the IDARE (Spielberger et al., 1971), which measures state and trait anxiety in adolescents and adults. The correlation coefficients obtained for the A-State scales in a group of 44 male and 44 female tenth-grade students were .87 for boys and .91 for girls. The concurrent validity coefficients for the A-Trait scales were .66 for males and .72 for females.

The equivalence of the STAIC and the IDAREN is indicated by a correlation of .79 between the Spanish and English A-State scales for boys ($N = 27$), and a correlation of .77 for girls ($N = 41$). For the Spanish and English A-Trait scales, the correlation was .76 for boys and .77 for girls.

CONSTRUCT VALIDITY OF THE IDAREN IN BEHAVIOR MODIFICATION RESEARCH

Bauermeister and his students are currently involved in a research program designed to evaluate the relative efficacy of behavior modification procedures for producing behavioral, affective, and attitudinal changes in children and adults with irrational avoidance responses. One of the aims of this research program is to determine whether the behavioral, emotional, and attitudinal components of avoidance response patterns are differentially affected as a function of type of psychotherapeutic intervention and level of cognitive development of the subjects. The results of a recently completed study are now described.

Elementary school girls between the ages of 9 and 11 years were exposed to different modeling and control conditions in the treatment of avoidance behaviors to white albino, laboratory rats (Bauermeister & Ouslán, 1974). The subjects were selected on the basis of their performance on a behavioral approach test that consisted of 21 discrete performance tasks involving increasingly more threatening interactions with three male albino rats. The performance tasks ranged from standing 20 ft from three rats that moved freely on a chair to remaining seated for a 10-sec period in a 3 × 3 ft enclosed area in which the rats could also move freely.

The approach test was immediately terminated when a subject refused to comply with the instructions for a particular performance task. The score was the number of tasks successfully completed. Those subjects who succeeded in lifting one of the rats with gloved hands for 30 sec (score of 10) were eliminated from the study.

In the pretreatment phase of this study, the A-State scale of the IDAREN was administered immediately after the subject's arrival in the experimental room, that is, before the subject was informed of the nature of the approach test or of the presence of the rats in the room. The A-State scale was readministered after the subject indicated her refusal to comply with the instructions for a performance task, that is, immediately after the termination of the approach test. Subjects were asked to respond to the A-State scale by indicating how they felt while attempting to perform the last step of the approach test.

After termination of the approach test, the subjects were administered the IDAREN A-Trait scale, a self-description scale, a fear of rats scale, a rat attitude scale, and a rat repugnance scale. The self-description scale (SDS) consisted of 11 bipolar adjective rating scales. The subjects' self-descriptions were assessed in terms of the evaluative dimensions of the semantic differential technique. The fear of rats scale (FRS) consisted of a 7-point scale in which the subject was asked to rate her fear of rats.

The rat attitude scale (RAS) consisted of six subscales describing various possible interactions with rats such as keeping rats at home, handling rats, and unexpectedly observing a rat during a picnic in the countryside. Subjects were instructed to rate each item on a 7-point scale that indicated strong enjoyment at one end, strong dislike on the other, and indifference at the scale midpoint. This scale is similar in content to one developed by Bandura, Blanchard, and Ritter (1969) for measuring attitudes toward snakes in college students.

The rat repugnance scale (RRS) was specially constructed for this study to measure the common expression of repugnance or loathing ("asco" in Spanish) among Puerto Rican children and adults when referring to their descriptions of their reactions toward rats, some insects, and reptiles. The RRS consists of seven rating scales in which subjects are asked to evaluate their repugnance toward various anatomical parts of rats (eyes, paws, tail, skin, whiskers, nose, and ears).

The correlations between the IDAREN state and trait anxiety measures and the behavioral, affective, and attitudinal measures are reported in Table 5. The A-State scores obtained upon the subjects' arrival in the experimental room did not correlate with the approach

TABLE 5 Correlations between the A-State and A-Trait scales of the IDAREN and other measures during the pretreatment phase

	A-State		A-Trait
	Upon arrival	Approach test	
Approach scores	−.10	−.36*	−.25
Fear of rats scale (FRS)	00	.35*	.57*
Rat attitude scale (RAS)	−.03	−.44*	−.38*
Rat repugnance scale (RRS)	−.03	.29	.36*
Self-description scale (SDS)	−.13	−.30	−.41*
A-Trait scale	.15	.43*	−

*$p < .05$.

scores or with the other scales. However, significant correlations in the predicted direction were found between A-State scores obtained upon termination of the approach test and approach scores and with FRS, RAS, and IDAREN A-Trait scores. The A-Trait scale was also significantly correlated with all of these scales, but not with the approach scores. However, the A-Trait scale correlated significantly with the self-description scale, whereas the A-State scale did not.

During the treatment phase of the study, one group of girls received a "participant-mastery modeling" (PMM) procedure in which a nonanxious model (therapist) was observed interacting gradually with the three white rats while performing the 21 steps of the approach test. The therapist subsequently encouraged and guided the subject and provided physical assistance in performing similar interactions with the rats (Bandura, Blanchard, & Ritter, 1969).

A second group of subjects participated in a "participant-coping modeling" (PCM) procedure. This treatment condition was similar to the PMM, except that the model initially expressed anxiety and fear toward rats, followed by verbalizations designed to help the subject to cope effectively with her anxiety and avoidance behaviors. In this treatment condition, the coping, verbalizing model displayed moderate amounts of anxiety and fear while performing the initial steps of the approach test, but also expressed cognitive activities involved in developing coping skills (Meichenbaum, 1971).

There were two control groups in this study, a placebo treatment condition and a no-treatment condition. The placebo group (P) observed the therapist modeling how to draw on a blackboard. The control group (C) did not receive any kind of modeling procedure and participated only in the evaluation phases of the experiment.

Upon completion of the treatment phase (a 40-min group session and a maximum of six additional 20-min individual sessions), the subjects were readministered the behavioral approach test and the same set of scales that were given during the pretreatment phase of the study. The IDAREN A-State scale was administered at the point of the uncompleted performance task during the pretreatment evaluation phase so that the levels of A-State prior to and following treatment could be meaningfully compared. The A-State scale was also administered immediately after the last performance task attempted or completed during the posttreatment evaluation phase.

The relative efficacy of the treatment condition was assessed by means of a 4 × 2 repeated-measures, factorial design (Winer, 1962). The main effects of treatment type and phase (pretreatment versus posttreatment) and the treatment × phase interaction were significant for the approach test, A-State while performing the approach behaviors, and the FRS, RAS, and RRS measures.

The mean approach scores obtained by the subjects in each of the four experimental conditions during the pretreatment and posttreatment phases of the experiment are presented in Figure 1A. Subjects in the PCM and PMM modeling treatments achieved comparable performance gains, while no significant differences were found between the placebo and control groups. The PCM and PMM groups were found to differ significantly in approach behavior from the two control groups.

Figure 1B presents the mean A-State scores associated with approach responses for subjects in the four experimental groups before and after the treatment phase of the experiment. The Post 1 scores reflect the anxiety arousal of subjects following the uncompleted performance task during the pretreatment evaluation. Thus, Pre and Post 1 state anxiety measures were obtained for the same approach response. The Post 2 measure reflects the subjects' anxiety arousal during the final performance task of the approach test or during the last task attempted.

It can be observed in Figure 1B that subjects who received the modeling treatments showed the greatest decrements in A-State during the posttreatment assessment phase. These decrements were maintained during the Post 2 measurement in spite of the fact that most subjects were performing the most threatening tasks of the approach test. The placebo group showed a slight decrease in state anxiety from pretreatment to posttreatment, while the control group showed no decrement in Post 1 and even an increase in A-State during the Post 2 measurements. However, none of the changes in state anxiety for the control and placebo groups were statistically significant, although the decrements for the modeling groups were highly significant ($p < .01$).

The A-Trait scores were also subjected to a 4 × 2 repeated-measures factorial design. As expected, no significant findings were obtained in this analysis. It should be noted that the treatment conditions were not directed toward modifying anxiety proneness in children. Similar findings were obtained in the analysis of the SDS scores.

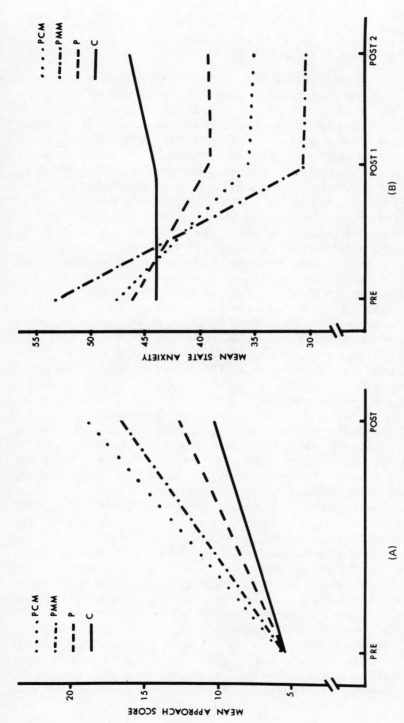

FIGURE 1 (A) Mean pretreatment and posttreatment approach scores for the four experimental groups. (B) Mean A-State scores for the four experimental groups associated with approach responses at the point of the uncompleted performance task before treatment (Pre), for this same performance task after treatment (Post 1), and for the final performance task (or the last task attempted) after treatment (Post 2).

81

SUMMARY AND CONCLUSIONS

In the series of studies that have been described, we have endeavored to develop a Spanish form of the State-Trait Anxiety Inventory for Children (STAIC) that would be useful for research with Puerto Rican children. Hopefully, the IDAREN can also be used to measure anxiety in children from other Spanish-speaking national and cultural groups, thus providing the means for cross-cultural research on state and trait anxiety. The evidence that has been presented suggests that the Spanish form of the STAIC (IDAREN), although still in an experimental stage, can be developed into an excellent instrument for measuring A-State and A-Trait in Spanish-speaking children.

Important phases in the construction of the IDAREN included: obtaining the assistance and recommendations of Spanish literature professors, child psychologists, and teachers; interviewing children from different socio-economic backgrounds; and conducting two separate sets of empirical studies in which internal consistency, reliability, and validity of the Spanish scale were evaluated, as well as the equivalence of the IDAREN and English STAIC.

Reasonably high item-remainder correlation coefficients were obtained for most of the items in the IDAREN A-State and A-Trait scales for both males and females. The median item-remainder correlations for both scales, and for male and female subjects, ranged from .33 to .49 and were comparable to those reported by Spielberger et al. (1973) for the STAIC. High alpha correlations were also obtained for the IDAREN A-State and A-Trait scales, comparable also to those reported by Spielberger et al. (1973) for the STAIC. These data are indicative of the homogeneity of individual items in the IDAREN and the high internal consistency of the A-State and A-Trait scales.

The stability of the IDAREN A-Trait scale was documented in the test-retest correlations obtained for boys and girls (.74 and .73) over an interval of 3 weeks. Additional evidence of the stability of the IDAREN A-Trait scale was obtained by Bauermeister for the group of girls who participated in the behavior modification study described earlier. The A-Trait scale was administered to these subjects at 6- and 18-week intervals. The stability coefficients were .70 and .75, respectively.

Test-retest correlations for the IDAREN A-State scale were lower than those for the A-Trait scale. Since the A-State scale was designed to be sensitive to the influence of unique situational factors that typically change over time, lower stability coefficients were expected. However, the A-State test-retest correlations in the present study (.67 and .50) were substantially higher than those reported by Spielberger et al. (1973) for the STAIC (.31 and .47). The higher stability coefficients obtained in the present study might be due to the fact that the data on which these test-retest correlations are based were collected during the last 3 weeks of the semester while students were preparing for final exams.

Evidence bearing on the construct validity of the IDAREN A-State scale is available from the point-biserial correlations and t tests obtained for the norm and test conditions. The mean A-State scores were considerably higher in the test condition than in the norm condition for both males and females. With one exception, the mean score for each A-State item was also significantly higher in the test condition. It is interesting to note that item-remainder coefficients were also higher in the test condition, and this was particularly true for those items with the lowest item-remainder coefficients in the norm condition. Spielberger et al. (1970) reported similar findings for adolescents and adults with the STAI.

By contrast, no significant differences were found in mean A-Trait scores in the test and norm conditions. Point-biserial correlations for each of the A-Trait items with experimental conditions were also essentially zero. Thus, the IDAREN A-Trait scale was not influenced by situational stress, as would be expected to be the case for a relatively stable personality trait.

The concurrent validity of the IDAREN is difficult to assess in view of the fact that there are no other available instruments to measure state and trait anxiety in Puerto Rican children. However, concurrent validity was indirectly established by administering the IDAREN and the IDARE in a counterbalanced order to a group of tenth-grade students. The magnitude of the correlation coefficients obtained between these two scales suggested that the children and adult forms of the inventory measure similar constructs in tenth-grade students.

Evidence of the equivalence of the Spanish and English forms of the STAIC is provided by the high correlations obtained between the IDAREN and the STAIC in bilingual elementary school children. These correlations ranged from .76 to .79, indicating that the IDAREN provides scales for measuring state and trait anxiety in Spanish-speaking children that are very similar to the English STAIC A-State and A-Trait scales.

The findings of the behavior modification study reported in this chapter contribute further to the construct validity and concurrent validity of the IDAREN A-State and A-Trait scales. In this study, pretreatment and posttreatment A-State scores were influenced by the treatment conditions. Significant decreases in state anxiety were obtained for the groups in the modeling treatment conditions, and there were no significant changes in state anxiety in the placebo and control conditions. Furthermore, during the approach test, state anxiety was significantly and negatively correlated with the approach test and rat attitude scores and positively correlated with fear of rats. These findings are in close theoretical correspondence with the rat approach scores obtained for the four groups.

On the other hand, the IDAREN A-Trait scores remained essentially unchanged throughout the study. This was consistent with the fact that the modeling treatment conditions were addressed to reducing state anxiety reactions to rats and not to altering the children's anxiety proneness in general.

Further research is needed to determine if the IDAREN, which was developed to measure anxiety in Puerto Rican children, can be used with other national cultural groups. The IDAREN was constructed with the hope that its availability will serve to stimulate cross-cultural research on anxiety phenomena with children in Latin American countries. The IDAREN A-State scale should prove useful as an indicator of the level of transitory anxiety experienced by children in counseling and psychotherapy situations. The scale should be especially useful as a measure of the effectiveness of modeling, desensitization, and counterconditioning procedures in behavior therapy, as was illustrated in the study described in this chapter.

The IDAREN A-Trait scale may be used for research purposes to select children who vary in anxiety proneness, or as a clinical screening device for detecting neurotic behavioral tendencies in elementary school children. The IDAREN A-Trait scale should also prove useful in measuring the effectiveness of clinical treatment procedures designed to reduce neurotic anxiety in children.

REFERENCES

Azpeitia, E. *Los efectos de las condiciones de fracaso y no fracaso en ansiedad-estado de sujetos que difieren en ansiedad-rasgo.* Unpublished master's thesis, University of Puerto Rico, 1971.

Bandura, A., Blanchard, E. B., & Ritter, B. Relative efficacy of desensitization and modeling approaches for inducing behavioral, affective, and attitudinal changes. *Journal of Personality and Social Psychology*, 1969, *13*, 173–199.

Bauermeister, J. J., & Colón, N. Rendimiento Académico en función del nivel de ansiedad-rasgo, sexo y habilidad general. *Revista Interamericana de Psicología*, 1974, *8*, 53–67.

Bauermeister, J. J., & Ouslán, A. *Comparación de los efectos de modelado en niños.* Paper presented at the meeting of the Interamerican Society of Psychology, Bogotá, Colombia, December, 1974.

Collado-Herrell, I. *Apperceived pain thresholds and anxiety levels in heroin addicts.* Unpublished master's thesis, University of Puerto Rico, 1971.

Cronbach, L. J. Coefficient alpha and the internal structure of tests. *Psychometric*, 1951, *16*, 297–335.

Hull, C. L. *Principles of behavior.* New York: Appleton-Century, 1943.

López-Garriga, M. M. *Ansiedad y dogmatismo y su relación con la opción vocacional.* Unpublished master's thesis, University of Puerto Rico, 1973.

Martínez, A., & Spielberger, C. D. The relationship between state-trait anxiety and intelligence in Puerto Rican psychiatric patients. *Revista Interamericana de Psicología*, 1973, *7*, 199–214.

Meichenbaum, D. H. Examination of model characteristics in reducing avoidance behavior. *Journal of Personality and Social Psychology*, 1971, *17*, 298–307.

Nazario, E. *Ansiedad-estado y memorización de dígitos en función del nivel de ansiedad-rasgo y las condiciones experimentales de fracaso y no fracaso.* Unpublished master's thesis, University of Puerto Rico, 1973.

Rivera-Santiago, J. A. *The effects of physical and psychological threat in A-State for Puerto Rican high school students who differed in A-Trait.* Unpublished master's thesis, University of Puerto Rico, 1973.

Spence, K. W. A theory of emotionally based drive (D) and its relation to performance in simple learning situations. *American Psychologist*, 1958, *13*, 131–141.

Spielberger, C. D. Theory and research on anxiety. In C. D. Spielberger (Ed.), *Anxiety and behavior.* New York: Academic Press, 1966.

Spielberger, C. D. Anxiety as an emotional state. In C. D. Spielberger (Ed.), *Anxiety: Current trends in theory and research* (Vol. 1). New York: Academic Press, 1972. (a)

Spielberger, C. D. Current trends in theory and research on anxiety. In C. D. Spielberger (Ed.), *Anxiety: Current trends in theory and research* (Vol. 1). New York: Academic Press, 1972. (b)

Spielberger, C. D., Edwards, C. D., Lushene, R. C., Montuori, J., & Platzek, D. *Preliminary Test Manual for the State-Trait Anxiety Inventory for Children.* Palo Alto, Calif.: Consulting Psychologist Press, 1973.

Spielberger, C. D., González, F., Martínez, A., Natalicio, L. F., & Natalicio, D. S. Development of the Spanish edition of the State-Trait Anxiety Inventory. *Interamerican Journal of Psychology*, 1971, *5*, 145–158.

Spielberger, C. D., Gorsuch, R. L., & Lushene, R. E. *Manual for the State-Trait Anxiety Inventory.* Palo Alto, Calif.: Consulting Psychologist Press, 1970.

Villamil, B. *Desarrollo del Inventario de Ansiedad Estado y Rasgo para Niños.* Unpublished master's thesis, University of Puerto Rico, 1973.

Winer, B. J. *Statistical principles in experimental design.* New York: McGraw-Hill, 1962.

III

RESEARCH ON ANXIETY IN DIFFERENT CULTURES

7

The Anxiety-Arousing Effect of Taboo Words in Bilinguals

Fernando Gonzalez-Reigosa
Florida International University

Bilingualism in individuals who have some degree of fluency in more than one language is generally recognized as a critical factor in their personality adjustment and emotional reactions. This study is concerned with the anxiety reactions of bilinguals to saying taboo words in their two languages.

The literature relevant to this investigation comes from two separate areas of psychological research: (1) studies on the anxiety-arousing effects of taboo words, and (2) research on the language-mediated emotional reactions of bilinguals.

The emotional significance of a specific word for a particular individual generally depends on the individual's personal values and his developmental history. Strong aversion and the concomitant emotional arousal evoked by obscene words have been attributed to the unpleasant feelings attached to these words in the course of the socialization of the child. Reprimands and punishment result when a child verbalizes an obscene word, and this

This study is an extension of the dissertation submitted to Florida State University for the Ph.D. by Fernando Gonzalez-Reigosa under the supervision of Charles D. Spielberger.

subsequently causes anxiety over anticipated punishment when such words are encountered later. Since this happens to almost all children, the use of obscene words is suppressed or becomes considerably reduced (Ferenczi, 1916).

In the psychological literature obscene words have been referred to as "taboo words." This terminology implies that these words are emotionally arousing because using them can result in punishment and/or other unpleasant consequences. The emotional arousal elicited by taboo words was first investigated within the context of studies of "perceptual defense." This term was used by Bruner and Postman (1947), to describe the operation of a process that resulted in higher tachistoscopic recognition thresholds for anxiety-laden words as compared to neutral words. They suggested that a person "unconsciously" attempts to delay recognition of anxiety-provoking stimuli.

In a study in which the recognition thresholds for taboo and neutral words were compared, McGinnies (1949) found that thresholds for taboo words were substantially higher than for neutral words. He attributed the higher thresholds of the taboo words to the operation of perceptual defense. Howes and Solomon (1950) suggested an alternative explanation in terms of the suppression of responses. In general, their response suppression hypothesis postulates that taboo words are recognized just as readily as neutral words, but that subjects are reluctant to say taboo words aloud, a factor that artifactually increases recognition thresholds.

Logical and experimental evidence have subsequently supported the response suppression hypothesis (Allport, 1955; Bitterman & Kniffin, 1953; Nothman, 1962; Postman, Bronson, & Gropper, 1953; Solomon & Howes, 1951; Spielberger, 1956; Walters, Banks, & Ryder, 1959; Whittaker, Gilchrist, & Fisher, 1952; Zajonc, 1962; Zigler & Yospe, 1960). A clear example of response suppression is reported in a study by Nothman (1962). He found that subjects had longer delays in responding to taboo words than to neutral words where the mode of response was oral, but not when a written response was required. Nothman interprets his result as indicating that, through a cultural conditioning process, individuals learn that the consequences of saying a taboo word are much more severe than writing it. This interpretation implies that punishment had been associated with saying the taboo word in the past, and that when the subject says the taboo word in the present he experiences anxiety because he anticipates being punished. Any attempt to study the emotional reactions evoked by the taboo words must distinguish between anxiety as a transitory state and a relatively stable personality trait. Spielberger (1972) has defined state and trait anxiety as follows:

> State anxiety (A-State) may be conceptualized as a transitory emotional state or condition of the organism that varies in intensity and fluctuates over time. This condition is characterized by subjective

feelings of tension and apprehension and activation of the autonomic nervous system. Level of A-State should be high in circumstances that are perceived by an individual to be threatening, irrespective of objective danger; A-State intensity should be relatively low in nonstressful situations, or in circumstances in which existing danger is not perceived as threatening.

Trait anxiety (A-Trait) refers to relatively stable individual differences in anxiety proneness; that is, to differences in the disposition to perceive a wide range of stimulus situations as dangerous or threatening, and in the tendency to respond to such threats with A-State reactions. A-Trait may also be regarded as reflecting individual differences in the frequency with which A-States have been manifested in the past and in the probability that such states will be experienced in the future. (p. 39)

Gonzalez-Reigosa (1971) investigated the effect of saying taboo and neutral words on A-State and reaction times for male subjects who differed in A-Trait. He found that high A-Trait subjects experienced higher levels of A-State intensity when saying taboo words than when saying neutral words. These results were interpreted as supporting the general hypothesis that saying taboo words is perceived as more threatening by high A-Trait individuals than by persons who are low in A-Trait.

The findings of research on taboo words suggest that these words evoke anxiety because they have been associated with punishment in the past. If this is the case, the reaction of a bilingual individual to a taboo word will depend upon his experiences associated with the language in which the word is verbalized.

LANGUAGE-MEDIATED EMOTIONAL RESPONSES IN BILINGUALS

Differential subjective experiences and changes in the ways of responding when speaking different languages are common occurrences among bilinguals. For example, Lowie (1945), an Austrian immigrant in the United States, wrote in his memoirs:

> The popular impression that a man alters his personality when speaking another language is far from ill grounded. When I speak German to Germans I automatically shift my orientation as a social being. (p. 249)

Ervin (1964) asked French-born bilinguals living in the United States to tell TAT stories in French and English and found that they gave very different responses to the same pictures according to the language of the response. The French stories contained more themes of rejection, verbal aggression, autonomy, aggression against siblings, and isolation, while achievement themes were more common in the English stories.

Del Castillo (1970) reported that psychotic symptoms in bilingual patients are more easily detected when psychiatric interviews are conducted in the patient's mother tongue rather than in the second language. These findings seem to indicate that the patient's more primitive emotional world is more readily expressed in the mother tongue. Following this same line of thought, Sechrest, Flores, and Arellano (1968) suggested that Philippino students who wanted to hide their emotions conversed in a second language. Adding support to this point of view, Sechrest and his colleagues (1968) reported anecdotal evidence that became available to them when married Philippinos were asked to state in which language they made love. All of them seemed to find the idea of communicating their most intimate emotions in languages other than Tagalog, their mother tongue, to be quite amusing, even though many of them habitually spoke English even at home.

The importance that the differential emotional involvement of bilinguals in their two languages has in therapy is clearly seen in the following cases in which the author was the therapist. The first case involves Sylvia, a young professional woman. Sylvia sought counseling because after several years of marriage she felt she had been "pushed" into an extramarital relationship. The relationship, although enjoyable, was the source of a good deal of anxiety.

Even though our therapeutic sessions were conducted in Spanish, the patient tried to avoid dealing with the emotional impact of her behavior by reverting to English every time she had to describe her encounter with her lover.

The patient's avoidance attempts served the therapist in two ways. First, he was able to identify emotionally sensitive areas, and, second, by forcing the patient to use Spanish, he helped her to assume responsibility for her behavior and its emotional consequences, thus facilitating a rational solution.

A more dramatic instance of bilingualism as an essential factor in therapeutic interventions is the case of Tony, a young Cuban, 20 years of age, 15 of which have been spent residing in the United States. He was a participant in a therapy group in which the author was the facilitator. The majority of the group members were Anglo males between the ages of 20 and 45.

From the first session it was obvious to the members of the group that Tony possessed an extraordinary command of the English language, an extensive vocabulary, a precise syntax, and flawless pronunciation. His command of this language was markedly superior to that of the other members of the group who were amazed that an alien could surpass them in their own language. Tony always had the correct phrase to describe the processes observed by the group, the proper indication, and the adequate suggestion. However, the admiration that the group felt for Tony promptly turned into frustration because Tony only observed but did not participate. Tony explained his problems like someone would explain a philosophical theory, without an iota of emotional involvement. There was no feeling or emotion in his conflicts, no contact with the pain that these should be generating. Tony hid behind a wall of words and therefore made himself inscrutable.

Finally, the facilitator decided to try to break down this wall and prohibited Tony from speaking in English. The Tony that the group now saw surprised all the participants. No longer the self-confident, fluent, cool, calm, and collected young man to which they were accustomed, he was now a stumbling individual who portrayed all the emotions, frustrations, and insecurities of an overgrown boy who had not yet succeeded in cutting the strings that tied him to his parents. He also seemed to feel inadequate in satisfying his young wife.

These changes marked the beginning of therapeutic progress for Tony. Even though the participants could not understand the words Tony was speaking because they were in Spanish, they felt that Tony was communicating with them for the first time. For the bilingual facilitator, who understood Spanish, Tony now reflected and expressed the long-repressed emotions of childhood. His way of speaking Spanish was primitive and awkward, since it was the direct and emotionally expressive language of a 5-year-old boy rather than that of a young man.

It is in the language learned as a child that one's earliest experiences are coded and labeled. These first experiences have traditionally been considered to be of paramount importance in shaping the personality and behavior of individuals. Expressions in the mother language are the first ones to be rewarded or punished, and it is in this language that feedback is offered. Weinrich (1953) speculates that stimuli whose emotional quality stems from childhood will arouse stronger emotions when experienced with relation to the mother tongue than in the second language. If this is the case, it may be expected that the anxiety-arousing effects of taboo words, whose aversive quality apparently stems from childhood experiences, will be greater for words in the mother tongue than for words in a second language.

THE ANXIETY-AROUSING EFFECT OF TABOO WORDS IN BILINGUALS

Ferenczi (1916) observed that the anxiety arousal caused by obscene or taboo words decreased when they were pronounced in a foreign language. Similarly, Ernest Jones (1953–1957), in his biographical study of Sigmund Freud, noted that the founder of psychoanalysis referred to an incident in which he saw his mother nude with the Latin words "mater nuda," presumably in order to avoid the anxiety associated with relating his observation in his own language.

Sollee (1963) studied differential tachistoscopic recognition thresholds in response to taboo and neutral words among Tagalog-English bilingual school children in the Philippines. She divided her subjects into two groups: (1) those who had learned Tagalog at home and were exposed to English at a later time, and (2) those who first learned English at home and learned Tagalog later in other settings. Six taboo words (for example, breast, belly) and six neutral words were tachistoscopically presented to the children in both Tagalog and English. Thresholds were obtained by means of increasing the time of exposure until the child said the word. "Defense" scores were obtained for each child by subtracting the sum of the thresholds for the six neutral words from the sum of the thresholds for the six taboo words. Each child received a defense score for English words and a defense score for Tagalog words.

Sollee found that defense scores were positive in both languages, indicating that thresholds for taboo words were higher than for neutral words. She also found that defense scores were higher in the mother tongue than in the second language. This latter finding is of critical importance for the present investigation. It suggests that the mother tongue, the vehicle of punishment during childhood, the period of life of greater emotional susceptibility, played a major role in mediating the anxiety reactions evoked by taboo words.

The main purpose of the present study was to investigate the effect of saying taboo words in two languages on A-State and reaction times for Spanish-English bilingual males who differed in A-Trait level and in degree of proficiency in their second language. Since the differential reaction of bilinguals to words in their two languages may also be attributed to their proficiency in each language, this variable was also considered. The subjects' mother tongue was Spanish, and their second language was English.

Method

Subjects The subjects were 152 Spanish-English bilingual male students at the Miami-Dade Community College. Spanish was the mother tongue for all the subjects. From the total sample, 40 subjects who were high in English proficiency and 40 who were low in English proficiency were selected to participate in this study.

Stimulus words and apparatus There were 30 stimulus words, 10 in each of the following categories: neutral Spanish, taboo English, and taboo Spanish. The neutral Spanish list consisted of a Spanish translation of the 10 neutral words used in an earlier study (Gonzalez-Reigosa, 1971). These words were originally selected from the neutral words used by McGinnies (1949).

The taboo English words were also previously used in the earlier study. Seven of these words were taken from McGinnies (1949) and three from Zajonc (1962). The taboo Spanish words consisted of a translation of the words in the taboo English list.

The Spanish translation of the taboo words was prepared by four English-Spanish bilingual judges. The judges (a psychologist, a social worker, and two college students) were asked to equate each English word with two

Spanish words that were approximately equivalent in the following characteristics: (1) denotative meaning, (2) connotative meaning and strength, (3) familiarity, and (4) length (difference not to exceed two letters).

Ratings of discomfort for each of the 20 Spanish taboo words were obtained from 30 native speakers of Spanish. Ratings of discomfort for the 10 English taboo words had previously been obtained (Gonzalez-Reigosa, 1971) from 30 native speakers of English. The mean discomfort index for each of the English words was compared with the discomfort ratings of its two alternate Spanish translations, and the translation having the more similar discomfort index was chosen for the Spanish taboo word list. The difference between the discomfort indices of the taboo English words and those of their Spanish translations was analyzed by a paired difference design test (Mendenhall, 1963) and was found to be nonsignificant ($t = .05$).

The words were printed in black capital letters and presented one-at-a-time by means of a double-mirror exposure box. A lamp was used in exposing the stimulus words and an electrical stopwatch used in measuring reaction times were simultaneously activated by the experimenter. Both the lamp and the stopwatch were turned off by a voice-operated switching circuit activated by the subject's oral responses.

Experimental measures The experimental measures consisted of instruments designed to assess state and trait anxiety and English proficiency.

The anxiety measures employed in this study were the A-State and A-Trait scales of the Spanish edition of the State-Trait Anxiety Inventory (STAI-SX) (Spielberger, Gonzalez-Reigosa, Martines-Urrutia, Natalicio, & Natalicio, 1971). The STAI-SX provides a Spanish translation of the STAI (Spielberger, Gorsuch, & Lushene, 1970). The STAI-SX A-Trait scale asks the subject to describe how he generally feels; the STAI-SX A-State scale asks the subject to describe how he feels at a particular moment in time. The A-Trait scale was used to assign subjects to the high and low trait anxiety groups. The A-State scale was used to measure the level of A-State intensity evoked by saying different types of words.

TABLE 1 Stimulus words

Neutral Spanish	Taboo Spanish	Taboo English
Casa (House)	*Barriga*	Belly
Baile (Dance)	*Bruja*	Bitch
Niño (Child)	*Basura*	Filth
Vidrio (Glass)	*Kotex*	Kotex
Río (River)	*Pene*	Penis
Sueño (Sleep)	*Violó*	Raped
Luz (Light)	*Ramera*	Whore
Cambio (Trade)	*Huevos*	Balls
Música (Music)	*Himen*	Hymen
Claro (Clear)	*Púbico*	Pubic

The language skills rating scale   A Language Skills Rating Scale required each subject to rate his language abilities. Each subject rated his speaking, reading, writing, and listening comprehension skills in Spanish and in English on the following 4-point rating scale: (1) Poor, (2) Fair, (3) Good, (4) Very Good. Proficiency scores for each language were obtained by summing each subject's self-rating on each of the four rating scales. Almost all of the subjects rated themselves as very good on the Spanish Proficiency Rating Scale (score of 16). Only the English proficiency scores were considered in this study.

The reaction time test of bilingualism   A technique devised by Johnson (1953) was used as a measure of language fluency. It requires subjects to produce as many different words as they can in one language within a limited period of time. A variety of measures of proficiency have been derived using Johnson's procedure, of which the simplest is based on counting the number of words.

The investigation was conducted in two separate stages. In the first stage, bilingual subjects who were high and low in English proficiency were selected.

Bilingual subjects who were in the upper and lower third of the distribution of English proficiency scores on the Language Skills Rating Scale were considered high and low in English proficiency. High proficiency (HP) subjects had scores of 12 and above; low proficiency (LP) subjects had scores of 7 and below. The Reaction Time Test of Bilingualism was used as a secondary measure of subject selection. High and low English proficiency groups were defined by splitting the subjects at the median number of English words. Subjects whose scores in the Reaction Time Test of Bilingualism were inconsistent with those in the Language Skills Rating Scale were not selected.

In the second stage, subjects were tested individually. The neutral Spanish list was presented first to all subjects. The taboo Spanish and taboo English lists were presented in counterbalanced order, with half of the subjects saying the taboo Spanish words first and the remaining subjects saying the taboo English list first.

Reaction times were measured for each word, and A-State measures were obtained after the subject responded to each of the three word lists. State anxiety (A-State) scores and reaction time were the dependent variables. High and low trait anxiety groups were defined by splitting the subjects at the median for the distribution of STAI A-Trait scales, which was 34.5.

On the basis of A-Trait and proficiency scores, the following four experimental groups were constituted: HA-HP ($N = 20$); HA-LP ($N = 18$); LA-HP ($N = 20$); LA-LP ($N = 20$). Since the number of subjects in these groups was unequal, two subjects were randomly deleted from the HA-HP, LA-HP, and LA-LP groups, in order to have 18 subjects in each cell.

RESULTS

Effect of Saying Taboo and Neutral Words on State Anxiety

Measures of state anxiety were obtained immediately after the subjects responded to each word list (neutral Spanish, taboo Spanish, and taboo English). The means and standard deviations for these three A-State scores are presented in Table 2 for the four experimental groups and for the total group.

The STAI A-State data were evaluated by a three-factor analysis of variance (ANOVA) in which proficiency (P) and trait anxiety (A-Trait) were between-subjects variables, and type of words (Lists) was the within-subjects variable. In this analysis, the main effects of Lists ($F = 11.44$, $p < .001$) and A-Trait ($F = 29.00$, $p < .001$) were statistically significant. Neither the proficiency main effect nor any of the interactions involving the proficiency variable were significant. Thus, A-State scores apparently were not influenced by English proficiency.

The main effects of Lists and A-Trait effects are graphically presented in Figure 1. As may be noted in this figure, in the context of the means reported in Table 2 for the total group, the Lists main effect suggested that A-State scores were higher for the taboo Spanish words than for either the taboo English words or the neutral words. The significant A-Trait main effect indicated that the A-State scores of the HA-Trait subjects were consistently higher for all three lists than those of the LA-Trait subjects.

Comparison of A-State Scores for the Neutral and Taboo Word Lists

In order to further clarify the differences in A-State scores for the three word lists, the A-State scores for the neutral Spanish list and the taboo Spanish list were evaluated as a function of A-Trait and proficiency. A similar analysis was carried out for the taboo Spanish and taboo English lists and for

TABLE 2 Mean A-State scores for taboo and neutral words

Group	N	Neutral-Spanish		Taboo-Spanish		Taboo-English	
		Mean	SD	Mean	SD	Mean	SD
HA-HP	18	38.28	8.85	42.67	9.26	38.83	7.92
HA-LP	18	40.56	7.19	43.56	8.56	40.83	7.27
LA-HP	18	31.06	5.77	33.83	7.26	32.39	6.40
LA-LP	18	30.33	6.01	32.33	8.59	30.39	7.01
Total	72	35.06	8.23	38.10	9.71	35.61	8.26

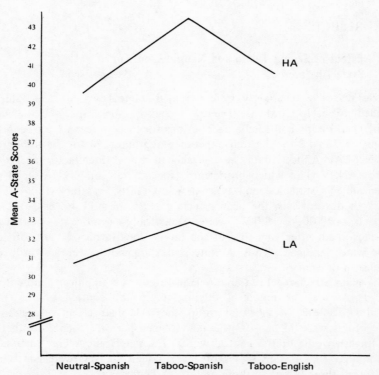

FIGURE 1 Mean A-State scores for taboo and neutral words for HA- and LA-Trait subjects.

TABLE 3 Summary of the analysis of variances of A-State scores for pairs of lists

Source	df	Neutral / Taboo Spanish / Spanish		Taboo / Taboo Spanish / English		Neutral / Taboo Spanish / English	
		MS	F	MS	F	MS	F
Proficiency (P)	1	2.01	<1	0.84	<1	5.44	<1
A-Trait (A)	1	3164.06	29.32*	3071.01	29.59*	2652.25	21.47
P × A	1	65.34	<1	91.84	<1	110.25	1.31
Error (b)	68	107.91		103.76		84.27	
Lists (L)	1	333.06	24.90*	222.51	11.67*	11.11	<1
P × L	1	10.56	<1	0.84	<1	5.44	<1
A × L	1	15.34	1.15	22.56	1.18	0.69	<1
A × P × L	1	0.84	<1	5.84	<1	2.25	<1
Error (w)	68	13.38		19.07		17.07	

*p < .001.

the neutral Spanish and taboo English lists. The results of the analyses for each of these pairs of lists are summarized in Table 3.

The significant A-Trait main effect in all three analyses indicated that the A-State scores of the HA-Trait subjects were consistently higher than those of LA-Trait subjects on each of the three word lists, as may be noted in Figure 1. The main effects of Lists was also significant in the two analyses that involved the taboo Spanish words, but not in the comparison of the neutral Spanish and taboo English words. As may be seen in Figure 1, A-State scores were higher for the taboo Spanish words than for either the neutral Spanish or taboo English words.

The absence of a significant Lists effect in the comparison of the neutral Spanish and taboo English words suggested that the level of A-State intensity evoked saying taboo words in English was no greater than the anxiety resulting from saying the neutral words. On the other hand, the finding that A-State scores for the taboo Spanish words were higher than for the taboo English words confirms the hypothesis that saying taboo words in one's mother tongue would evoke more anxiety than saying them in one's second language. Neither the proficiency effect nor any interaction involving the proficiency variable was significant in any of these analyses, as was the case in the overall ANOVA.

Comparison of the A-State Scores of HA-Trait and LA-Trait Subjects

Levels of A-State intensity for taboo and neutral words as a function of A-Trait were found to be nonsignificant for the median split analysis. A more sensitive test was carried out with subjects who scored in the extreme quartiles of the STAI A-Trait scores distribution. Eighteen subjects who scored 40 or above on the STAI A-Trait Scale were classified as HA-Trait, and 18 subjects who scored 30 or below comprised the LA-Trait group. The mean A-State scores for neutral Spanish and taboo Spanish words for the HA- and LA-Trait groups are presented in Figure 2. These data were evaluated by a two-factor ANOVA in which A-Trait was the between-subjects variable and Lists was the within-subjects variable. The most important finding was the significant A-Trait by Lists (A × L) interaction, $F = 5.47$, $p < .05$. When considered in the context of Figure 2, the A-Trait by Lists interaction indicated that the HA-Trait subjects showed a greater increase in A-State scores for the taboo words than the LA-Trait subjects.

Effect of Order of Saying Spanish and English Taboo Words on A-State

It may be recalled that in the present study the order in which the Spanish and English taboo words were presented was counterbalanced. Half of

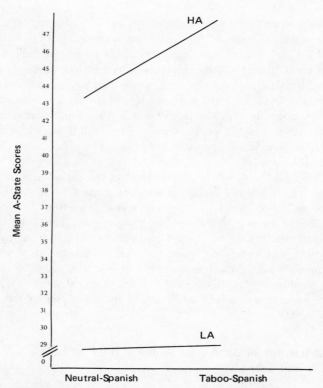

FIGURE 2 Mean A-State scores for neutral Spanish and taboo
Spanish words for HA-Trait and LA-Trait subjects
who scored in the extreme quartiles of the A-Trait
scores distribution.

the subjects were given the taboo Spanish words first (Order 1), and the
remaining subjects were given the taboo English words first (Order 2).
However, to investigate the possibility that order might have influenced the
A-State scores, an additional analysis was conducted to evaluate the effects of
order on A-State.

On the basis of A-Trait scores, proficiency scores, and order, eight
experimental groups were defined as follows: HA-HP/Order 1 ($N = 10$);
HA-HP/Order 2 ($N = 10$); HA-LP/Order 1 ($N = 10$); HA-LP/Order 2 ($N = 8$);
LA-HP/Order 1 ($N = 10$); LA-HP/Order 2 ($N = 10$); LA-LP/Order 1 ($N = 10$);
and LA-LP/Order 2 ($N = 10$). Because the number of subjects in the
HA-LP/Order 2 group was only eight, it was necessary to eliminate two
subjects at random from each of the other groups in order to have equal cell
frequency.

The A-State scores for the eight experimental groups were evaluated by a
four-factor ANOVA in which A-Trait, proficiency, and order were the

between-subjects variables, and Lists was the within-subjects variable. Neither the main effect of order nor any of the interactions involving order as a variable was statistically significant. The main effects of both A-Trait and Lists were essentially the same as in the analyses previously reported. Thus, the order of saying the Spanish and English taboo words did not appear to influence changes in A-State.

Reaction Times for Taboo and Neutral Words

A reaction time score was derived for each subject for each of the three word lists. These scores were based on the sums of the reaction times of the 10 words in each list.

The means and standard deviation of the reaction time scores for neutral Spanish, taboo Spanish, and taboo English words are presented in Table 4. Separate scores are reported for the HA-HP, HA-LP, LA-HP, and LA-LP groups, as well as for the total sample. These data were evaluated by a three-factor ANOVA in which trait anxiety (A-Trait) and proficiency (P) were the between-subjects variables, and Lists was the within-subjects variable. The only significant finding in this analysis was the proficiency main effect ($F = 6.77$, $p < .05$). The mean reaction times for taboo and neutral words for the HP and LP subjects are presented in Figure 3, in which the main effect of proficiency is reflected in the fact that HP subjects consistently responded faster than the LP subjects to each of the three types of words.

In order to compare the data for reaction time with the A-State findings, separate ANOVAs were computed for the neutral Spanish and the taboo English pairs of lists. As in the overall ANOVA for reaction times, the only significant finding in these three analyses was the main effect of proficiency ($Fs = 5.66$, 7.01, and 6.74, $p < .05$). When considered along with Figure 3, these findings indicated that subjects with high English proficiency responded faster to the neutral Spanish, taboo Spanish, and taboo English words than low proficiency subjects.

TABLE 4 Mean reaction times for taboo and neutral words

Group	N	Neutral Spanish		Taboo Spanish		Taboo English	
		Mean	SD	Mean	SD	Mean	SD
HA-HP	18	902.39	147.15	908.16	125.34	887.17	134.51
HA-LP	18	951.89	158.70	989.67	242.22	991.27	192.50
LA-HP	18	867.39	161.85	875.67	165.47	873.06	198.46
LA-LP	18	973.27	169.44	989.94	159.85	997.44	176.64
Total	72	923.73	161.57	940.83	181.80	937.23	182.88

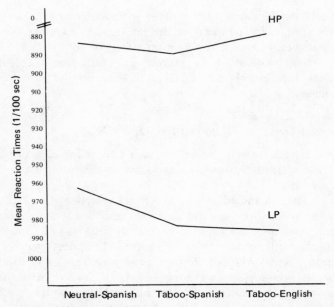

FIGURE 3 Mean reaction times for taboo and neutral words
for high and low proficiency subjects.

DISCUSSION

The emotional reactions of Spanish-English bilingual subjects to saying taboo and neutral words in their mother tongue (Spanish) and taboo words in their second language (English) were examined. Taboo Spanish words evoked higher levels of A-State intensity than either the neutral Spanish or the taboo English words.

It was found that in their mother tongue subjects showed higher levels of A-State while saying taboo words than while saying neutral words. This finding is consistent with the findings reported by Gonzalez-Reigosa (1971) and provides support for the hypothesis that saying taboo words is anxiety arousing (Ferenczi, 1916; Nothman, 1962).

The finding that subjects showed higher A-State scores for taboo words in their mother tongue than in their second language is also consistent with Ferenczi's observation that the emotional arousal evoked by taboo words decreases when they are pronounced in a foreign language, and with the findings reported by Sollee (1963), in which recognition thresholds for taboo words in the mother tongue were higher than for taboo words in the second language.

A related but unexpected finding was that the A-State intensity aroused by saying taboo words in the second language was no greater than the anxiety aroused by saying neutral words in the mother tongue. This finding was in accord with the comments made by many subjects during the debriefing session. These subjects spontaneously expressed that even though they knew the meaning of the taboo English words, they did not feel any emotional reaction while saying them, whereas this was not so for the taboo Spanish words. These subjects reported that this experience was a common everyday occurrence and not limited to the experimental session. The fact that the taboo words in the second language were not anxiety arousing provides support for Weinrich's (1953) contention that stimuli whose emotional quality stems from childhood (such as taboo words) arouse stronger emotions when experienced in relation to the mother tongue. Similarly, the hypothesis that an individual's more primitive emotional world is more readily expressed and assessed in terms of the mother tongue (Ervin, 1964; Sechrest, Flores, & Arellano, 1968; Del Castillo, 1970) was supported by these findings.

Since it was found that for these subjects taboo English words were not anxiety arousing, the most meaningful evaluation of changes in A-State as a function of A-Trait was the comparison between A-State scores for taboo Spanish and neutral Spanish words. The F test for this analysis was not significant when subjects were assigned to the HA- and LA-Trait groups on the basis of a median split. When a more sensitive test was conducted with subjects who scored in the quartile extremes on the distribution of A-Trait scores, it was found that the anxiety evoked in the HA-Trait subjects while saying taboo words was markedly higher than while saying neutral words. In contrast, LA-Trait subjects showed almost no difference in levels of A-State for the taboo and neutral words. When considered in the context of the trait-state anxiety theory (Spielberger, 1972), this finding appears to indicate that while HA-Trait subjects regard the verbal expression of taboo words as threatening, the LA-Trait subjects do not.

In examining the relationship between A-Trait and the threatening quality of stimuli that are capable of eliciting A-States, Spielberger (1966) says:

> A-Trait is assumed to reflect residues of past experiences that in some way determine individual differences in anxiety proneness, i.e., in the disposition to see certain types of situations as dangerous and to respond to them with A-States. Those experiences that have most influence on level of A-Trait probably date back to childhood, involving parent-child relationships centering around punishment situations. Level of A-Trait is not expected to influence A-State responses to all stimuli, only to particular classes of stimuli. (p. 18)

It may be recalled that Ferenczi (1916) and Nothman (1962) attributed the anxiety-arousing effect of taboo words to the fact that an individual who has been punished as a child for saying taboo words will anticipate punishment when he says one of these words later in life. Within these two frameworks, taboo words appear to belong to the class of stimuli whose threat value results from punishment situations dating back to childhood and, as such, are able to evoke elevations of A-State intensity in HA-Trait subjects.

An interesting point concerning the outcome of this study is the fact that proficiency in English did not influence the anxiety aroused by saying taboo words in that language. This finding suggests that the source of threat in a taboo word does not reside in the knowledge of the language or in knowing what a particular taboo word means. In this respect, it will be recalled that many subjects reported feeling no anxiety while saying a taboo word in the second language, even though they knew the meaning of the word.

When comparing the absence of an effect of English proficiency on the anxiety evoked by taboo words said in English and the marked differences in A-State for taboo words in English and Spanish, it is evident that the age at which the language was learned, rather than proficiency, is the critical variable influencing language-mediated emotional responses; hence, the importance of the mother tongue as the verbal vehicle of an individual's emotional world has been emphasized by this study.

The absence of a differential effect of taboo and neutral words on reaction time suggests that reaction times may be subject to the influence of variables other than emotional arousal. It may be speculated that a subject's mental set on what was expected of him in terms of speed of response and also his attitude toward the experimenter may affect his response latencies. In any case, the finding that the reaction time measures for the three types of words were highly intercorrelated indicates that the subjects responded to the stimuli in an idiosyncratic manner, in which each subject consistently tended to respond quickly or slowly to the three types of words.

The most important result with reference to reaction times, which is consistent with the previously reported finding, was the effect of proficiency on response latencies: subjects who were high in English proficiency consistently responded faster to all three types of words than did those who were low in English proficiency. This finding suggests the operation of a general factor relating proficiency in foreign languages to the ability to respond rapidly to written stimuli. The data obtained in this study do not allow for the identification of this general factor. It is possible that the nature of this factor may reside in differences in intelligence, but this is a hypothesis that needs to be empirically tested.

REFERENCES

Allport, F. H. *Theories of perception and the effect of structure.* New York: John Wiley & Sons, 1955.

Bitterman, M. E., & Kniffin, C. W. Manifest anxiety and "perceptual defense." *Journal of Abnormal and Social Psychology*, 1953, *48*, 248–252.

Bruner, J. S., & Postman, L. Emotional selectivity in perception and reaction. *Journal of Personality*, 1947, *16*, 69–77.

Del Castillo, J. C. The influence of language upon symptomatology in foreign-born patients. *Journal of Psychiatry*, 1970, *127*, 242–249.

Ervin, S. Language and TAT content in bilinguals. *Journal of Abnormal and Social Psychology*, 1964, *68*, 500–507.

Ferenczi, S. *Contributions to psychoanalysis.* Boston: Badger, 1916.

Gonzalez-Reigosa, F. *The anxiety arousing effect of taboo words.* Unpublished Master's Thesis, Florida State University, Tallahassee, Florida, 1971.

Howes, D. H., & Solomon, R. L. A note on McGinnies' "Emotionality and perceptual defense." *Psychological Review*, 1950, *57*, 229–235.

Johnson, G. B. Bilingualism as measured by a reaction time technique and the relationship between a language and an average IQ. *Journal of Genetic Psychology*, 1953, *82*, 3–9.

Jones, E. *Sigmund Freud: Life and work* (3 vols.). London: Hogarth Press, 1953–1957.

Lowie, R. A case of bilingualism. *Word*, 1945, *1*, 249–259.

McGinnies, E. Emotionality and perceptual defense. *Psychological Review*, 1949, *56*, 244–251.

Mendenhall, W. *Introduction to statistics.* Belmont, Calif.: Wadsworth, 1963.

Nothman, F. H. The influence of response conditions on recognition thresholds for taboo words. *Journal of Abnormal and Social Psychology*, 1962, *51*, 427–433.

Postman, L., Bronson, W. C., & Gropper, G. L. Is there a mechanism of perceptual defense? *Journal of Abnormal and Social Psychology*, 1953, *48*, 215–224.

Sechrest, L., Flores, L., & Arellano, L. Language and social interaction in bilingual culture. *Journal of Social Psychology*, 1968, *78*, 215–224.

Sollee, N. A. *A study of perceptual defense involving bilinguals: An experiment.* Unpublished Master's Thesis, University of the Philippines, Quezon City, 1963.

Solomon, R. L., & Howes, D. S. Word frequency, personal values and visual duration threshold. *Psychological Review*, 1951, *53*, 256–270.

Spielberger, C. D. The effects of stuttering behavior and response set on recognition thresholds. *Journal of Personality*, 1956, *25*, 33–45.

Spielberger, C. D. Theory and research on anxiety. In C. D. Spielberger (Ed.), *Anxiety and behavior.* New York: Academic Press, 1966.

Spielberger, C. D. *Anxiety: Current trends in theory and research.* New York: Academic Press, 1972.

Spielberger, C. D., Gonzalez-Reigosa, F., Martinez-Urrutia, A., Natalicio, L. F. S., & Natalicio, D. S. Development of the Spanish edition of the State-Trait Anxiety Inventory. *Revista Interamericana de Psicologia*, 1971, *5*, 145–158.

Spielberger, C. D., Gorsuch, R. L., & Lushene, R. E. *Manual for the State-Trait Anxiety Inventory.* Palo Alto, Calif.: Consulting Psychologist Press, 1970.

Walters, R. H., Banks, R. K., & Ryder, R. R. A test of the perceptual defense hypothesis. *Journal of Personality*, 1959, *27*, 47–55.

Weinrich, U. *Languages in contact.* The Hague: Mouton, 1953.

Whittaker, E. M., Gilchrist, J. C., & Fisher, J. W. Perceptual defense or response suppression? *Journal of Abnormal and Social Psychology*, 1952, *47*, 732–733.

Zajonc, R. B. Response suppression in perceptual defense. *Journal of Experimental Psychology*, 1962, *64*, 206–214.

Zigler, E., & Yospe, L. Perceptual defense and the problem of response suppression. *Journal of Personality*, 1960, *28*, 222–239.

8

A Repertory Grid Study of Anxiety in Greek Psychiatric Patients

Aris Liakos
John Papacostas
Costas Stefanis
Department of Psychiatry, University of Athens

Scientists and clinicians are confronted with a diversity of views in the study of anxiety. Many authors characterize anxiety as a "concept" or "construct" (Beck, 1972; Endler, 1975; Sarason, 1972). Clinicians are interested in pathological anxiety, psychoanalysts view anxiety as a product of conflicting intrapsychic forces, personality theorists consider individual differences in anxiety proneness as a personality trait, and neurophysiologists concern themselves with hormonal and neural mechanisms. Biochemists try to understand anxiety's contribution to blood chemistry, existentialists are interested in the experiential aspects of anxiety, and learning theorists view anxiety as a conditioned response.

Complex models have been proposed by investigators who regard anxiety as a confluence of more fundamental emotions. Cognitive appraisal is considered to be an essential component of anxiety by investigators who stress the importance of the individual's perception of stressful situations (Lazarus, Averill, & Opton, 1970). Some theorists contend that ambiguity and semantic confusion in anxiety research has resulted from the failure to recognize that there are several different types of anxiety concepts (Spielberger, 1966, 1972).

The diversity of views with regard to the nature of anxiety is also reflected in the measurement techniques that are employed by various investigators. Anxiety is assessed by such diverse measurement procedures as introspective reports, observer ratings, analysis of fantasy in projective personality tests, GSR fluctuations, EEG tracings, and the presence of adrenalin in the blood and of steroids in the urine.

In commenting on a study by Izard (1972), which attempted to provide evidence that anxiety is composed of many simpler emotions, Levitt (1972) concluded that it was a "fascinating study in semantics." However, there is a lack of research on anxiety in which appropriate techniques of measurement were employed. If a diversity of conceptions of anxiety is evident in the minds of the various investigators, such diversity should presumably also exist in the minds of the persons who experience anxiety. It would, therefore, seem desirable to investigate this possibility, and we have attempted to do this in the present study.

This study is presented in four main parts. In the first part, we briefly discuss Kelly's (1955) personal construct theory and summarize the repertory grid technique for the measurement of the conceptual structures employed in this research. In the second part, the results of an investigation of the anxiety-producing situations or elements of our anxiety grid are reported. In the third part, we report an investigation of constructs used by our subjects to evaluate anxiety situations. Finally, in the fourth part, we discuss the implications and meaning of our findings in relationship to other approaches to the study of anxiety.

KELLY'S PERSONAL CONSTRUCT THEORY AND METHODS OF APPLICATION

A formal detailed description of personal construct theory, with its fundamental postulate and its elaboration in eleven corollaries, as well as clinical applications, is presented in Kelly's (1955) two-volume work. Further elaborations of the theory are presented in a series of articles (Kelly, 1958, 1961, 1963, 1964, 1965). Comments and summaries of the theory have been offered by Banister (1962), Sechrest (1963), Mischel (1964), Warren (1964), and Kelly (1969).

According to personal construct theory, all human beings are concerned with the prediction and control of their environment. The basic philosophical assumption of personal construct theory is that there are many alternative ways to construe the world. In the process of adapting to the environment, each individual develops his own unique pattern of personal constructs (individuality corollary). Human processes, according to the theory's fundamental postulate, are "psychologically channelized by the ways in which [the person] anticipates events" (Kelly, 1955). The anticipation of events is accomplished by "construing their replication" (construction corollary).

Constructs are bipolar structures (dichotomy corollary). Their poles may be emergent (immediately perceived) or submerged. Each person chooses the pole of a construct which "seems to him more suitable for extension and clarification of his system" (choice corollary; Kelly, 1955).

Constructs are "based on simultaneous awareness of likeness and differences" (Kelly, 1955) among the objects or events that are evaluated and that are called *elements*. Constructs have a limited range of elements to which they can be applied (range corollary), and they are organized into a network of interrelationships forming the person's construct system (organization corollary). This system is continuously modified in the course of the successive replication of events (experience corollary). However, the modifications of a person's construct system are limited by the capability of his constructs to admit newly perceived elements (modulation corollary).

A variety of apparently incompatible construct subsystems may be employed by a person to evaluate similar sets of elements (fragmentation corollary). While personal constructs and construct systems are unique for each person, there are similarities between the systems and constructs of different persons (commonality corollary). An individual may partially construe the construction processes of another person and, in that way, play a role in the social processes involving the other person (sociality corollary).

According to Kelly (1955), events and objects can be appreciated, and appear real and meaningful, only when an individual's construct system allows him to assimilate or interpret them. Each construct has a "range of convenience," that is, "all those things to which the user would find its application useful." Some constructs are represented by words and others are not (preverbal constructs). The subject may have a high or low "level of cognitive awareness" for the constructs that are used in his patterns of construction. Some constructs are more important than others, and they may include other constructs as elements in their range of convenience (superordinate constructs). Thus, the distinction between elements and constructs seems to be artificial. Constructs may become elements, and vice versa. Anxiety is the "awareness that the events with which one is confronted lie mostly outside the range of convenience of his construct system."

In this brief outline of personal construct theory and the aspects of the theory necessary to understand the methodology of our work, we see that Kelly's theory places great importance on individual conceptual structures. Each person, in his own right, can be the sole object of investigation in the evaluation of his construct system. The evaluation of the personal constructs of a particular individual is accomplished by the grid method.

The Grid Method of Exploring Construction Processes

If we ask a person to classify a set of elements by his personal repertory of constructs, a repertory grid is produced. Grids are forms of sorting tests. They differ from common sorting tests, however, as they have evolved as a technique for investigating the construction processes that are defined by

Kelly's personal construct theory. The sorting materials, or sorting categories, are the elements of the grid whose nature depends on the area of the investigation. The categories may be people, objects, illnesses, political parties, emotions, and so on. The elements can be provided by the investigator in cases where a comprehensive range of them may be easily selected—political parties, for example—or they may be produced by the subjects. This becomes necessary in cases where an extensive range of elements may exist with the possibility that the elements provided by the investigator may be outside the range of convenience of the constructs of the subject. The following example will illustrate this. Let us suppose that the elements of a grid were types of meals. If we ask an American to evaluate curry, chow mein, paella, keftedes, or other exotic dishes, he might be unable to do so, but he would have no difficulty with hamburgers, hot dogs, fried potatoes, and the like.

In general, constructs should be elicited from the subjects. Or in cases where the investigator provides them, he must ensure that they are useful in the construct system of the subject. Various techniques for eliciting constructs have been employed, and one of the most frequently used is the *triad method.* According to this method we place three elements in front of the subject (typed on cards), and the subject is asked to specify in what important way two of them are alike, and thereby different from the third. Once the subject produces a construct, the procedure is repeated with different combinations of elements until an adequate number of constructs has been elicited.

While various ways of grid administration have been described, the most common is the ranking method. The subject is asked to rank order a set of elements using one of his constructs. He repeats this procedure using all the elicited constructs in turn until the grid is completed.

Analysis of Grids

The basic assumption in grid analysis is that a statistical relationship between two constructs in a given subject reflects a psychological relationship between them. Computer programs have been developed for analysis of grids based on principal component analysis (Slater, 1967; Hope, 1966). Other simple indices like Spearman rhos or relationship scores have been used to investigate the links between constructs or their relative importance in the subjects' construct system.

A relationship score between two constructs (Banister & Mair, 1968) is calculated by squaring their rank order correlation—calculated from the similarity of element placement by the two constructs—multiplied by 100. Relationship scores provide a measure of the percentage variance in common between the two constructs.

The intensity of relationship score of a subject for a given grid is the sum of *all* relationship scores of the grid (Banister, 1965). If we add the relationship scores of a construct with every other construct of the grid, we get the intensity score of the construct. This measure shows the amount of variance of the grid that is accounted for by the construct and may be considered a measure of the importance of the construct in the person's construct system.

OBTAINING THE ELEMENTS OF THE ANXIETY GRID

For the purpose of investigating the construct system of a given subject, the constructs and elements of this person are used. However, no simple method exists for the comparison of persons or groups using this method. In order to do this, a grid with standard elements and constructs is needed. An example of such a grid is the grid test of schizophrenic thought disorder developed by Banister and Francella (1966, 1967). To construct such a grid, there is no standard methodology other than the principles and theory that have been described earlier. As stated previously, before administering a grid we must ensure that all elements are within the range of convenience of the constructs used by the subjects and, in addition, that the constructs are within their construct systems.

The first thing that must be decided upon is the *elements* of the grid. In the investigation of construct systems of anxiety, the elements could be anxiety-producing situations or conditions. We asked subjects to produce such elements in the first phase of our investigation. We could have provided a range of elements that we thought were representative, as is often done in grid construction, but this would have assumed that the elements provided by us were within the range of convenience of the subjects' constructs. Given the variety and diversity of anxiety-producing situations, this assumption would be questionable.

Subjects and Method

Since our anxiety grid should be useful for clinical purposes, we asked a sample of neurotics and a sample of normal controls to provide the elements. The first sample consisted of 13 neurotics under treatment as inpatients ($N = 10$) or outpatients ($N = 3$) by the University of Athens Psychiatric Department (Eginition Hospital). The diagnosis recorded in the hospital records was the criterion for the selection of patients. Patients with doubtful diagnosis or evidence of organic disease were not included. Seven of the patients were male and six female. Their mean age was 37.07 (SD = 14 years). The sample of controls consisted of normal persons selected from the community who were free of any symptoms of mental disorder, and who were comparable in age and came from the same socioeconomic background as the patients. Of the 12 controls, six were male and six female, with a mean age of 34 years (SD = 8.2 years). The two samples did not significantly differ in age and sex as evaluated by statistical tests.

Each subject was asked to specify 10 situations or conditions that produce anxiety in him. A total of 250 elements were produced by the two samples. These were tabulated and a comparison of their frequency was made for the two groups of subjects. The effects of age, sex, and education on the frequency of appearance of elements was also tested.

In tabulating the elements, we noted a great diversity in the wording and content. Indeed, not a single pair of identical elements could be identified among the 250 produced. Therefore, in order to tabulate the elements, the following procedure was used. Two of the authors studied the elements carefully and tried to extract the main theme from each of them. This procedure yielded 43 different themes or categories, as listed in Table 1. We then asked two psychiatrists in our department to classify all of the elements into one of the 43 categories. The psychiatrists did this independently and were unaware of the purpose of the research. We added a forty-fourth category, "unclassifiable to any of the above," for elements that the judges could not classify in any of the 43 categories. The two judges agreed on 187 elements (74.8%), and only these reliable elements were used in the analyses that follow.

Results

The number of patients and controls who used each of the 44 categories is indicated in Table 1. No significant differences were found between the two groups when the 4 squares method of χ^2 was used to estimate differences. Next, the two samples were combined, and the effects of sex, age, and education were tested for each of the 44 categories. The mean age (35.6 years) and the mean number of years of education (9.3) were the cut-off points for the separation of the two groups.

With regard to sex, there was a difference in only one of the 44 categories: "difficulties with children." Only 2 of the 13 male subjects (15%) used this category in comparison with 10 of the 12 female (83%) ($\chi^2 = 11.54$; $p < .001$). Since some of the subjects were not married, or had no children, we tested the effect separately for married subjects with children and found a similar result. Two of the 6 married men with children used elements in this category as compared with 10 of the 11 married women with children ($\chi^2 = 6.78$; $p < .001$).

Age had an effect only on the category, "death." In the group of 15 subjects under the age of 35, only one used this category in comparison to 4 of 10 subjects who were over 35 years of age ($\chi^2 = 4.16$; $p < .05$).

Education had an effect only on the category, "Examinations." Of the 13 subjects with over 9 years of education, 6 used this category as compared with 1 of 12 subjects with less than 9 years of education ($\chi^2 = 4.4$; $p < .05$).

TABLE 1 Classification of anxiety elements (numbers of subjects who included the 44 categories in the range of convenience of their constructs)

	Neurotics (N = 13)	Controls (N = 12)	Total (N = 25)
1. Death	3	2	5
2. Illness	7	6	13
3. Unpleasant news	1	1	2
4. Difficulties with parents	1	1	2
5. Difficulties with spouse	6	3	9
6. Difficulties with children	7	5	12
7. Home responsibilities	1	1	2
8. Examinations	3	4	7
9. Economic difficulties	5	8	13
10. Difficulties with work	5	7	12
11. Social contact with unknown people	1	3	4
12. Threatening natural phenomena	1	3	4
13. Waiting	4	1	5
14. Sexual relations	3	2	5
15. Inadequacy	2	–	2
16. Difficulties with persons outside the family	1	1	2
17. Someone in authority	3	–	3
18. Difficulties with the boss	–	1	1
19. Dependence on others	–	2	2
20. Interference of others in my affairs	–	2	2
21. Accidents	4	–	4
22. Surgical operations	–	1	1
23. Insomnia	–	1	1
24. Lack of time	–	1	1
25. Senescence	–	–	–
26. Political situations	–	2	2
27. War	–	1	1
28. Injustice	1	–	1
29. Obligations	1	–	1
30. Adaptation	–	–	–
31. Lack of control of reality	–	1	1
32. Lack of self-control	–	2	2
33. To have to comply	–	1	1
34. Difficulties of understanding	–	2	2
35. Unfavorable criticism	–	1	1
36. Failure	1	1	2
37. Conflicting desires	–	1	1
38. Doubt	1	–	1
39. Uncertainty	1	–	1
40. Metaphysical phenomena	–	1	1
41. Physical appearance	1	–	1
42. Perfection	2	–	2
43. Traveling	–	3	3
44. Unclassifiable to any of the above categories	8	5	13
Total	74	77	151

OBTAINING THE CONSTRUCTS OF THE ANXIETY GRID

Subjects and Method

During this phase of the research, the following 10 elements from the 44 categories identified in the previous phase were used: (1) work difficulties, (2) illnesses, (3) the opposite sex, (4) waiting, (5) someone in authority, (6) failure, (7) home responsibilities, (8) social contacts, (9) difficulties with parents, (10) threatening natural phenomena.

In selecting these elements, categories of nonuniversal relevance (for instance, children, spouse, death, examinations) were avoided. We tried to include only those categories that were frequently used and to cover as wide a range as possible. The 10 standard elements were typed on cards and were used to elicit constructs from each subject in two new samples of neurotics and controls.

The procedure for eliciting constructs was the triad method described above. Three of the elements—illnesses, failure, and social contacts—were presented to the subject, who was asked to specify in what important way two of these elements were alike and thereby different from the third element. The procedure was repeated with different combinations of elements until the subject produced 10 constructs. All subjects used the 10 constructs that they provided to rank order each one of the 10 standard elements, and thus each subject completed one grid. Constructs were classified in the same way as were the elements during the previous phase of the investigation. We obtained 46 different construct categories during this phase. Grids were analyzed with a specially prepared computer program to obtain intensity scores for every construct used by the subjects.

During this phase, all subjects completed the Greek Form of the State-Trait Anxiety Inventory (STAI) (Spielberger, Gorsuch, & Lushene, 1970). The scale was translated independently by three bilingual persons. There was complete agreement among the translators on most items, but where there was disagreement on a specific item, differences were resolved by the consensus of the translators after thorough discussion of the linguistic connotations of the key words.

TABLE 2 Age and education of the neurotics and controls

	Neurotics (N = 26)		Controls (N = 17)			
	M	SD	M	SD	t	p
Age	32.8	10.5	29.17	9.87	1.25	NS
Years of education	8.73	3.4	10.35	3.51	1.48	NS

TABLE 3 The STAI scores of the samples

	Neurotics (N = 26)		Controls (N = 17)			
	M	SD	M	SD	t	p
State anxiety	55.60	10.4	39.69	9.69	5.053	.001
Trait anxiety	51.23	10.0	40.41	7.45	3.80	.001

The sample of neurotic patients consisted of 26 subjects (15 male, 11 female), and the sample of controls consisted of 17 subjects (7 male, 10 female). The neurotics and controls did not differ significantly in age and years of education, as is shown in Table 2.

Results

The mean STAI scores for the neurotics and controls are reported in Table 3. These scores are similar to the scores obtained in the administration of the STAI to other populations of neurotic and normal subjects (Spielberger et al., 1970). The STAI-GX state and trait anxiety scales significantly discriminated between the two groups.

Table 4 lists the 46 categories of constructs that were obtained and the number of neurotic and control subjects who provided constructs belonging to each category. As may be noted in Table 5, the only construct given by a significantly larger number percentage of neurotics was, "Has to Do with Guilt." Nineteen neurotic subjects (73%) produced this category in comparison with only 5 controls (29%) ($\chi^2 = 7.96; p < .01$). There was also a tendency for the neurotics to use the constructs, "has to do with depression" and "may have good results," more often than the controls. Conversely, a significantly higher percentage of controls produced constructs that were difficult to classify.

We next tested the effects of sex, age, and education on the frequency of use of the 46 categories of constructs. Table 6 shows the effect of sex. Significantly more male subjects used the construct categories, "has to do with money," "has to do with guilt," and "needs help from someone else." In contrast, significantly more females used the construct categories "every day anxiety" and "may have unpleasant results."

The number of constructs that the raters could not classify within the 45 construct categories was related to age and level of education. Subjects over 31 years of age produced a significantly smaller number of constructs (22%) that could not be classified than did subjects under 31 years of age (56%) ($\chi^2 = 4.40; p < .05$). More educated subjects produced a significantly higher number of unclassifiable constructs (41%) than subjects with less education (5%). The better educated subjects also used the category, "personal anxiety"

TABLE 4 Classification of anxiety constructs

	Neurotics ($N = 26$)	Controls ($N = 17$)	Total ($N = 43$)
1. Produced by ourselves	2	0	2
2. Internal	2	0	2
3. Due to my character	2	4	6
4. Personal	5	5	10
5. Objective	4	3	7
6. Has to do with relatives	6	2	8
7. Has to do with social contact	9	5	14
8. Has to do with money	5	4	9
9. Normal	3	1	4
10. Accounted for	1	0	1
11. The cause is known	2	0	2
12. Has to do with guilt	19	5	24
13. Has to do with duty	1	0	1
14. Everyday (anxiety)	10	4	14
15. Vague	8	2	10
16. Has to do with depression	11	3	14
17. Has to do with fear	7	4	11
18. Fear of death	2	2	4
19. Has to do with anguish	3	1	4
20. Has to do with luck	1	1	2
21. Has to do with love	2	2	4
22. Has to do with failure	3	1	4
23. Has to do with inadequacy	1	3	4
24. Has to do with nerves	1	0	1
25. Has to do with insecurity	2	1	3
26. Difficult	4	3	7
27. Intolerable	1	0	1
28. Ugly	1	0	1
29. Bad	1	1	2
30. Worse	4	2	6
31. Heavy	2	0	2
32. Light	2	3	5
33. Preferable	4	1	5
34. Interesting	5	2	7
35. May have good results	5	0	5
36. May have unpleasant results	5	7	12
37. You could deal with it yourself	4	4	8
38. Could be overcome	6	3	9
39. I know how to deal with it	2	1	3
40. Needs help from someone else	6	2	8
41. You may avoid it	2	3	5
42. The result is unknown	2	1	3
43. We don't know what we are going to face	1	0	1
44. Concerns me	3	0	3
45. Needs special care	5	1	6
46. Unclassifiable to any of the above categories	5	13	18
Total	182	97	281

TABLE 5 Differences between neurotic subjects and controls in the use of constructs

Construct	Neurotics ($N = 26$)		Controls ($N = 17$)		χ^2	p
	N	$\%$	N	$\%$		
12. Has to do with guilt	19	73	5	29	7.96	.005
16. Has to do with depression	11	42	3	18	2.48	.10
35. May have good results	5	19	0	0	3.69	.10
46. Nonclassified constructs	5	19	13	76	13.83	.001

significantly more often (59%) than persons with less education (24%) ($\chi^2 = 5.40$; $p < .025$).

We next examined the constructs that accounted for the largest amount of variance in the grid for each subject, that is, those constructs with the highest intensity scores. According to Kelly, these constructs are the most important, or "superordinate." Table 7 shows the distribution of super-ordinate constructs in the 46 construct categories.

To determine if quantitative measures of important anxiety constructs could be related to other anxiety measures, such as state and trait anxiety as measured by the STAI, correlations of the intensity scores with STAI A-State and A-Trait scales were computed, and these are shown in Table 8. The correlation of the STAI score with intensity score is also shown in Table 8, separately for the neurotics and controls, and for the two groups pooled together. While the correlations shown in Table 8 were not statistically significant, the correlation for neurotics was consistently negative and the correlation for controls positive. Furthermore, this pattern was evident for both important (superordinate) constructs and for the intensity scores of the subjects.

TABLE 6 The effect of sex on the frequency of construct categories

Construct	Male ($N = 22$)		Female ($N = 21$)		χ^2	p
	N	$\%$	N	$\%$		
8. Has to do with money	8	36.4	1	6.5	6.48	.025
12. Has to do with guilt	17	77.2	7	8.4	8.41	.005
14. Everyday (anxiety)	2	9.0	11	11.3	11.29	.001
36. May have unpleasant results	3	13.6	9	4.6	4.55	.05
40. Needs help from someone else	7	31.8	1	5.2	5.19	.025

TABLE 7 Distribution of important constructs

	Neurotics (N = 26)	Controls (N = 17)	Total (N = 43)
2. Internal	1		1
4. Personal	1		1
7. Has to do with social contact	3	1	4
14. Everyday (anxiety)	1		1
16. Has to do with depression	4	1	5
17. Has to do with fear	2		2
18. Fear of death		1	1
19. Has to do with anguish	1		1
23. Has to do with inadequacy		1	1
25. Has to do with insecurity	1		1
26. Difficult	1	2	3
27. Intolerable	1		1
28. Ugly	1		1
30. Worse		1	1
31. Heavy		1	1
33. Preferable		1	1
36. May have unpleasant results	1		1
37. You could deal with it yourself		1	1
40. Needs help from someone else	1		1
44. Concerns me	1	2	3
46. Unclassifiable to any of the above categories	1	1	2
Constructs rejected because of disagreement of raters	5	4	9

TABLE 8 Correlation of the STAI scores with intensity scores of the grids and intensity score of important constructs

	Grid intensity scores		
	Neurotics (N = 26)	Controls (N = 17)	Neurotics and Controls (N = 43)
State anxiety	−.18	.21	.00
Trait anxiety	−.13	.20	.00

	Important construct intensity scores		
	Neurotics (N = 26)	Controls (N = 17)	Neurotics and controls (N = 43)
State anxiety	−.07	.19	.04
Trait anxiety	−.08	.19	.02

SUMMARY AND CONCLUSIONS

Sarason (1972) has stressed the importance of situational, cognitive, and perceptual factors in anxiety research, pointing out that much research is needed to fill the gap in present knowledge. The present investigation attempts to fill a small part of the gap. It was performed in the Greek language, and some of the expressions used by our subjects were difficult to translate. As construction systems of anxiety vary from person to person one should expect differences between persons who belong to different sociocultural environments. While one should be cautious in trying to draw conclusions of universal relevance from the results of this investigation, similarities exist and some general points may be made.

The first thing that became apparent is the great diversity and variety of anxiety-producing situations. As expected, each subject appeared to have his own almost unique anxiety-producing situation range. It was necessary to simplify elements into broader categories, to classify them, in order to discover some similarities. Older subjects mentioned "death" more often, female subjects were more concerned about "anxiety related to children," and better educated subjects reacted more to "examinations." While the majority of elements concerned external events, some seemed to stem from the subject himself such as "inadequacy," "lack of self-control," "conflicting desires," "doubt," "uncertainty," and "perfection." These findings suggest that anxiety-producing situations may be classified as resulting from either internal or external sources of stress (Spielberger, 1966; Lader & Marks, 1971).

Other authors have stressed the importance of anxiety-producing situations for anxiety research (Mandler, 1959; Endler, et al., 1962; Levitt, 1967). We would like to add that, in studying the individual, one should try to understand his *personal* sources of anxiety. But when studying groups of people, great difficulty arises in deciding on a *representative* set of anxiety-producing situations that has relevance for all subjects. When one tries to focus on a specific source, things may be easier. It would be easier, for example, to select a representative set of elements in order to develop a test anxiety grid.

As dimensions of anxiety-producing situations, individual constructs are diverse. By grouping constructs together, some differences between neurotics and controls in their preference of constructs became evident. Neurotics used the construct "has to do with guilt" more than normals and also showed a greater tendency to use the construct "has to do with depression." They also tended to use the construct "may have good results" less than normals.

Effects of sex and education were also evident in the preference of constructs. Males used the constructs "has to do with guilt," "has to do with money," and "needs help from someone else" more than females. Females used the construct "may have unpleasant results" more than males. Educated subjects used the construct "personal" more than persons with relatively little education.

When one looks at categories in general, familiar dimensions emerge that remind us of various theories of anxiety. "Due to my character," "produced by ourselves," and "has to do with inadequacy," for example, focus on the personality aspects of anxiety. "Normal," "everyday," "needs special care," "needs help from someone else," and "vague" are constructs expressing the clinician's views. Other categories like "may have good results" and "interesting" remind us of anxiety as a drive. Associations of anxiety constructs with other emotions—such as "has to do with guilt," "depression," and "fear"—are widespread.

Some constructs are more like elements in that they are associated with anxiety-producing situations such as "has to do with relatives" and "social contacts." Personal construct theory provides for this possibility in that constructs that become elements are considered as subordinate. A similar observation applies to anxiety elements that appear more like constructs than like anxiety-producing situations. Thus, if one looks at constructs in their raw form (as produced by subjects), every diverse scientific theoretical view of anxiety appears to be represented. We may then conclude that we were justified in our expectation that the divergent views about anxiety in the minds of scientists are also represented in the minds of individuals who experience anxiety.

In conclusion, the grid technique and the underlying theory employed in this study provided a good method for investigating individual subjects' constructions of anxiety. One would eventually like to have a tool suitable for groups of people, and this work may be considered as a necessary preliminary step toward that end. In the present investigation we mainly concerned ourselves with the *content* analysis of an anxiety grid, and very little attention was directed toward quantitative analysis. If one chooses a well-selected set of standard constructs to use in further investigation, quantitative analysis of the constructs of *groups* of neurotics in comparison to controls will become possible. The authors have used a similar procedure to develop an illness grid from which quantitative scores can be derived that discriminated between parents of schizophrenics and physically ill patients (Liakos, Papacostas, & Stefanis, 1975). If the constructions of anxiety are different for neurotics and normals, an anxiety grid with standard constructs can be developed that would yield quantitative scores to discriminate neurotics from normal controls.

REFERENCES

Banister, D. Personal construct theory: A summary and experimental paradigm," *Acta Psychologica*, 1962, *20*, 104.

Banister, D. The genesis of schizophrenic thought disorder: Re-test of the serial invalidation hypothesis." *British Journal of Psychiatry*, 1965, *111*, 377–382.

Banister, D., & Francella, F. A grid test of schizophrenic thought disorder. *British Journal of Social Psychology*, 1966, *5*, 95.

Banister, D., & Francella, F. *A grid test of schizophrenic thought disorder: A standard clinical test.* Barnstaple: Psychological Test Publication, 1967.

Banister, D., & Mair, J. M. M. *The evaluation of personal constructs.* New York and London: Academic Press, 1968.

Beck, A. T. Comments on Dr. Epstein's paper. In C. D. Spielberger (Ed.), *Anxiety: Current trends in theory and research* (Vol. 2). New York and London: Academic Press, 1972.

Endler, N. S. A person-situation interaction model for anxiety. In C. D. Spielberger and I. G. Sarason (Eds.), *Stress and anxiety* (Vol. 1). Washington, D.C.: Hemisphere/Wiley, 1975.

Endler, N. S., Hunt, J. McV., & Rosenstein, A. J. An S-R inventory of anxiousness. *Psychological Monographs*, 1962, *76*, 1–30.

Hope, K. Cos and cosmos: Consideration on Patric Slater's monograph "The principal components of a repertory grid." *British Journal of Psychiatry*, 1966, *112*, 1115–1163.

Izard, C. E. Anxiety: A variable combination of interacting fundamental emotions. In C. D. Spielberger (Ed.), *Anxiety: Current trends on theory and research* (Vol. 1). New York and London: Academic Press, 1972.

Kelly, G. A. *The psychology of personal constructs* (Vols. 1 & 2). New York: Norton, 1955.

Kelly, G. A. Man's construction of his alternatives. In G. Lindzey (Ed.), *The assessment of human motives.* New York: Rinehart, 1958.

Kelly, G. A. Theory and therapy in suicide: The personal construct point of view. In N. Farberow & E. Shneidman (Eds.), *The cry for help.* New York: McGraw-Hill, 1961.

Kelly, G. A. *A theory of personality.* New York: Norton, 1963.

Kelly, G. A. The language of hypnosis. *Journal of Individual Psychology*, 1964, *20*, 137.

Kelly, G. A. The strategy of psychological research. *B. P. S. Bull.*, 1965, *18*, 1.

Kelly, G. A. In B. A. Maher (Ed.), *Clinical psychology and personality: The selected papers of George Kelly.* New York and London: John Wiley & Sons, 1969.

Lader, M., & Marks, I. *Clinical anxiety.* London: Heinemann Medical Books, 1971.

Lazarus, R. S., Averill, E. M., & Opton, E. M. Towards a cognitive theory of emotions. In M. Arnold (Ed.), *Third International Symposium of Feelings and Emotions.* New York: Academic Press, 1970.

Levitt, E. E. *The psychology of anxiety.* Indianapolis: Bobbs-Merrill, 1967.

Levitt, E. E. Comments on Dr. Izard's paper. In C. D. Spielberger (Ed.), *Anxiety: Current trends in theory and research* (Vol. 1). New York: Academic Press, 1972.

Liakos, A., Papacostas, J., & Stefanis, C. A repertory grid investigation of the concept of illness by parents of schizophrenic patients. *British Journal of Psychiatry*, 1975, *126*, 354–359.

Mandler, G. Stimulus variables and subject variables: A caution. *Psychological Review*, 1959, *6*, 145–149.

Mischel, T. Personal constructs, rules and the logic of clinical activity. *Psychological Review*, 1964, *71*, 180.

Sarason, I. G. Experimental approaches to test anxiety: Attention and the uses of information. In C. D. Spielberger (Ed.), *Anxiety: Current trends in theory and research* (Vol. 2). New York and London: Academic Press, 1972.

Sechrest, L. B. The psychology of personal constructs: George Kelly. In J. M. Wepman & R. W. Heine (Eds.), *Concepts of personality.* Chicago: Aldine, 1963.

Spielberger, C. D. Theory and research on anxiety. In C. D. Spielberger (Ed.), *Anxiety and behavior.* New York: Academic Press, 1966.

Spielberger, C. D. Conceptual and methodological issues in research on anxiety. In C. D. Spielberger (Ed.), *Anxiety: Current trends in theory and research* (Vol. 2). New York: Academic Press, 1972.

Spielberger, C. D., Gorsuch, R. L., & Lushene, R. E. *Manual for the State-Trait Anxiety Inventory.* Palo Alto, Calif.: Consulting Psychologists Press, 1970.

Warren, N. Constructs, rules and the explanation of behaviour. In N. Warren (Ed.), *Brunel construct theory seminar report.* Brunel University, 1964.

9

State and Trait Anxiety in Italian Cardiac and Dermatological Patients: Clinical and Cross-Cultural Considerations

P. Pancheri
A. Bernabei
M. Bellaterra
S. Tartaglione
Istituto di Psichiatria della Universita di Roma

The present study is based on a rather new conceptual distinction in psychological research on anxiety: state anxiety versus trait anxiety. From a conceptual point of view, there are important differences between personality states and personality traits. Personality states have been defined as temporal cross sections in the life-stream of a person (Spielberger, 1966, 1972). Personality traits are generally defined in terms of individual differences in tendencies to react or to behave in a specified manner. The response dispositions associated with a personality trait are latent until a particular situation activates them.

The state-trait distinction has been most productive in anxiety research. State anxiety has been defined as a transitory emotional state characterized by feelings of tension and apprehension and by increased autonomic nervous system (ANS) activity (Spielberger, 1972). In contrast, trait anxiety is the probability, stronger or weaker depending on the individual, that anxiety states will be experienced in response to stresses in one's social environment. Persons who are high in trait anxiety are more prone to perceive relations with other persons as more threatening and to respond with more frequent and more intense elevations in state anxiety.

STATE-TRAIT ANXIETY ASSESSMENT

Techniques for the measurement of personality traits are better developed than procedures for the assessment of personality states. In part, this difference seems to reflect the psychometric and methodological difficulties encountered in measuring inner feelings and experiences that vary in intensity and fluctuate over time. The problem of empirically evaluating the construct validity of self-report inventories that purport to measure transitory states requires different psychometric assumptions than those that have proved successful in measuring personality traits.

The State-Trait Anxiety Inventory (STAI) was developed by Spielberger, Gorsuch, and Lushene (1970). The STAI A-State scale consists of 20 items that require the subject to rate present anxiety feelings. The STAI A-Trait scale consists of 20 items that require subjects to rate symptoms of anxiety in terms of the frequency with which they are experienced. On both scales, the subject rates each item on a 4-point scale. The scale points for the A-State scale are: (1) not at all; (2) somewhat; (3) moderately so; (4) very much so. For the A-Trait scale, the choices are: (1) almost never; (2) sometimes; (3) often; (4) almost always. The STAI A-State scale measures transitory anxiety. The STAI A-Trait scale reflects individual differences in the frequency and the intensity of anxiety states and associated behaviors.

An important characteristic of the STAI scales is the brevity of administration. A long test might interfere with performance and would be less sensitive to variations that occur in a time shorter than that needed to take the test. Evidence of the construct and concurrent validity and the reliability of the STAI A-Trait and A-State scales may be found in the investigations that are described and the references cited in the Test Manual (Spielberger et al., 1970).

ANXIETY AS PROCESS: DEFENSE MECHANISMS AND PSYCHOSOMATIC DISORDERS

According to Spielberger (1972), the arousal of anxiety states involves a process that can be described as follows: external stimuli (i.e., stressors) or internal stimuli (i.e., inner feelings, thoughts, unconscious life pressures), interpreted by cognitive appraisal as threatening, evoke anxiety states. Once aroused, the intensity and persistence of anxiety states depend on individual differences in anxiety proneness, previous experiences in dealing with similar stimuli, and the strength and duration of external and internal stimuli. In this process unconscious defense mechanisms are also involved. Usually, the stronger or more effective the defense mechanism, the lower is the level of free-floating state anxiety.

One important unconscious psychological defense mechanism is conversion. Conversion reactions may be regarded as demonstrating a connection between psychological and somatic states that results from the arousal of the autonomic nervous system (ANS) as a somatic response to external stressors or internal stimuli. In psychosomatic disorders, conversion processes and psychogenic ANS activation contribute to the development of psychosomatic symptoms.

It is quite obvious that one can only measure what can be observed. Constructs about psychological defense mechanisms such as conversion are widely accepted and used, but such mechanisms are inferred rather than directly observed. On the other hand, people can be asked to describe, by means of an inventory, their own feelings and behaviors. Responses to personality inventories thus provide an empirical approach to the measurement of affective states.

MEASUREMENT OF ANXIETY IN CARDIAC AND DERMATOLOGY PATIENTS

The procedures used by investigators interested in psychosomatic research include behavioral-clinical, psychosocial, personological, and biological approaches. In our opinion, a major problem in current psychiatric research is that while much new data have been collected, this field lacks a comprehensive and widely accepted psychological system with generally accepted constructs. In this chapter we propose to employ, as a system of reference, a trait-state theory of anxiety (Spielberger, 1966, 1972).

The first goal of this study was to collect normative data on state and trait anxiety for an Italian population, and to compare Italians with Americans from a cross-cultural standpoint. The availability of these normative data was essential to the second goal of the study, which was the assessment of A-State and A-Trait in Italian cardiac and dermatological patients.

Developing the Italian Form of the STAI

The choice of the STAI as an assessment device in this study was based on two main considerations. First, this inventory was specifically designed to assess the central constructs of Spielberger's (1966, 1972) trait-state anxiety theory. Second, the STAI has been employed with promising results in studies of emotional factors associated with medical and surgical interventions (e.g.,

De Long, 1970; Edwards, 1969; Spielberger, Auerbach, Wadsworth, Dunn, & Taulbee, 1973).

As the first step in this research, the STAI was translated into Italian by the Psychology Service and the clinical staff of the Istituto di Psichiatria della Universita di Roma. The translation of any personality inventory from the original language always raises methodological problems that need to be resolved in order to make the normative data comparable from a cross-cultural standpoint. For example, different normative values may reflect real differences among the populations compared, or may be cross-cultural artifacts that result when the translation of each item does not exactly fit the original meaning of the item.

Since language is dependent upon the sociocultural framework in which it was developed, the less technical the language that is used in a personality test, the more difficult will be the exact correspondence between terms in different languages. Thus, a technical translation can be highly reliable, while the translation of a popular novel with many slang terms or the literal translation of a poem may be almost impossible. In the case of the translation of a personality inventory, the linguistic content and form of each item in the original language are chosen from among many other similar forms because they are best suited for measuring the personality trait. Therefore, any change in form or content is likely to modify the response of the patient to that item.

In most cases it is not difficult to find the word or sentence that has approximately the same exact meaning in both languages, but in some cases a concept, a quality, or a feeling that is easily expressed with a single word in one language needs a whole sentence in its translation into another language. Moreover, when, as in the case of the STAI, there are many items directed to the measurement of the same psychological dimension, even slight differences in meaning among items may become very important and influence test scores.

The Italian translation of the STAI was carried out by a group of three psychiatrists, each with a good knowledge of English and with substantial experience in the practice of psychiatry with Italian patients. The accuracy of the translation was checked by means of a "back translation" from Italian into English, made by a bilingual American psychologist with no previous knowledge of the STAI. As a result of this work, it was found that the 40 STAI items could be grouped into three different categories from the standpoint of the exactness of the translation:

1. Items whose Italian translation closely fitted with the original English form.
2. Items with content that caused problems for the translators because of the difficulty of finding words in Italian that corresponded to the content of the English words.

3. Items with a linguistic form that could not be translated from English into Italian without changing the grammatical construction of the item.

Examples of STAI items that could be translated literally into Italian are indicated in the top section of Table 1. The Italian translation of these items fits exactly with the English content in that the back translation gives the same wording as the original item in English. The total number of STAI items of this type was 29.

Examples of the second category of items are given in the middle portion of Table 1. For such items, the translators had to formulate words with similar meaning to replace English words like "upset" and "blue" for which there was no corresponding "twin-word" in Italian. The number of items belonging to this group was 8. In developing the Italian form of the STAI, it was decided that the closest single Italian word, or two or three similar terms, would be used to define, as precisely as possible, the original English term.

Examples of the third category of items are given in the bottom portion of Table 1. For such items, word-to-word translation was not possible because the equivalent Italian terms were not available and changes in the linguistic structure of the item were also required. It may be noted that the back translations were somewhat different from the original items. Fortunately, there were only three items of this type, all involving American idioms. Moreover, as may be noted in the back translations of the items in Table 1, it was possible to capture the essential content of the English item in the Italian translation.

TABLE 1 Examples of STAI items translated into Italian

Item category	Original STAI item in English	Italian translation	Back translation
Items for which literal translation was possible	1. I feel calm.	*Mi sento calmo.*	I feel calm.
	2. I feel secure.	*Mi sento sicuro.*	I feel secure.
	17. I am worried.	*Sono preoccupato.*	I am worried.
Items with no corresponding "twin word" in Italian	6. I feel upset.	*Mi sento turbato.*	I feel troubled (or disturbed).
	35. I feel blue.	*Mi sento stanco e depresso.*	I feel tired and depressed.
Items that required changes in linguistic form	14. I feel "high strung."	*Mi sento molto teso.*	I feel very tense.
	25. I am losing out on things because I can't make up my mind soon enough.	*Spesso perdo delle occasioni perche non riesco a decidermi abbstanza in fretta.*	I miss opportunities because I can't decide quickly enough.

During the translation, it was noticed that when the content of the original English items was very similar, the Italian translation for such items was exactly the same. For example, the best translation for item 5 ("I feel at ease.") was "mi sento a mio agio," but the same translation was also perfectly appropriate for item 10 ("I feel comfortable."). Therefore, for item 5, it was decided to alter the Italian translation to "mi sento tranquillo," which, though not a literal translation, has essentially the same meaning.

Collecting Normative Data

The collection of normative data for populations that differ socioculturally and linguistically brings other important methodological problems. The method usually followed, when an inventory is translated and adapted to another language, is to administer it to a normal population whose demographic characteristics (age, sex, educational level) are as close as possible to those of the original normative population. It should be pointed out, however, that the comparability of two populations in cross-cultural research may depend upon variables that are difficult to take into account.

For example, there may be strong cultural differences in some countries between different geographical areas, and, therefore, the same college population is likely to be scarcely comparable if assessed in different parts of the country. A college population in northern Italy is more similar, from a cross-cultural standpoint, to a French or Swiss population than to Sicilians because of historical and cultural factors. Similarly, there are important cultural differences between the northern and southern states in the United States. Thus, important differences may be reflected in normative data for which the psychological meaning cannot be entirely attributed to cross-cultural factors.

In the present study, the STAI data for the normative sample were based on 370 normal subjects (165 males, 205 females). The males were mostly military draftees plus a few college undergraduates. The normal females were all undergraduate college students. The age range for the normative sample was 20 to 27 years. The data for the normal sample in the present study are the first norms obtained for the STAI in Italy.

The means and standard deviations of scores on the STAI A-State and A-Trait scales for normal Italian males and females are reported in Table 2. For comparison purposes, STAI means and SDs for U.S. college students, as reported in the STAI Test Manual (Spielberger et al., 1970), are also presented in Table 2.

Comparison of Cardiac and Dermatological Patients With Normals in State and Trait Anxiety

One of the goals of this study was to examine state and trait anxiety in two classic psychosomatic disorders, skin problems and heart disease, and to

TABLE 2 STAI A-Trait and A-State means for Italian normals and
U.S. college students

		A-Trait		A-State	
	N	Mean	SD	Mean	SD
Italian males	165	39.53	9.25	40.17	10.01
Italian females	205	46.10	11.53	45.20	12.37
U.S. males	253	37.68	9.69	36.35	9.65
U.S. females	231	38.25	9.14	35.12	9.25

compare patients suffering from these disorders with each other and with normal subjects. The subjects were 370 normals (165 males, 205 females), 282 dermatological patients (154 males, 128 females), and 78 cardiac patients (57 males, 21 females).

The dermopaths were out-patients receiving treatment at the Casualty Department of the San Gallicano Hospital in Rome. The cardiopaths were all in-patients of the Cardiological Department of the San Camillo de Lellis Hospital, also in Rome. Fifty-one of the cardiac patients were equipped with pacemakers. Patients were chosen for testing without any regard to the specific clinical diagnosis subsumed under the general categories of dermopath and cardiopath.

Each subject was tested individually. The examiner introduced himself as a staff member of the Psychology Service of the I.P.U.R. It was explained that the Psychology Service was interested in the emotional problems of dermatological or cardiac patients in order to understand them better and to help other patients with similar problems who must undergo therapy in the future. After a brief interview, in which age, educational level, and willingness to participate in the study were determined, the STAI A-State and A-Trait scales were administered with standard instructions.

In Table 3, STAI means and SDs for dermopaths and cardiopaths, each sample considered as a whole and by sex, are reported. Cardiopaths with pacemakers are also compared to those without pacemakers. As may be noted in Table 3, females in all groups were consistently higher than males in A-State and A-Trait and cardiopaths tended to be higher than dermopaths in A-Trait.

In Table 4, *t* tests and level of statistical confidence for differences between A-State and A-Trait means for normals versus dermopaths, normals versus cardiopaths, and males versus females are reported. The differences between A-State means for dermopaths and normals were significant, but the difference between cardiopaths and normals was not. For A-Trait, the difference between the means of cardiopaths and normals was statistically significant, while the difference between the means of dermopaths and

TABLE 3 STAI A-Trait and A-State means for dermopaths
and cardiopaths

Groups	N	A-Trait		A-State	
		Mean	SD	Mean	SD
All dermopaths	282	43.32	9.08	44.99	10.46
Males	154	41.55	9.15	43.22	10.16
Females	128	45.45	8.55	47.13	10.45
All cardiopaths	78	45.78	9.42	44.87	10.86
Males	57	43.78	9.17	43.40	10.52
Females	21	51.19	8.02	48.85	11.01
With pacemaker	52	47.21	10.19	46.05	11.90
Without pacemaker	26	42.84	7.21	42.15	8.10

normals was not. The normal females were significantly higher than the normal
males in both state and trait anxiety (see Table 3).

DISCUSSION OF RESULTS

The differences in STAI means among Italian and American normals that
may be observed in Table 2 must be considered from a cross-cultural point of
view. The higher STAI A-Trait scores for the Italian sample appears to
indicate that anxiety states and associated behaviors are more frequently
experienced by Italian subjects. On the basis of a single self-report measure,
however, for which item content is focused on symptoms or feelings without
regard to external stressors or internal stimuli, it is obviously not possible to
provide a coherent interpretation of these differences in anxiety.

Clearly, cross-cultural factors may have differentially affected test-taking
attitudes in the Italian and American samples. In general, the Italian
population seems to be more overt in complaining of anxiety feelings. We
speculate that Italian social and interpersonal situations tolerate, or reinforce,
more overt expressions of anxiety feelings and associated behaviors than does
the American culture, and this would seem to be especially true in females.

TABLE 4 Level of statistical confidence of differences between
A-State and A-Trait means for normal male and female
dermopaths and cardiopaths

Subject group	A-Trait		A-State	
	t	p	t	p
Dermopaths–Normals	.090	n.s.	2.348	<.02
Cardiopaths–Normals	2.150	<.05	1.396	n.s.
Normal females–Males	6.072	<.01	4.321	<.01

The results of previous cross-cultural studies with the Minnesota Multiphasic Personality Inventory have shown that Italian subjects, when compared to German-speaking populations, tended to report more depression and anxiety feelings (Pancheri, 1973).

In the analysis of the STAI performance of cardiopaths and dermopaths, the most prominent findings were: first, dermopaths had significantly higher mean A-State scores than normals, while cardiopaths did not differ from normals in A-State; and, second, cardiopaths had significantly higher mean A-Trait scores than normals, while dermopaths and normals did not differ in A-Trait. It should be noted that the cardiac patients were presumably experiencing high levels of stress when they were tested. Acute failure of cardiac functioning had resulted in their hospitalization, and their medical condition was considered serious. In addition, hospitalization itself is often experienced as anxiety arousing. When tested, the cardiopaths were no more anxious than normals as reflected in their A-State scores, but they reported that they usually experienced more anxiety than normals as may be noted in their A-Trait scores.

The results indicated that dermopaths, who were tested when they submitted to a routine physical exam in a casualty department, were higher in A-State than the cardiac patients and much more anxious than normals. In contrast, the dermopaths reported they usually experienced no more anxiety (A-Trait) than normals and were considerably lower in A-Trait than the cardiopaths. In medical practice it is well known that dermopaths are generally tense, nervous persons who have a low threshold for anxious reactivity. Indeed, the hypothesis of a psychological etiology for dermatological diseases originated from this evidence. On the other hand, a low level of A-State in cardiopaths during hospitalization is actually not too surprising. In cardiological departments, physicians often observe seriously ill persons who have no anxiety or only very mild emotional upset.

Beyond the psychometric evidence, what are the interpretive implications of our findings from a psychodynamic point of view? For cardiopaths, hospitalization itself might contribute to a lower level of A-State. It is possible that good nursing and medical care and improvement in the patient's physical condition could explain the low level of anxiety. While such factors might explain the low anxiety that is sometimes observed in cardiopaths, it is an unlikely explanation for the results of the present study. The physical condition of many of our patients, all hospitalized for serious cardiac diseases, was still very critical, and they were tested before any significant clinical improvement could be demonstrated.

It has been noted that the defense mechanisms toward anxiety become very strong in cardiopaths during an acute failure of cardiac functioning. These defenses serve to protect the individual from free-floating anxiety and related arousal of the autonomic nervous system and help to preserve the homeostatic balance that is necessary for survival. We have also observed that cardiopaths use their disease to symbolize the need for inhibition and repression of disturbing affects, as happens in hysteria with conversion symptoms. Acute cardiopaths may also obtain emotional gratification from their illness.

The anxiety reactions of dermopaths can be interpreted in three ways. First, the high A-State scores of dermopaths reflect their reaction to an illness that mars and diminishes the individual's bodily appearance, damages his self-image and adequacy in interpersonal relations, and results in self-denigration that is reflected in negative test-taking attitudes. Second, from a more sophisticated point of view, dermopaths seem to be characterized by less-developed defensive mechanism than cardiopaths. In general, they have fewer personal resources for coping with the threat to their self-image that is evoked by their illness. Third, assuming a theory that skin disease is psychologically determined, the dermopathic condition itself may be interpreted as reflecting the immediate expression (conversion) of state anxiety in individuals whose psychological defense mechanisms are relatively inefficient.

From a psychoanalytic point of view, when anxiety feelings are evoked by uncontrollable id forces, or result from self-destructive superego forces, the probability is increased that reductions in the intensity of these anxiety states will serve as a reinforcement for the defense mechanisms that are involved in conversion reactions. We may speculate that the incidence of psychosomatic diseases in a given population will be related to the average level of free-floating anxiety and to the defense mechanisms that are inculcated by a particular culture. At this time these are work-in-progress hypotheses, and further empirical evidence is needed.

REFERENCES

De Long, R. D. *Individual differences in patterns of anxiety arousal, stress-relevant information, and recovery from surgery.* Unpublished doctoral dissertation, University of California, Los Angeles, 1970.

Edwards, K. R., Jr. *Psychological changes associated with pregnancy and obstetric complications.* Unpublished doctoral dissertation, University of Miami (Florida), 1969.

Pancheri, P. *Measurement of emotion: Transcultural aspects.* International Interdisciplinary Symposium on Parameters of Emotions, Stockholm, June 4–6, 1973.

Spielberger, C. D. Theory and research on anxiety. In C. D. Spielberger (Ed.), *Anxiety and behavior.* New York: Academic Press, 1966.

Spielberger, C. D. Conceptual and methodological issues in anxiety research. In C. D. Spielberger (Ed.), *Anxiety* (Vol. 2). New York: Academic Press, 1972.

Spielberger, C. D., Auerbach, S. M., Wadsworth, A. P., Dunn, T. M., & Taulbee, E. S. Emotional reactions to surgery. *Journal of Consulting and Clinical Psychology*, 1973, *40*, 33–38.

Spielberger, C. D., Gorsuch, R. L., & Lushene, R. E. *Manual for the State-Trait Anxiety Inventory.* Palo Alto, Calif.: Consulting Psychologists Press, 1970.

IV

CROSS-CULTURAL RESEARCH ON ANXIETY

10

Test Anxiety and General Anxiety in Mexican and American School Children

R. Diaz-Guerrero
National University of Mexico

W. H. Holtzman, R. Diaz-Guerrero and J. Swartz, in collaboration with L. Lara Tapia, L. Laosa, M. L. Morales, I. Reyes Lagunes, and D. B. Witzke (1975), have recently completed a cross-cultural longitudinal study of personality development in Mexico and the United States. In this study, data were systematically obtained for Mexican and American children on a number of tests, among them, Sarason's Test Anxiety Scale for Children (TASC), and the Holtzman Inkblot Test (HIT). One of the variables measured by the HIT is anxiety in fantasy (Ax).

C. D. Spielberger (1966, 1972) has critically discussed the theory and measurement of anxiety and has painstakingly elaborated the fundamental concepts of state and trait anxiety that were introduced by Cattell (Cattell & Scheier, 1961). He has also developed brief, reliable, and validated scales of state and trait anxiety for both adults (Spielberger, Gorsuch, & Lushene, 1970) and children (Spielberger, 1973). The availability of these scales in both English and Spanish now permits the systematic exploration of anxiety phenomena in these two language worlds.

This chapter has two major objectives: first, to report results obtained from the systematic administration of the TASC to Mexican and American school children as a function of sex, age, and social class; and, second, to report results obtained for variable Ax from the HIT in the context of the findings with the TASC. These findings will then be used in formulating intracultural and cross-cultural hypotheses regarding state and trait anxiety.

METHODOLOGY

The Measures

The Test Anxiety° Scale for Children (TASC) was developed by Sarason and his associates (Sarason, Davidson, Lighthall, Waite, & Ruebush, 1960). The TASC is a 30-item questionnaire that was specifically designed to measure test anxiety in children. A typical TASC item is: "When the teacher asks you to get up in front of the class and read aloud, are you afraid that you are going to make some bad mistakes?"

Subsequent to the initial development of the TASC, additional items were added to comprise a lie scale (LSC, 11 items) and a defensiveness scale (DSC, 27 items). The final TASC contained 67 items that were individually answered by every child. One point on the LSC is scored when a child answers negatively to questions such as: "Do you ever worry?" The DSC is scored in the same manner. A typical DSC item is: "Since you started school, have you ever felt like crying?" Although the TASC was designed to measure children's test anxiety, it is also considered a convenient and useful instrument for studying the properties of anxiety in general.

The HIT, a highly reliable inkblot technique, was developed by Holtzman, Thorpe, Swartz, and Herron (1961). The HIT anxiety score, Ax, is one of the 23 variables that are measured by this test.

Subjects

The sample consisted of a total of 392 children, half of them Mexican and half American, who were in the first, fourth, or seventh grade when the study began. The initial testing took place within 15 days of the birthday of each child. The Mexican and American children were precisely paired by sex, socioeconomic level, and school grade at the time they were initially tested.

The 196 pairs consisted of 56 pairs for whom the initial age was 6.7 years, 75 pairs whose initial age was 9.7 years, and 65 pairs with an initial age of 12.7 years. The data reported in this chapter correspond to the initial administration of each test. For the HIT, the initial testing took place in the first year of the study; for the TASC, the same children were tested in the second year of the study.

TABLE 1   Mean scores on the test anxiety scale, the lie scale, and the defensive scale for the three age groups

Age groups[a]	TASC score*	LSC score***	DSC score**
8.7 years	13.99	4.52	11.18
11.7 years	13.71	3.05	9.98
14.7 years	12.28	2.71	9.05

[a]Median age of children when they were initially tested. Note: maximum scores for each scale were: TASC = 30; LSC = 11; DSC = 27.

*$p < .1000$.
**$p < .0015$.
***$p < .0001$.

RESULTS

The data for the TASC subscales were evaluated in analyses of variance in which the variables were the two cultures, high and low social class, sex, and age. Results for the TASC anxiety scale proved to be highly significant for culture, socioeconomic level, and sex. None of the interactions among these variables resulted in significant F tests.

Table 1 reports the results by age groups for the three component TASC scales. It can be seen that there was a trend for the TASC scores to decrease with age, but this trend was significant at only the .10 level of confidence. The differences for the LSC and the DSC as a function of age were highly significant. For these two scales, scores decreased significantly with age regardless of culture, sex, or socioeconomic class.

Table 2 shows that the Mexican subjects scored higher on all three TASC scales than the American subjects did. The difference was largest for the TASC—a remarkable 7-point difference—and relatively small, but still significant, for the DSC.

Table 3 shows that, regardless of culture, subjects from the lower socioeconomic class scored higher on the test anxiety scale than those from

TABLE 2   Mean scores on the test anxiety scale, the lie scale, and the defensiveness scale for Mexican and American children

Culture	TASC score***	LSC score**	DSC score*
Mexicans	16.85	4.03	10.63
Americans	9.81	2.82	9.50

*$p < .0158$.
**$p < .0005$.
***$p < .0000$.

TABLE 3 Mean scores on the test anxiety scale, the lie scale, and
the defensiveness scale by socioeconomic level

Socioeconomic level	TASC score***	LSC score*	DSC score**
Low	14.66	3.94	9.86
High	12.00	3.46	10.63

*$p < .8336$.
**$p < .3771$.
***$p < .0003$.

the upper socioeconomic level. There were no differences in the LSC and DSC
scores as a function of socioeconomic level.

In Table 4, it can be seen that, regardless of culture, girls scored higher
on the TASC. The girls also scored slightly below the boys on the LSC and
DSC, but these differences were still significant.

Finally in Table 5, we can observe an interesting third-order interaction of
culture by age and sex in the test anxiety scale. This interaction approached
significance and can be usefully discussed in terms of our hypotheses about
the relation between anxiety and culture. Mexican girls apparently contributed
more to the sex difference previously reported than did the American girls
and showed a stronger tendency for their TASC scores to diminish with age.

TABLE 4 Mean scores on the test anxiety scale, the lie scale, and
the defensiveness scale for girls and boys

Sex	TASC score***	LSC score**	DSC score*
Girls	14.60	3.07	9.50
Boys	12.10	3.78	10.60

*$p < .0283$.
**$p < .0232$.
***$p < .0008$.

TABLE 5 Mean scores on the test anxiety scale by age and
sex for Mexican and American children

Age groups	Mexican		American*	
	Boys	Girls	Boys	Girls
8.7	15.94	21.09	10.43	8.52
11.7	14.37	18.80	9.48	12.21
14.7	14.67	16.24	7.80	10.43

*$p < .0513$.

A similar but smaller tendency was also perceptible in the case of the American males. Thus, the trend previously noted for TASC scores to decline with age was due primarily to the Mexican girls.

DISCUSSION

In 1966, when the TASC was first administered in the cross-cultural study conducted by Holtzman and his co-workers (1975), it was the best available instrument for measuring anxiety in children. With regard to test anxiety, Cronbach (1970) had the following to say:

> Threats are ever present in testing: a delinquent fears that his punishment will depend on the test results; a child fears that a poor intelligence rating will disappoint his parents and diminish their affection; a college girl fears that failure will force her to leave her campus friends and return to the farm; an anxious patient fears that a test will prove him insane. Fears such as these can be listed without end. (p. 63)

Spielberger (1973) has recently contributed to the measurement of anxiety by developing the State-Trait Anxiety Inventory for Children (STAIC). The STAIC A-State scale is transsituational and thus eliminates uneconomical efforts to construct anxiety measures for each specific stress situation. With the STAIC and its explicit underlying theory, it is now possible to explore the anxiety component for a large number of psychological processes. Furthermore, the demonstrated reliability of the Spanish form of the STAI and its comparability with the English form (Diaz-Guerrero & Spielberger, 1975; Spielberger, Gonzalez-Reigosa, Martinez-Urrutia, Natalicio, & Natalicio, 1971), and the availability of the first validity studies with the Spanish adult form (e.g., Martinez-Urrutia & Spielberger, 1973) make this test attractive for intra- and cross-cultural studies.

The use of inkblots as a psychological technique attempts to measure clinical anxiety phenomenologically. Originally pioneered by Rorschach, the Holtzman et al. (1961) Inkblot Test is a more objective approach to measuring anxiety in fantasy. Hill (1972) points out that the anxiety score on the HIT follows upon the original work by Elizur (1949) who defined anxiety as an inner state of insecurity that may take the form of fears, phobias, lack of self-confidence, extreme shyness, ideas of reference, and marked sensitivity. With regard to the HIT Ax score, Hill says: "The anxiety score reflects the level of anxiety and implies a long-term personality characteristic of the individual rather than a transitory reaction to stress" (1972, p. 126).

Holtzman et al. (1975) have reported that nearly all of the reliable variance of the HIT Ax score was shared in common with a number of other HIT scores. In this cross-cultural study, the sample consisted of 900 children, distributed in six groups of approximately 150 subjects of three different ages in the two cultures. All subjects were tested once each year for six consecutive years. Thus, it was possible to observe changes in the Ax scores relative to a number of individual differences over an extended time period in Mexican and American children.

In previous normative studies, it was found that the Ax score was frequently a follower variable for Factor 1 and a marker variable for Factor 3 of the HIT (Holtzman et al., 1961). Factor 1 is generally interpreted as indicative of well-organized ideational activity, good imaginative capacity, well-differentiated ego boundaries, and awareness of conventional concepts. Factor 3 is indicative of psychopathology.

Holtzman et al. (1975), in the cross-cultural study described earlier, found that the Ax score load was generally low for Factor 1, but differed according to the different age groups in the two cultures. For the two oldest groups (seventh graders), regardless of culture, the Ax score was highly associated with Factor 1. On the other hand, Ax appeared as a marker variable for all age groups for Factor 3 in both cultures. In contrast with studies on normal and psychotic adults where Factors 1 and 3 appear as independent dimensions, for children and adolescents Factor 3 tended to be correlated with Factor 1 particularly for the seventh-grade children in both cultures.

Up to now, no correlations have been reported between Ax scores and either A-Trait or A-State as measured by the STAI (Spielberger et al., 1970). However, in their cross-cultural study of Mexican and American children, Holtzman et al. (1975) found that American children scored consistently higher on anxiety than Mexican children regardless of age, social class, or sex. The mean HIT Ax score for Americans was 9.1 compared to only 5.6 for the Mexican children. Thus, while Mexican children showed greater test anxiety than Americans, American children obtained higher scores on symbolic anxiety as measured by the Ax than did Mexican children.

Hill appears to be right when she states that, since Ax is scored on the basis of symbolic contents, neither the presence nor the absence of anxiety may be considered as a sign of weakness of the ego. It is important to determine how well one deals with anxiety in order to specify if the personality is healthy or not. This may explain the failure to find correlations between the Ax measure and the TASC, the LSC, or the DSC in this cross-cultural study.

No cross-cultural study of Mexican and American children has been conducted as yet with Spielberger's trait and state anxiety scales, so we do not know how these scales compare. A preliminary Spanish form of the STAIC was administered by Hernandez Cuesta (1972) to 209 high school students between 14 and 16 years of age and almost equally divided by sex. The A-Trait and A-State scores for males were 37.12 and 32.41, respectively, while the females scored 39.32 on A-Trait and 31.68 on A-State. Mean anxiety scores for the Mexican children were lower, particularly for A-State, than the norms reported for junior high school students in the United States.

The mean scores for U.S. males were 39.37 and 36.99 for A-Trait and A-State, respectively. For U.S. females the A-Trait and A-State scores were 41.61 and 37.57, respectively (Spielberger, 1973).

It has been clearly demonstrated that, regardless of culture, subjects from lower socioeconomic levels consistently score higher in anxiety, and that females tend to score higher in anxiety than males. It is important, therefore, to take sociocultural and socioeconomic variables into account in explaining the variance in anxiety scores. Furthermore, it seems likely that differences in anxiety mediated by sex, culture, and social class are related to relevant "sociocultural premises" (Diaz-Guerrero, 1975) that are prominent in different countries as well as in different social classes.

On the basis of the evidence presented in this chapter, several specific hypotheses can be formulated for cross-cultural studies of trait and state anxiety:

1. Mexican elementary and high school students will obtain higher anxiety scores than Americans when A-State is measured during school examinations.
2. Mexican elementary and high school children will have lower state anxiety scores than American children in typical social interaction situations.
3. Difference between males and females in A-State with reference to school examinations will be greater in Mexico than in the United States; that is, Mexican females will be relatively higher in A-State than Mexican males as compared to males and females in the United States.

More work is needed with regard to the meaning of trait anxiety in different cultures before specific cross-cultural hypotheses may be entertained. It would appear, however, that Mexican school children would be somewhat lower in A-Trait scores than American children, but higher in test anxiety scores.

These hypotheses are consonant with the interpretation that Holtzman et al. (1975) have given to results for the TASC that are summarized in this paper. In a culture where affiliative obedience toward adult authorities is intense, objective tests and exams represent a much greater threat for children. Mexican children, particularly girls, do not find effective ways of coping with exam situations among their store of responses because most of their responses are designed to please adults. Furthermore, they are even more afraid than American children of disappointing their parents and teachers.

On the other hand, the North American culture, with its stress on competitive achievement and self-sufficient individualism, is more consonant with objective exams. Therefore, the availability of appropriate responses of American children to test situations is more adequate. Regarding Hypothesis 2, as a consequence of the greater affiliative interdependence in Mexican children, the resolution of anxiety through close interpersonal relationships with adults results in a less-threatening and friendlier social environment. In general, Mexican children in standard social situations will show less A-State and, consequently, will be lower in A-Trait than their North American counterparts.

It will be interesting to test these hypotheses in cross-cultural research. Given the obvious pertinence to the problems of mental health and neurosis in all cultures, cross-cultural investigations of test anxiety and state and trait anxiety should be given high priority.

REFERENCES

Cattell, R. B., & Scheier, I. H. *The meaning and measurement of neuroticism and anxiety.* New York: Ronald Press, 1961.

Cronbach, L. J. *Essentials of psychological testing* (3rd ed.). New York: Harper & Row, 1970.

Diaz-Guerrero, R. *Psychology of the Mexican culture and personality.* Austin: University of Texas Press, 1975.

Diaz-Guerrero, R., & Spielberger, C. D. *IDARE Inventario de Ansiedad: Rasgo-Estado.* Mexico City: El Manual Moderno, S.A., 1975.

Elizur, A. Content analysis of the Rorschach with regard to anxiety and hostility. *Journal of Projective Techniques*, 1949, *13*, 247–284.

Hernandez Cuesta, U. *Angustia y familia tradicional.* Tesis de Doctorado, U.N.A.M., 1972.

Hill, E. F. *The Holtzman inkblot technique.* London: Jossey-Bass, 1972.

Holtzman, W. H., Diaz-Guerrero, R., Swartz, J. D., Lara Tapia, L., Laosa, L., Morales, M. L., Reyes Lagunes, I., & Witzke, D. B. *Personality development in two cultures.* Austin and London: University of Texas Press, 1975.

Holtzman, W. H., Thorpe, J. S., Swartz, J. D., & Herron, E. W. *Inkblot perception and personality.* Austin: University of Texas Press, 1961.

Martinez-Urrutia, A., & Spielberger, C. D. The relationship between state-trait anxiety and intelligence in Puerto Rican psychiatric patients. *Revista Interamericana de Psicologia*, 1973, *11*, 3–4.

Sarason, S. B., Davidson, K. S., Lighthall, F. F., Waite, R. R., & Ruebush, B. K. *Anxiety in elementary school children.* New York: John Wiley & Sons, 1960.

Spielberger, C. D. Theory and research in anxiety. In C. D. Spielberger (Ed.), *Anxiety and behavior.* New York: Academic Press, 1966.

Spielberger, C. D. Anxiety as an emotional state. In C. D. Spielberger (Ed.), *Anxiety: Current trends in theory and research* (Vol. 1). New York: Academic Press, 1972.

Spielberger, C. D. *Manual for the State-Trait Anxiety Inventory for Children.* Palo Alto, Calif.: Consulting Psychologist Press, 1973.

Spielberger, C. D., Gonzalez-Reigosa, F., Martinez-Urrutia, A., Natalicio, L. F. S., & Natalicio, D. S. Development of the Spanish edition of the State-Trait Anxiety Inventory. *Interamerican Journal of Psychology*, 1971, *5*, 145–157.

Spielberger, C. D., Gorsuch, R. L., & Lushene, R. E. *Manual for the State-Trait Anxiety Inventory.* Palo Alto, Calif.: Consulting Psychologist Press, 1970.

11

Multidimensional Aspects of State and Trait Anxiety: A Cross-Cultural Study of Canadian and Swedish College Students

Norman S. Endler
York University, Toronto, Canada

David Magnusson
University of Stockholm, Sweden

The existence of cultural differences is an obvious truism, but one becomes really aware of these differences through first-hand experiences with

This study was assisted under Grant No. 391 from the Ontario Mental Health Foundation, Grant No. S73-1110 from the Canada Council and by a J. B. C. Watkins Leave Fellowship from the Canada Council (W73 0350) to N. S. Endler, and by a grant from the Swedish Council for Social Science Research to D. Magnusson. Most of the work with respect to the Swedish sample was conducted at the Psychological Laboratories, University of Stockholm, where N. S. Endler was on sabbatical (1973-1974) as a Visiting Scholar (Professor) and where D. Magnusson was on sabbatical (1973-1974) from his duties as Professor and Director of the Laboratories. The assistance of Karin Dittmer, Bo Ekehammar, Marilyn Okada, and Daisy Schalling is gratefully acknowledged. Requests for reprints should be sent to Norman S. Endler, Department of Psychology, York University, 4700 Keele Street, Downsview, Ontario, Canada, M3J 1P3.

143

another culture. One of the first experiences one encounters is the feeling of anxiety, based primarily on the fact that one does not know how to cope with the new situation. After experience with the new culture, however, the initial level of anxiety with respect to the novelty or ambiguity of the situation is generally reduced. Nevertheless, through cross-cultural experiences one becomes more aware of the universality of anxiety and the fact that anxiety is a fundamental human emotion. Despite its universality, the question can still be raised as to whether there are cultural differences with respect to the level and nature of the anxiety experience. A major goal of the present study is to compare Canadian and Swedish college students with respect to various aspects of anxiety.

Anxiety, which has been defined in many different ways, has both theoretical and practical importance. Lewis (1970), in discussing the characteristics of anxiety, states that "*it is an emotional state, with the subjectively experienced quality of fear or a closely related emotion* (terror, horror, alarm, fright, panic, trepidation, dread, scare)" (p. 77). Furthermore, according to Lewis, the emotion is unpleasant and directed toward the future, is out of proportion to the threat, and involves subjective and manifest bodily disturbances. Hopefully, an understanding of the construct of anxiety will help alleviate some of its deleterious effects and will also contribute to theoretical developments.

There has been an increase in research on anxiety from three articles in 1927 to over 200 in 1966, according to Lewis (1970). Since 1950, 5,000 articles and books on anxiety have been published, according to Spielberger (1972), with diverse attempts at comprehensive theories and differing methodological formulations. Nevertheless, when it comes to definition, the concept of anxiety is still ambiguous. Indeed, the title of Lewis's (1970) paper is "The Ambiguous Word 'Anxiety'". At various times, anxiety has been conceptualized as a response, a stimulus, a trait, a motive, and a drive.

Before the Christian era, Cicero made a basic distinction between *angor* and *anxietas.* According to Cicero, "*angor* is transitory, an outburst; *anxietas* is an abiding predisposition" (as quoted in Lewis, 1970, p. 62). This fundamental distinction between *state anxiety*, a transitory emotional condition, and chronic or *trait anxiety*, a relatively stable personality characteristic, has been recently elaborated by Cattell and Scheier (1958, 1961), and by Spielberger (1966, 1972). Spielberger has suggested that conceptual and empirical confusion in anxiety research derives from a failure to differentiate between trait anxiety and state anxiety.

Spielberger, Gorsuch, and Lushene (1970) conceive of state anxiety (A-State) as a *transitory* emotional state characterized by "feelings of tension, and apprehension and heightened autonomic nervous system activity" (p. 3). Trait anxiety (A-Trait), on the other hand, refers to *stable* individual differences in anxiety proneness. That is, high A-Trait individuals should experience greater A-State arousal than low A-Trait individuals under threatening conditions, but not under neutral or innocuous conditions (Spielberger, 1972).

Endler, Magnusson, Ekehammar, and Okada (1976) have empirically investigated the relationship between A-Trait and A-State for a sample of Swedish college students. Since Spielberger's (1972) theory implies that under neutral conditions A-State and A-Trait are relatively independent of one another, Endler et al. (1976) attempted to test this proposition empirically. For the Swedish college students, A-State and A-Trait were highly correlated under neutral conditions. A major goal of the present study was to extend the Endler et al. (1976) study. The relationship between A-State and A-Trait under neutral conditions was evaluated for a sample of Canadian college students and compared with the results obtained for the Swedish college students. If, in fact, A-Trait and A-State are highly correlated under nonstressful conditions, then it would not be justified to treat them as two distinct concepts.

Another problem of major interest in the present study was the unidimensionality of both A-Trait and A-State. Although trait anxiety is a relatively stable characteristic, it does not appear to be unidimensional (Ekehammar & Magnusson, 1973; Endler, 1975a; Endler & Okada, 1975), and Endler et al. (1976) have reported evidence for the multidimensional nature of A-Trait for Swedish college students.

Typical A-Trait inventories such as the Spielberger et al. (1970) STAI A-Trait scale and the Taylor (1953) Manifest Anxiety Scale (MAS) yield omnibus or general measures of anxiety that relate primarily to ego-threatening or interpersonal aspects of A-Trait. Endler and Shedletsky (1973) found, for example, that the STAI A-Trait scale was more highly correlated with the interpersonal ego threat situations of the S-R Inventory of Anxiousness (Endler, Hunt, & Rosenstein, 1962) than with the subscales that measured ambiguous threats or physical danger situations. Similarly, Endler and Okada (1974, 1975), using the S-R Inventory of General Trait Anxiousness (GTA), found that the STAI A-Trait scale was more highly correlated with the GTA interpersonal ego-threat scale than with the GTA physical danger scale. The present investigation examines the multidimensional nature of A-Trait for both Canadian and Swedish college students.

In examining the relationship between A-Trait and A-State, it is necessary to consider the nature of the evocative situations in the context of possible person-by-situation interactions (Endler & Hunt, 1969; Endler, 1975a). Furthermore, in order for trait anxiety and a particular stressful situation to have an interactive effect on the arousal of A-State, the component (or dimension) of A-Trait must be congruent with the stressful situation (Endler & Okada, 1975; Shedletsky & Endler, 1974; Endler, 1975a, 1975b). Furthermore, in some situations it is possible to arouse one aspect of A-State (e.g., autonomic and physiological responses) but not others (e.g., avoidance responses), which suggests that A-State may also be multidimensional. Endler et al. (1976) found evidence of the multidimensionality of A-State for Swedish college students. The present study examined the multidimensionality of A-State as assessed by both the STAI (Spielberger et al., 1970) and the BRQ (Endler & Okada, 1974, 1975; Hoy & Endler, 1969) for both Canadian and Swedish college students.

In the present study, three major problems were investigated: the empirical relationship between A-State and A-Trait; the dimensionality of A-State and A-Trait; and a cross-cultural comparison of Canadian and Swedish college students with respect to levels of state and trait anxiety and the multidimensionality and relationship between A-State and A-Trait. These problems were evaluated using data from two state anxiety and two trait anxiety measures with samples of Swedish and Canadian college students. The use of different measures enabled us to investigate and cross-validate the problems under consideration.

METHOD

Subjects

The subjects were 54 male and 105 female undergraduate students enrolled in psychology courses at the University of Stockholm, Sweden, and 48 male and 71 female undergraduate students enrolled in psychology courses at Atkinson (evening) College, York University, Canada. All of the Canadian subjects were administered the two trait measures, but only 74 of them (30 males, 44 females) completed both measures. In general, the Canadian subjects were older than the Swedish subjects.

Anxiety Measures

Trait anxiety Two self-report trait anxiety inventories were used. One of these was a revised form of the S-R Inventory of General Trait Anxiousness (GTA) (Endler & Okada, 1974, 1975). The GTA samples four general situations, each situation having 15 modes of response. Each subject was asked to report the *intensity* of his own reaction to the situation in question on a five-point scale, ranging from "not at all" (1) to "very much" (5). Positively stated items are scored in the reverse direction to indicate the presence of anxiety. The general situations were: "You are in situations involving interaction with other people" (which implies being judged by others); "You are in situations where you are about to or may encounter physical danger"; "You are in a new or strange situation"; and "You are involved in your daily routines" (see Table 5). Modes of response included items such as "enjoy these situations," "feel nervous," and "have an uneasy feeling." (For a list of the 15 modes of response, see Table 6.)

The other self-report measure of trait anxiety used in this study was the A-Trait scale of the State-Trait Anxiety Inventory (STAI-T) (Spielberger et al., 1970). The STAI-T is a 20-item scale (see Table 7) that asks people to respond according to how they generally feel. The subject rates the *frequency* of his reactions on a 4-point scale ranging from "almost never" to "almost always." The positively stated items are scored in the reverse direction to indicate the presence of anxiety.

State anxiety Two self-report measures of state anxiety were used. One of these was a modified form of the Behavioural Reactions Questionnaire (BRQ) (Hoy & Endler, 1969). The subjects were asked to complete the BRQ for the situation "How do you feel at this particular moment." For this situation, the subject is instructed to rate the intensity of his reaction to 21 anxiety responses (see Table 9) using a 5-point scale ranging from "none" to "very much" for the negatively stated items and "very much" to "none" for the positively stated items. The anxiety responses included such items as "heart beats faster," "want to avoid this situation," and "feel nervous."

The A-State scale of the State-Trait Anxiety Inventory (STAI-S) (Spielberger et al., 1970) was also used to measure state anxiety. This 20-item self-report questionnaire (see Table 10) asks the subject to respond according to how he feels "at this moment." The subject rates the *intensity* of his reaction on a 4-point scale ranging from "not at all" to "very much so." The positively stated items are scored in the reverse direction to indicate the presence of anxiety.

Translation of the Scales into Swedish

The four state and trait anxiety scales were translated from English into Swedish by three researchers—one native English-speaker and two native Swedish-speakers. Since a basic construct in the original language (e.g., English) does not necessarily have the exact connotative meaning in the new language (e.g., Swedish), the translation was initially conducted situation-by-situation and reaction-by-reaction. We attempted to obtain a meaning as close to the original version as possible, and some of the scales were subsequently revised slightly in order to cover the entire domain of situations and reactions that were included in the original versions of the questionnaires.

Administration of the Anxiety Measures and Treatment of the Data

Swedish sample The state and trait data were administered on two separate occasions, in a lecture room, with a time interval of 1 week between data collections. There was no experimental attempt to induce anxiety. On the first occasion half of the subjects took the BRQ followed by the GTA and the other half of the subjects took the STAI-S followed by the STAI-T. The state measure (BRQ or STAI-S) was always administered first. On the second occasion, this order was reversed, and all subjects were administered all four forms, that is, the two state measures and the two trait measures. A code number was used for each subject so that all inventories were completed anonymously.

Canadian sample   The state and trait data were collected on one occasion, in a lecture room. There was no experimental attempt to induce anxiety. Some subjects were administered all four inventories and completed them in the following order: BRQ followed by STAI-S, followed by STAI-T, followed by GTA. Other subjects were only administered the trait measures and completed the STAI-T first, followed by the GTA.

Data Treatment (Both Samples)

Trait anxiety   The STAI-T was analyzed with respect to individual item scores and to total scores across items. (Positively stated items were scored in the reverse direction to indicate the presence of anxiety.) The GTA was analyzed with respect to situation scores, obtained by summing across reactions, and to reaction scores, obtained by summing across situations. For both trait scales, the data for males and females were treated separately. Means, standard deviations, and internal consistency reliabilities expressed as alpha coefficients (Cronbach, 1951) were computed for the STAI-T total scores, and for each of the four GTA situation scales. Sex and cross-cultural differences were evaluated in two-way analyses of variance of the A-Trait scores.

Product-moment correlation coefficients were computed to determine the relationship between the trait anxiety scales, and principal components factor analyses (with unity in the diagonals) were computed separately for the GTA situation scales, the GTA reaction scales, and the STAI-T reaction scales (items). A scree curve was plotted for the eigenvalues greater than unity, and the main criterion for determining the number of significant factors was based on observing where the curve suddenly dropped. Factors were chosen for rotation only if they contributed substantially to the explained variance. For the GTA situation scales, it was necessary to rotate factors with eigenvalues lower than 1 because the second factor contributed substantially to the explained variance and made psychological sense. The varimax method was used to rotate the factor solutions to simple structure.

State anxiety   The BRQ and STAI-S were both analyzed with respect to item scores and total scores. The positively stated items were scored in the reverse direction to indicate the presence of anxiety. Means, standard deviations, and internal consistency reliabilities (alpha coefficients) were computed for the total scores. Sex and cultural differences were evaluated by means of a two-way analysis of variance of the A-State scores.

Product-moment correlation coefficients were computed to determine the degree of relationship between the STAI-S and BRQ, and principal components factor analyses (using unity in the diagonals) were computed separately for the STAI-S and BRQ scales, and for the nine pairs of items common to the STAI-S and BRQ. A scree curve was plotted for the eigenvalues and the number of significant factors was then determined by observing where the curve suddenly dropped. Factors were chosen for rotation only if they contributed substantially to the explained variance. The varimax method was used to rotate the factor solutions to simple structure. Because of the small size of the Canadian sample, the A-State data for males and females were combined for the correlational analyses and factor analyses.

Product-moment correlation coefficients were also computed to determine the degree of relationship between the state and trait anxiety scales. Principal components factor analyses were computed for the total scale scores of the state and trait scales, including each of the four GTA subscales. The factorial procedure was the same as above.

RESULTS

Cross-Cultural and Sex Differences in Trait and State Anxiety

Trait measures The means and standard deviations for Swedish and Canadian males and females for the four GTA trait scales (interpersonal, physical danger, ambiguous or novel, and daily routines), and for the STAI A-Trait scale are presented in Table 1. A two-way analysis of variance, with sex and culture as the independent variables, was computed separately for each of the A-Trait scores. There were no significant F ratios for the interpersonal ego threat GTA. For the GTA physical danger threat, the sex $(F_{(1,274)} = 6.84, p < .01)$ and culture $(F_{(1,274)} = 9.82, p < .01)$ main effects were significant. Females reported significantly higher physical danger A-Trait scores $(\bar{X} = 57.58)$ than males $(\bar{X} = 54.19)$, and Swedish students reported higher physical danger A-Trait scores $(\bar{X} = 57.91)$ than the Canadians $(\bar{X} = 53.86)$. For the ambiguous GTA, the significant effect for culture $(F_{(1,274)} = 8.91, p < .01)$, indicated that the Swedish students reported higher A-Trait scores on this scale $(\bar{X} = 41.65)$ than the Canadians $(\bar{X} = 38.03)$. For the innocuous GTA, the F ratio for the sex main effect was significant $(F_{(1,274)} = 6.02, p < .05)$, indicating that the males reported higher innocuous GTA scores $(\bar{X} = 28.98)$ than females $(\bar{X} = 26.47)$. The means in Table 1 also indicate that, for both the Canadian and the Swedish samples, males and females reported the greatest anxiety on the GTA for the physical danger situation, followed by the ambiguous (novel) situation, then the interpersonal situation, and finally the daily routines situation.

TABLE 1   Means (M) and standard deviations (S.D.) on trait anxiety scales for Swedish and Canadian male and female college students

		Males		Females	
Trait anxiety scales		Swedish ($N = 54$)	Canadian ($N = 48$)	Swedish ($N = 105$)	Canadian ($N = 71$)
STAI-T	M	37.98	40.06	39.75	41.72
	S.D.	7.77	8.22	9.68	11.68
GTA: Interpersonal	M	34.52	32.38	33.81	32.86
	S.D.	9.25	9.79	9.78	12.69
GTA: Physical danger	M	55.74	52.65	60.09	55.07
	S.D.	9.71	10.83	8.76	12.52
GTA: Ambiguous (novel)	M	40.57	36.77	42.73	39.28
	S.D.	8.58	7.54	11.13	9.34
GTA: Daily routines	M	29.57	28.40	26.79	26.14
	S.D.	8.46	9.31	7.30	8.26

Note. Sex differences. Based on the analysis of variance results, females were significantly more anxious than males for the physical danger GTA and STAI-T. For the innocuous GTA, males were significantly more anxious than females.

Cultural differences. Based on the analysis of variance results, Swedish students were significantly more anxious than Canadian students for physical danger GTA and ambiguous GTA, and significantly less anxious than Canadian students for STAI-T.

The analysis of variance computed for the STAI-T scores resulted in significant main effects for both sex and culture ($F_{(1,274)} = 4.12$, $p < .05$, and $F_{(1,274)} = 5.41$, $p < .05$, respectively). From the mean scores reported in Table 1, it is apparent that females reported higher A-Trait ($\bar{X} = 41.33$) than males ($\bar{X} = 39.02$), and that the Canadian students reported higher A-Trait scores ($\bar{X} = 41.50$) than the Swedish students ($\bar{X} = 38.85$). The

TABLE 2   Means (M) and standard deviations (S.D.) on state anxiety scales for Swedish and Canadian male and female college students

		Males		Females	
State anxiety scale		Swedish ($N = 54$)	Canadian ($N = 30$)	Swedish ($N = 105$)	Canadian ($N = 44$)
STAI-S	M	36.43	33.83	35.08	38.11
	S.D.	9.17	7.41	9.06	8.92
BRQ	M	37.20	32.60	36.20	37.23
	S.D.	9.81	7.20	9.36	15.39

Note. Sex differences. Based on the analysis of variance results, it was apparent that Canadian females were significantly more anxious than Canadian males for the STAI-S. No BRQ differences were found.

Cultural differences. No significant differences were found for either the BRQ or STAI-S.

alpha coefficient reliabilities for all of the trait measures were high, ranging from .88 to .95.

State measures The means and standard deviations for males and females, for both the Swedish and Canadian samples, for the STAI state and BRQ state scales are presented in Table 2. A two-way analysis of variance (sex × culture) was computed for the BRQ and STAI state scores. There were no significant F ratios for the BRQ. For the STAI A-State scale, a significant interaction was found for sex × culture ($F_{(1,229)} = 4.75$, $p < .05$). Subsequent multiple comparisons on the means indicated that the Canadian females reported higher A-State ($\overline{X} = 38.11$) than Canadian males ($\overline{X} = 33.83$). Alpha coefficients of reliability for the state measures ranged from .82 to .96.

Intercorrelations among the Anxiety Measures

The product-moment correlations between the trait measures (the STAI-T and the four GTA measures) for the Swedish ($N = 159$) and Canadian ($N = 119$) samples are presented in Table 3. These correlations are for the total samples, but are based on the means of the male and female correlations. The correlations of the A-Trait scales were moderate to low, ranging from .58 to .15 for the Swedish sample and from .42 to −.03 for the Canadian sample.

The STAI-T scale correlated highest with the GTA interpersonal ego threat scale for both Canadians ($r = .41$) and Swedes ($r = .58$), whereas the correlation between the STAI-T and GTA physical danger was relatively low, being $r = .33$ for Canadians and $r = .30$ for Swedes. The lowest correlations, as shown in Table 3, were between GTA physical danger and GTA daily routines for both samples ($r = −.03$ for Canadians and $r = .15$ for Swedes). There is a clear tendency for higher intercorrelations among the A-Trait scales (7 out of 10) for the Swedish sample than for the Canadian sample. The

TABLE 3　Correlations among trait anxiety scales for total sample (based on means of male and female correlations) for Swedish (above the diagonal) and Canadian (below the diagonal) samples

Scales	STAI-T 1	Interpersonal 2	Physical danger 3	Ambiguous 4	Daily routines 5
STAI-T		.58	.30	.48	.56
GTA: Interpersonal	.41		.21	.49	.48
GTA: Physical danger	.33	.27		.34	.15
GTA: Ambiguous (novel)	.15	.42	.38		.39
GTA: Daily routines	.31	.35	−.03	.35	

Note. Swedish sample ($N = 159$); Canadian sample ($N = 119$).

TABLE 4 Correlations between trait and state anxiety scales for Swedish and Canadian
college students

Trait anxiety	Swedish sample ($N = 159$)		Canadian sample ($N = 74$)	
	STAI-S	BRQ	STAI-S	BRQ
STAI-T	.69	.53	.67	.65
GTA: Interpersonal	.42	.59	.49	.74
GTA: Physical danger	.19	.25	.38	.19
GTA: Ambiguous (novel)	.44	.44	.41	.32
GTA: Daily routines	.51	.46	.32	.24

relatively low intercorrelations of the STAI-T with each of the four GTA trait
scales provide some evidence for the multidimensionality of trait anxiety.

The correlations between the BRQ and STAI measures of state anxiety
were $r = .53$ for the Swedish sample and $r = .59$ for the Canadian sample.
(Because of the small sample size for the Canadian sample, the data for males
and females were combined.) As parallel test reliability coefficients, these
correlations are low, accounting for between 25 to 36 percent of the common
variance. When the BRQ and STAI-S scores were based on the nine common
items (rather than on all the items) the correlations between BRQ and STAI-S
were $r = .69$ for the Canadian sample and $r = .57$ for the Swedish sample. The
correlation for the Canadian sample was higher than for the Swedish sample,
but the BRQ and STAI-S data were collected on the same day for the
Canadians, while for the Swedish students there was a 1-week interval between
the administration of the two state scales.

The correlations between the state and trait measures are reported in
Table 4. Note that the correlations between the STAI A-Trait and A-State
measures ($r = .69$ for Sweden and $r = .67$ for Canada) are markedly higher
than the correlations between the two state measures, BRQ and STAI-S,
reported above ($r = .53$ for Sweden and $r = .59$ for Canada). The correlations
between the BRQ and the physical danger, ambiguous, and daily routines
GTA trait scales are lower than the correlation between BRQ state and GTA
interpersonal ego threat scale (see Table 4). The correlations between the BRQ
and the noninterpersonal scales of the GTA (i.e., physical danger, ambiguous,
and daily routines) as reported in Table 4 are lower than the correlations
between the two state measures (BRQ and STAI-S) reported above.

Factor Analysis of Trait Anxiety Measures

GTA situation scales Table 5 presents, separately for males and females
in the Swedish and Canadian samples, the eigenvalues (unrotated) and
cumulative proportion of variance (unrotated) for the four situations as well
as the varimax rotated solutions for principal components factor analysis of

TABLE 5 Rotated factor analyses (varimax) of GTA situation scales for Swedish and Canadian male and female samples

Situation scales	Swedish males (N = 54)		Swedish females (N = 105)		Canadian males (N = 48)		Canadian females (N = 71)	
	I Interpersonal ego threat	II Physical danger	I Interpersonal ego threat	II Physical danger	I Interpersonal ego threat	II Physical danger	I Interpersonal ego threat	II Physical danger
1. You are in situations involving interaction with other people.	*.81*	.18	*.84*	.12	*.74*	.33	*.69*	−.24
2. You are in situations where you are about to or may encounter physical danger.	.07	*.95*	.06	*.96*	.13	*.96*	*.63*	*.63*
3. You are in a new or strange situation.	*.60*	*.51*	*.69*	.44	*.73*	.38	*.82*	−.02
4. You are involved in your daily routines.	*.86*	.01	*.80*	−.04	*.89*	−.09	.27	*−.86*
Eigenvalues (unrotated)	2.07	.89	2.03	.94	2.20	.86	1.63	1.20
Cumulative proportion of total variance (unrotated)	.52	.74	.51	.74	.55	.77	.41	.71

Note. Factor loadings ⩾ 0.50 are italicized.

the four GTA situation subscales. For both males and females in the Swedish and Canadian samples, two factors were rotated. The first factor appears to be interpersonal–ego threat and the second factor appears to be physical danger (safety). For the Canadian females, the daily routines situation also had a high negative loading on the second factor. For the three other subsamples, there was a moderate loading on the second factor for the ambiguous (novel) situation.

GTA reaction scales The varimax solutions from the principal components factor analyses of the 15 GTA reaction scales[1] for the male and the female Swedish and Canadian samples are presented in Table 6. The eigenvalues (unrotated) and cumulative proportion of variance (unrotated) are also presented in Table 6. On the basis of an inspection of the eigenvalues, two factors were rotated. The analyses were based on the 15 reaction scores summed across the four GTA situations.[2] The results in Table 6 indicate that the factor structures were very similar for both males and females in the Swedish and Canadian samples. The first factor was interpreted as a distress-tension (related to feelings) factor, and the second factor as an absence of curiosity (absence of exhilaration) factor.

STAI-T reaction scales Table 7 (males and females separately, Swedish sample) and Table 8 (males and females separately, Canadian sample) present the varimax solutions from principal components factor analyses of the 20 STAI-T reaction scales (see footnote 1). The eigenvalues (unrotated) and cumulative proportion of variance (unrotated) for the 20 items are also presented in Tables 7 and 8. Using these eigenvalues and plotting scree curves, it was decided that three factors should be rotated for each of the four subsamples (males and females for both Swedish and Canadian samples), and these are presented in Tables 7 and 8. When the criterion of eigenvalues greater than 1 was used, we obtained differing numbers of factors for the four subsamples, varying from three to five factors.

Although we have tentatively labeled the factors in Tables 7 and 8, the only firm conclusions that we can make are: first, STAI-T is multidimensional; second, the items that are related to *affect* or *feeling* seem to load on a different factor than those that are related to *cognitions* or *preoccupations*; and, third, the factor structure seems to be more relevant to method variance than to content variance. For example, positively worded items seem to group together as do the negatively worded items. Items that contain longer

---

[1] Factor loadings for the reversed (positively stated) items were reflected to negative values in order to indicate the absence of positive affect (i.e., to indicate the presence of anxiety).

[2] Factor analyses of the reaction scales were done for each situation separately. Two or three factors were obtained in all solutions, and the two-factor solutions were congruent with the factor structure presented in Table 6. In the three-factor solutions, which were common for males, the distress factor split into two factors that could be denoted somatic and psychic distress, respectively.

TABLE 6 Rotated factor analyses (varimax) of GTA reaction scales

Reaction scales	Swedish males (N = 54)		Swedish females (N = 105)		Canadian males (N = 48)		Canadian females (N = 71)	
	I Distress-tension	II Absence of curiosity	I Distress-tension	II Absence of curiosity	I Distress-tension	II Absence of curiosity	I Distress-tension	II Absence of curiosity
1. Seek experiences like this	-.06	-.79	.01	-.86	-.16	-.87	-.05	-.88
2. Feel upset	.84	.21	.79	.25	.76	.34	.83	.06
3. Perspire	.52	-.16	.62	-.20	.40	.29	.26	-.32
4. Feel relaxed	-.78	-.32	-.87	-.20	-.74	-.50	-.90	-.02
5. Have an "uneasy feeling"	.86	.27	.85	.32	.89	.19	.78	.22
6. Look forward to these situations	.08	-.86	-.06	-.85	-.18	-.92	-.17	-.85
7. Get fluttering feeling in stomach	.86	-.04	.79	.12	.81	.16	.80	-.03
8. Feel comfortable	-.27	-.83	-.51	-.59	-.75	-.53	-.87	-.24
9. Feel tense	.91	.06	.89	.10	.85	.31	.87	.04
10. Enjoy these situations	-.24	-.85	-.28	-.87	-.20	-.91	-.23	-.85
11. Heart beats faster	.78	-.01	.78	.08	.39	.09	.79	-.05
12. Feel secure	-.80	-.25	-.77	-.30	-.86	-.24	-.84	-.11
13. Feel anxious	.87	.20	.88	.14	.90	.09	.87	.15
14. Feel self-confident	-.76	-.30	-.74	-.30	-.87	-.13	-.73	-.08
15. Feel nervous	.91	.16	.90	.14	.92	.17	.90	.07
Eigenvalues (unrotated)	8.08	2.60 (0.89)	8.37	2.26 (0.89)	8.88	2.00 (1.05)	8.00	2.34 (0.97)
Cumulative proportion of total variance (unrotated)	.54	.71 (.77)	.56	.71 (.77)	.59	.73 (.80)	.53	.69 (.75)

Note. Factor loadings ≥ 0.50 are italicized.

155

TABLE 7 Rotated factor analyses (varimax) of STAI-T reaction scales for Swedish college students

Reaction scales	Males (N = 54)			Females (N = 105)		
	I Emotive (affective) discontent	II Distress preoccupation (cognitive)	III Neurotic depression (psychasthenia)	I Emotive (affective) discontent	II Distress preoccupation (cognitive)	III Avoidance-apathy
1. I feel pleasant.	*-.87*	-.05	-.16	*-.73*	-.28	-.11
2. I tire quickly.	.16	-.01	*.54*	.44	.28	.05
3. I feel like crying.	-.15	.00	*.57*	.33	*.53*	-.23
4. I wish I could be as happy as others seem to be.	.30	*.66*	-.28	.50	.26	*.59*
5. I am losing out on things because I can't make up my mind soon enough.	.45	.31	-.30	.16	.19	*.59*
6. I feel rested.	*-.78*	-.17	-.21	*-.75*	-.26	-.14
7. I am "calm, cool and collected."	*-.75*	-.12	-.39	*-.63*	-.41	-.22
8. I feel that difficulties are piling up so that I cannot overcome them.	.27	.50	-.23	.36	.39	.19
9. I worry too much over something that really doesn't matter.	.23	*.73*	.18	.37	*.64*	.30
10. I am happy.	*-.70*	-.13	-.01	*-.73*	-.07	-.22
11. I am inclined to take things hard.	.12	*.56*	.44	.18	*.86*	.00
12. I lack self-confidence.	*.56*	*.54*	.18	*.51*	.39	.35
13. I feel secure.	*-.60*	-.36	-.46	*-.72*	-.33	-.28
14. I try to avoid facing a crisis or difficulty.	.46	.37	-.14	.06	-.05	*.77*
15. I feel blue.	*.54*	.24	.30	*.70*	.30	-.01
16. I am content.	*-.80*	-.10	.09	*-.87*	-.09	-.02
17. Some important thought runs through my mind and bothers me.	.14	*.79*	.07	.21	*.77*	.18
18. I take disappointments so keenly that I can't put them out of my mind.	-.08	*.73*	.15	.17	*.70*	.36
19. I am a steady person.	-.36	-.06	*-.73*	-.49	*-.54*	.19
20. I become tense and upset when I think about my present concerns.	.47	.35	.47	*.57*	.42	.29
Eigenvalue (unrotated)	7.13 2.17	1.81 1.27	1.10 .98	8.61 1.49	1.37 1.04	.94
Cumulative proportion of total variance (unrotated)	.36 .47	.56 .62	.67 .72	.43 .50	.57 .62	.67

Note. Factor loadings > 0.50 are italicized.

TABLE 8 Rotated factor analyses (varimax) of STAI-T reaction scales for Canadian college students

Reaction scales	Males (N = 48)			Females (N = 71)		
	I Emotive (affective)	II Avoidance-apathy	III Preoccupation (cognitive)	I Emotive (affective)	II Distress preoccupation	III Avoidance-apathy
1. I feel pleasant.	*-.82*	.00	.03	-.46	-.20	-.50
2. I tire quickly.	.46	.21	.37	.27	.21	*.65*
3. I feel like crying.	.05	.44	-.03	*.57*	.37	.27
4. I wish I could be as happy as other seem to be.	-.08	-.08	*.58*	.48	*.69*	.12
5. I feel rested.	-.16	*.70*	-.17	.16	*.77*	.26
6. I am losing out on things because I can't make up my mind soon enough.	*-.70*	.10	-.22	-.28	.10	*-.67*
7. I am "calm, cool and collected."	*-.69*	-.09	-.41	-.26	-.33	*-.64*
8. I feel that difficulties are piling up so that I cannot overcome them.	*.52*	.07	-.11	.42	*.54*	.41
9. I worry too much over something that really doesn't matter.	.39	*.55*	.25	*.67*	.42	.11
10. I am happy.	*-.78*	-.15	-.29	*-.75*	-.21	-.43
11. I am inclined to take things hard.	.10	.15	*.84*	*.77*	.35	.00
12. I lack self-confidence.	.26	-.13	*.76*	.24	*.80*	.06
13. I feel secure.	*-.62*	.13	-.42	*-.72*	-.33	-.28
14. I try to avoid facing a crisis or difficulty.	-.10	*.82*	.06	-.01	.37	*.66*
15. I feel blue.	.19	*.75*	.10	*.64*	.26	.39
16. I am content.	*-.73*	-.04	-.04	*-.72*	-.04	-.50
17. Some important thought runs through my mind and bothers me.	.13	-.10	*.72*	*.63*	.13	.32
18. I take disappointments so keenly that I can't put them out of my mind.	.23	.31	*.62*	*.52*	.48	.44
19. I am a steady person.	*-.71*	-.04	-.25	*-.59*	-.11	*-.62*
20. I become tense and upset when I think about my present concerns.	.35	.12	*.55*	*.65*	.50	.26

Eigenvalues (unrotated) — Males: 6.31 2.39 2.05 1.82 1.24 ; Females: 10.28 1.55 1.12 .94

Cumulative proportion of total variance (unrotated) — Males: .32 .43 .54 .63 .69 ; Females: .51 .59 .65 .69

Note. Factor loadings > 0.50 are italicized.

157

sentences seem to group together. Both the Canadian and Swedish samples have similar factor structures, but somewhat different patterns.

Factor Analysis of State Anxiety Measures

Table 9 presents the varimax (rotated) solutions from the principal components factor analyses of the 21 BRQ reaction scales (see footnote 1) for the Swedish and Canadian samples (males and females combined). On the basis of the obtained scree curves, it was decided that three factors should be rotated for both samples. With the criterion of eigenvalues greater than 1, we obtained six factors for the Swedish sample and four factors for the Canadian sample. Since the factor patterns are somewhat different for the Canadian and Swedish samples, the only firm conclusions that we can make are: first, the BRQ is multidimensional; second, the items related to *physiological* reactions seem to load on a different factor than those related to *psychic distress*; and, third, positively worded items seem to group together, probably reflecting method variance rather than content variance.

Table 10 presents, for males and females combined, the varimax (rotated) solutions from the principal components factor analyses of the 20 STAI-S items (see footnote 1) for the Swedish and Canadian samples. Eigenvalues (unrotated) and cumulative proportion of variance (unrotated) are also presented. Using these eigenvalues and plotting scree curves, it was decided that three factors should be rotated for both the Swedish and Canadian samples. Although we have tentatively labeled the factors in Table 10, the factor patterns are different for the Swedish and Canadian samples. The only firm conclusions that we can make are: first, STAI-S is multidimensional; second, the first factor (emotive discontent), consisting primarily of positively worded items, seems to be similar for both samples; and, third, items that are positively worded seem to load on a different factor than those that are negatively loaded; therefore, part of the variance is due to method rather than to content.

In order to illuminate the relative importance of method and item content, principal components factor analyses were computed on the nine pairs of items common to the BRQ and STAI-S for both the Swedish and Canadian samples.[3] The results for these 18 items as well as the eigenvalues

---

[3] For the Swedish sample, half the subjects took the STAI-S one week and the BRQ the following week. For the other half this procedure was reversed. The Canadian samples were administered the BRQ, followed by the STAI-S, on one occasion. There are nine pairs of items that are common to both scales. The correlations between the BRQ and STAI-S, when the scores were based on the sum of the nine items, were $r = .57$ for the Swedish sample and $r = .69$ for the Canadian sample. For the Swedish sample, the correlation coefficients among corresponding BRQ and STAI-S item scores ranged from $r = .23$ to $r = .49$, with a mean of .38. For the Canadian sample, these correlations ranged from $r = .01$ to $r = .66$ with a mean of .44.

TABLE 9 Rotated factor analyses (varimax) of the BRQ for Swedish and Canadian college students

Scale	Swedish sample (N = 159)			Canadian sample (N = 74)		
	I Psychic distress uneasiness	II Physiological distress reaction	III Emotive (affective) discontent avoidance	I Emotive (affective) discontent	II Physiological distress reaction	III Autonomic distress
1. Hands feel moist	-.11	*.70*	.21	.07	.02	*.78*
2. Feel relaxed	-.34	*-.57*	-.20	*-.56*	-.35	*-.50*
3. Hands feel shaky	.06	*.59*	.08	.33	*.66*	.42
4. Feel self-confident	-.41	-.26	-.37	*-.67*	-.27	-.43
5. Feel like crying	.35	.16	.13	.13	.41	*.62*
6. Enjoy this situation	-.05	-.09	*-.79*	*-.80*	.07	-.09
7. Heart beats faster	.21	*.61*	.09	.11	*.57*	.45
8. Feel calm	-.45	*-.56*	-.33	*-.54*	-.45	-.42
9. Perspire	.02	*.67*	.04	.37	.02	*.76*
10. Feel comfortable	-.27	-.06	*-.77*	*-.65*	-.46	-.27
11. Feel frightened	.29	.38	.32	.08	*.82*	.27
12. Feel pleasant	-.45	-.12	*-.71*	*-.77*	-.30	-.06
13. Feel nervous	.47	*.51*	.31	*.55*	.41	.47
14. Feel secure	*-.50*	-.29	*-.54*	*-.71*	-.30	-.44
15. Feel upset	*.77*	.21	.07	.43	*.58*	.43
16. Mouth feels dry	.22	.47	-.05	.24	*.81*	-.01
17. Feel happy	*-.61*	.16	-.38	*-.82*	-.15	.00
18. Feel anxious	*.71*	.42	.25	*.53*	*.50*	.26
19. Have shortness of breath	*.56*	-.03	-.17	.07	*.82*	-.14
20. Have an uneasy feeling	*.60*	.39	.29	*.55*	.33	.38
21. Want to avoid this situation	-.10	.14	*.53*	.49	-.05	.38

Eigenvalues (unrotated) — Swedish: 7.14, 1.84, 1.43, 1.29, 1.23, 1.09; Canadian: 10.31, 2.10, 1.49, 1.13

Cumulative proportion of total variance (unrotated) — Swedish: .34, .43, .50, .56, .62, .67; Canadian: .49, .59, .66, .72

Note. Factor loadings ≥ 0.50 are italicized.

159

TABLE 10 Rotated factor analyses (varimax) of STAI-S reaction scales for Swedish and Canadian college students

Reaction scales	Swedish sample (N = 159)			Canadian sample (N = 74)		
	I Emotive (affective) discontent	II Agitated distress	III Tension worry	I Emotive (affective) discontent	II Tension worry	III Agitated distress
1. I feel calm.	-.47	-.42	-.37	-.75	-.05	-.15
2. I feel secure.	-.52	-.15	-.52	-.77	-.22	.26
3. I am tense.	.23	.68	.33	.00	.66	.41
4. I am regretful.	.07	.70	.05	.07	.18	.57
5. I feel at ease.	-.57	-.24	-.47	-.88	-.16	-.11
6. I feel upset.	.26	.24	.68	-.13	.67	.17
7. I am presently worrying over possible misfortunes.	.15	.13	.75	.45	.52	-.26
8. I feel rested.	-.57	-.23	-.49	-.52	.24	-.35
9. I feel anxious.	.24	.63	.42	.28	.72	-.03
10. I feel comfortable.	-.84	-.03	-.04	-.89	-.08	.01
11. I feel self-confident.	-.34	-.29	-.47	-.69	-.07	-.12
12. I feel nervous.	.19	.81	.31	.18	.76	.25
13. I feel jittery.	.16	.83	.12	.44	.46	.36
14. I feel "high strung."	.08	.37	.21	.16	.18	.73
15. I am relaxed.	-.52	-.32	-.46	-.83	-.17	-.25
16. I feel content.	-.68	-.23	-.31	-.73	-.03	-.27
17. I am worried.	.22	.26	.72	.10	.80	.27
18. I feel over-excited and "rattled."	.17	.37	.58	.04	.32	.76
19. I feel joyful.	-.82	-.13	-.12	-.66	-.09	.27
20. I feel pleasant.	-.74	-.22	-.36	-.69	-.14	-.18
Eigenvalues (unrotated)	8.97	1.85	1.05 .99 .95	7.19	3.26	1.64 1.43
Cumulative proportion of total variance (unrotated)	.45	.54	.59 .64 .69	.35	.52	.60 .68

Note. Factor loadings ≥ 0.50 are italicized.

and cumulative proportion of variance for the Swedish and Canadian samples are presented in Table 11. Two factors were rotated for each sample. For the Swedish sample, the first factor appears to be a STAI-S factor (consisting of all the STAI-S items) and the second factor a BRQ factor (consisting of all the BRQ items). These factors seem to be due to method variance. For the Canadian sample, the first factor consists of all the BRQ items plus the positively worded STAI-S items. The second factor loads on the negatively worded STAI-S items. Here again, method variance is important. (Note that for the Canadian sample the BRQ and the STAI-S data were obtained on the same occasion, while for the Swedish sample these data were obtained on two separate occasions.)

Factor Analyses of Trait and State Measures

Principal components factor analyses were computed separately for the Swedish and Canadian samples (males and females combined) for all the state and trait scales. Table 12 presents the eigenvalues (unrotated) and cumulative proportion of variance (unrotated), as well as the rotated factor matrices, for the Swedish and Canadian students.

Two factors were rotated for each sample. With respect to number and content, the factor pattern is very similar for the two samples. The first factor, interpersonal ego threat, accounting for about 50 percent of the total variance, has high loadings on both state measures (BRQ and STAI-S) and on all of the trait measures, except for GTA physical danger. The second factor, physical danger (safety) accounts for about 15 percent of the variance. The GTA ambiguous (novel) situation scale loads on both factors, especially for the Swedish sample. Empirically, state and trait anxiety do not appear to be separate factors.

DISCUSSION

Cross-Cultural and Sex Differences in Trait and State Anxiety

For both the Swedish and Canadian samples, females reported greater anxiety on the GTA physical danger situation and the STAI A-Trait scales than males. These results were similar to the findings reported by Endler and Okada (1974, 1975) and Oetzel (1966). However, for the innocuous GTA scale, the males reported higher anxiety than females.

For the physical danger and ambiguous GTA situations, the Swedish sample was more anxious than the Canadian sample. Perhaps Swedish students perceive ambiguous (novel) situations as more anxiety-provoking because Swedish society is less mobile than Canadian society. The Swedish students have fewer opportunities to encounter novel situations and may therefore

TABLE 11 Rotated factor analyses of items common to both the STAI-S and BRQ for Swedish and Canadian college students

| | Swedish sample (N = 159) | | Canadian sample (N = 74) | |
| | I | II | I | II |
Reaction scales	Emotive (affective) discontent (STAI-S)	Emotive (affective) discontent (BRQ)	Emotive (affective) discontent	General anxiety distress (STAI-S)
STAI-S				
1. Feel calm	-.70	-.32	-.67	-.31
2. Feel secure	-.73	-.26	-.71	-.31
3. Feel upset	.70	.14	-.23	.63
4. Feel anxious	.72	.14	.19	.76
5. Feel comfortable	-.58	-.04	-.77	-.30
6. Feel self-confident	-.60	-.30	-.65	-.19
7. Feel nervous	.68	.28	.10	.79
8. Feel relaxed	-.73	-.27	-.66	-.44
9. Feel pleasant	-.77	-.11	-.63	-.30
BRQ				
1. Feel calm	.14	-.78	-.85	.11
2. Feel secure	-.26	-.77	-.88	.04
3. Feel upset	.40	.52	.72	.05
4. Feel anxious	.36	.75	-.77	-.36
5. Feel comfortable	-.04	-.65	-.83	-.06
6. Feel self-confident	-.28	-.60	-.85	.15
7. Feel nervous	.12	.76	-.78	.07
8. Feel relaxed	-.28	-.62	-.81	.08
9. Feel pleasant	-.15	-.75	-.76	.10
Eigenvalues (unrotated)	7.48 2.21	1.24 .94	9.06 2.12	1.24
Cumulative proportion of total variance (unrotated)	.42 .54	.61 .66	.50 .62	.69

Note. Factor loadings ≥ 0.50 are italicized.

TABLE 12 Rotated factor analysis (varimax) of trait and state anxiety scales for Swedish and Canadian college students

Anxiety scales	Swedish sample (N = 159)		Canadian sample (N = 119)	
	I Interpersonal ego threat	II Physical danger (safety)	I Interpersonal ego threat	II Physical danger (safety)
STAI-S (state)	.79	.14	.70	.41
BRQ (state)	.74	.24	.80	.23
STAI-T (trait)	.78	.29	.74	.43
GTA: Interpersonal (trait)	.74	.19	.75	.26
GTA: Physical danger (trait)	.05	.94	.06	.92
GTA: Ambiguous or novel (trait)	.54	.53	.38	.56
GTA: Daily routines (trait)	.79	−.08	.71	−.35
Eigenvalue (unrotated)	3.63	.99	3.48	1.17
Cumulative Proportion of total variance (unrotated)	.52	.66	.50	.66

Note. Factor loadings ⩾ 0.50 are italicized.

perceive novel or ambiguous situations as more threatening than Canadian students. In contrast to the GTA results, the Canadian sample scored higher on the STAI-Trait scale than the Swedish sample.

In both Canada and Sweden, both male and female college students responded differentially to the four situations of the GTA, indicating the importance of situational factors (Magnusson, Gerzén, & Nyman, 1968; Endler & Magnusson, 1974). Both Canadian and Swedish college students reported the highest anxiety on the physical danger situation, followed by the ambiguous (novel) situation, the interpersonal ego threat situation, and finally the daily routines situation (see Table 1). These differences were similar to the results reported by Endler and Okada (1974, 1975) and provide evidence of the multidimensional nature of A-Trait. Physical danger (safety) situations involve a realistic threat and, therefore, are perceived as the most anxiety-provoking, whereas daily routines are usually not perceived as anxiety-provoking by normal college students. Interpersonal ego threat situations, which depend more on the psychological perception of the situation than on actual threat, apparently induce less anxiety than physical threat situations. Ambiguous or novel situations, which contain elements of both physical danger and psychic threat, induce more anxiety than pure interpersonal (social) situations, but less anxiety than pure physical danger situations.

There were no sex differences in state anxiety for the Swedish sample. Canadian females were higher in A-State than males as measured by the

STAI-S scale, but not on the BRQ measure of state anxiety. The results for the STAI A-State measure in the Canadian sample were congruent with findings reported by Oetzel (1966) that American females manifested higher anxiety than males.

There were no A-State differences between the Canadian and Swedish samples, and there was a remarkable similarity between the Canadian and Swedish college students with respect to their anxiety reactions in different kinds of situations.

Intercorrelations among the Anxiety Measures

The finding that the STAI-T had higher correlations with the GTA interpersonal ego threat situation than with the GTA physical danger situation was congruent with results reported by Endler and Shedletsky (1973), Endler (1975a), Shedletsky and Endler (1974), and Endler and Okada (1974, 1975), and indicates that the STAI-T is primarily a measure of interpersonal threat anxiety. The GTA physical danger situation had low correlations with all the other trait scales, suggesting that physical danger and interpersonal ego threat anxiety may well represent different facets of A-Trait. The differential correlations of the STAI-T with each of the four GTA trait scales and the relatively low intercorrelations of the four GTA scales, for both the Swedish and Canadian samples provide some additional evidence for the multi-dimensionality of A-Trait.

The correlations between the BRQ and STAI-S measures of state anxiety were comparable for both the Swedish sample ($r = .53$) and for the Canadian sample ($r = .59$). These are relatively low correlations for scales that presumably measure the same construct. Newmark (1972) studied the test-retest reliability of STAI-S after a 1-week interval and obtained correlations of .69 and .73 for males and females, respectively. In the present study, there was a 1-week interval for the Swedish sample, while for the Canadian sample the BRQ and STAI-S were administered on the same day. Therefore, it is possible for the Swedish sample, where the tests were administered at separate times in two nonthreatening situations, 1 week apart, that the state measures are sensitive to change. However, this would not account for the relatively low correlation for the Canadian sample where the BRQ and STAI-S were administered on the same day.

The correlations derived from scores based on the nine common items in two A-State measures were .57 for the Swedish sample and .69 for the Canadian sample. The correlation coefficients among corresponding BRQ and STAI-S items ranged from .23 to .49 (with a mean of .38) for the Swedish sample, and from .01 to .66 for the Canadian sample (with a mean of .44). In addition to low parallel test reliability, these results also indicate the existence of method variance (as opposed to content variance). The BRQ uses a 5-point scale and the STAI-S uses a 4-point scale, and these are anchor points for each individual BRQ item (e.g., heart beats faster, is keyed from "not at all" to "much faster") while the STAI-S items all have the same anchor points, ranging from "not at all" to "very much so."

The correlations between the state measures (STAI-S or BRQ) and the STAI-T were markedly higher (see Table 4) than the correlations between the two state measures. The correlations between STAI-T and STAI-S for the Swedish and Canadian subjects in the present study are higher than those reported by Spielberger et al. (1970) for U.S. college students, which varied between .44 and .55 for females, and between .51 and .67 for males.

The correlations between the BRQ and the GTA physical danger, ambiguous (novel), or daily routines scales were lower than the correlations between BRQ and the GTA interpersonal trait anxiety scale (see Table 4). The GTA physical danger situation scale had low correlations with both state anxiety measures. This is not surprising since the situations in which the data were collected (standard conditions) did not contain the anticipation of physical danger threat. The pattern of intercorrelations between state and trait measures were similar for the Swedish and Canadian samples.

The high correlations between the STAI trait and the state measures, and between GTA interpersonal and the state measures question the conceptual trait-state distinction in anxiety theory (Spielberger, 1966, 1972), at least under neutral or nonthreatening conditions. The differential correlations between state anxiety and the four subscales of the GTA provide further evidence for the multidimensionality of the GTA. The fact that the correlations between STAI-T and STAI-S were higher than the correlations between the two state measures is an interesting and puzzling result.

Factor Analysis of Trait Anxiety Measures

Factor analyses of the GTA trait anxiety situation scales yielded two situational factors for the Swedish and Canadian males and females. These factors (see Table 5), which were named interpersonal ego threat and physical danger (safety), are similar to the two factors found by Endler and Okada (1974, 1975). Basowitz, Persky, Korchin, and Grinker (1955) suggested the existence of two types of anxiety, *shame* anxiety and *harm* anxiety, which appear to be analogous to interpersonal anxiety and physical danger anxiety, respectively. The ambiguous or novel situation loaded on both factors for Swedish males, indicating that novelty or ambiguity can be anxiety-provoking with respect to both interpersonal ego-threatening situations and physical danger situations (Endler et al., 1962, using 11 situations, found a separate ambiguous factor). The daily routines situation loaded on the interpersonal factor for all samples, except Canadian females, perhaps suggesting that most daily routines involve social interactions with other people. These factor analytic results provide evidence for the multidimensionality of A-Trait.

Further evidence for the multidimensionality of trait anxiety comes from the factor analytic results of the 15 reaction scales of the GTA (see Table 6). For both the Swedish and Canadian samples, there were two reaction factors, distress-tension and absence of curiosity (absence of exhilaration). These results are essentially similar to those found by Endler and Okada (1974, 1975) and analogous to two of the three factors found by Endler et al. (1962).

In discussing Hebb's (1955) model with respect to performance as a function of arousal level, Day and Berlyne (1971) suggest that curiosity increases efficiency in performance, whereas anxiety and boredom decrease efficiency. They reason that curiosity is at a higher level of arousal than boredom and at a higher level than anxiety. Levitt (1967) suggests a negative relationship between anxiety and curiosity, and Day and Berlyne (1971) note that "anxious people tend not to be curious, and one could easily accept the converse that curious persons do not tend to become anxious" (p. 327). Therefore, the absence of curiosity factor (not wanting to "seek experiences like this" or not wanting to "look forward to these situations," and so on) appears to be a bona fide anxiety factor, which is at a lower level of arousal than the first factor (distress-tension). While these results attest to the multi-dimensionality of A-Trait, method variance might also contribute to the factor structure. Most of the items on Factor 2 are positively stated (reversed items), while those on Factor 1 are negatively stated.

The STAI-T also appears to be multidimensional (see Tables 7 and 8). However, both the number of factors and the psychological content of the factors were different for the two trait anxiety scales (GTA and STAI-T). On the STAI-T the items that are related to affect or *feeling* seem to load on a different factor than those that are related to *cognitive preoccupations*. To some extent, the factor structure seems to be based more on method variance than on content variance. Positively worded items seem to group together and negatively worded items seem to group together. In addition, items that contain longer sentences seem to group together. Although the Canadian and Swedish samples have similar factor structures, the patterns are somewhat different.

In summary, the factor analytic results of the trait anxiety scales indicate that trait anxiety should be seen as a *multidimensional* construct with respect to both situation and reaction components (see Endler & Hunt, 1969). Endler (1975a) has previously stressed this point in analyzing the STAI-T instrument. One practical consequence of these results is the recommendation that one should use anxiety inventories that sample both different situational domains and different types of anxiety reactions in order to provide a comprehensive description of a person's general trait anxiety pattern. This implies, among other things, the necessity for developing a classification of situations (see Magnusson, 1971, 1974).

Factor Analysis of State Anxiety Measures

Evidence for the multidimensionality of the BRQ measure of state anxiety comes from the factor analysis results of the BRQ reaction scales (see Table 9). Although the nature of the factors is not clear, it appears that the items that are related to *physiological* reactions seem to load on a different factor than those related to *psychic* distress. These results are analogous to the psychic and somatic components of the Multicomponent Anxiety Scale (A-Trait scale) reported by Schalling, Cronholm, and Asberg (1974), and to two of the factors (psychic anxiety and somatic anxiety) found by Ekehammar, Magnusson, and Ricklander (1974). Although there appear to be at least three factors for both the Swedish and Canadian samples, and the factor structure appears similar for both samples, the patterning with respect to specific item loadings is somewhat different for the two cultures. Some of the variance seems to reflect method variance rather than content variance, since positively worded items seem to group together.

The factor analyses of the STAI-S items (see Table 10) indicates the existence of at least three factors for both the Swedish and Canadian samples, with different factor patterns for Swedish and Canadian college students. Furthermore, the factor pattern and structure are different for the STAI-S and the BRQ. The STAI-S factor analysis yielded factors that could be interpreted only in terms of psychic anxiety, since this scale does not include any clear physiological response items, and positively worded items seem to load on a different factor than negatively loaded items, indicating the existence of method variance. Only the emotive discontent factor, consisting primarily of positively worded items, seems to be similar for both the Swedish and Canadian samples.

The factor analyses of the nine pairs of items common to both the BRQ and STAI-S (see Table 11) yielded two factors for both the Swedish and Canadian samples. However, much to our surprise, these factors appeared to reflect method variance rather than content variance.

The conclusions to be drawn from the factor analyses of the BRQ and the STAI-S is that state anxiety, like trait anxiety, is a multidimensional construct. Furthermore, these two scales appear to measure partially different aspects of state anxiety in that the factors that were identified in the present study were different for the two state instruments. Endler et al. (1976) factor analyzed the state anxiety data separately for the Swedish sample and found that even the number of factors differed for BRQ (four factors) and STAI-S (three factors). A practical consequence of the multidimensionality of state anxiety is that state anxiety instruments should sample different types of anxiety reactions, and the anxiety intensity should be determined for each type of reaction. This approach would provide a differentiated picture of a person's anxiety response pattern in a specific situation. It is congruent with the Endler and Hunt (1966, 1968, 1969) interaction model, which suggests that it is necessary to examine person-by-situation and person-by-reaction interactions in order to understand the construct of anxiety.

Factor Analyses of Trait and State Measures

The factor analyses of the scale scores for all the state and trait scales that were obtained in this study did not yield separate trait and state factors as expected (see Table 12). Both state and trait scales (with the exception of the GTA physical danger subscale) loaded heavily on one and the same factor. Two factors were obtained: an interpersonal ego threat factor (about 50 percent of the variance), on which both state and trait anxiety measures had high loadings, and a physical danger factor (about 15 percent of the variance). For the Swedish sample, the ambiguous situation scale loaded on both factors. These results are analogous to those found in the factor analysis of the GTA trait situation scales (see Table 5).

The empirical results in this study regarding state and trait anxiety are not congruent with the trait-state distinction in anxiety theory (Spielberger, 1966, 1972) from which it would have been expected that the trait and state scales would form separate trait and state factors, at least under neutral or standard conditions. It does not rule out the possibility that A-Trait and A-State may be separate entities under stressful conditions. However, it is clear that interpersonal ego threat and physical danger threat are separate factors.

CONCLUSIONS

1. The correlations and factor analyses of the state and trait anxiety scales do not *empirically* support the conceptual distinction between trait and state anxiety.
2. The state and trait anxiety scales used in the present study are multidimensional.
3. Both method variance and content variance contribute to the multidimensionality of the trait and state measures.
4. Although the internal consistency reliabilities of the state and trait measures are extremely high and therefore satisfactory, the stability coefficients for the state measures are not very satisfactory.
5. With respect to cultural differences, Swedish males and females combined report more physical danger and ambiguous (novel) trait anxiety and less STAI A-Trait anxiety than Canadian males and females combined.
6. With respect to sex differences, Swedish and Canadian females combined reported more anxiety on the STAI A-Trait scale and for the physical danger situation than Swedish and Canadian males combined. However, Swedish and Canadian males combined reported more anxiety for daily

routines than Swedish and Canadian females combined. Canadian females report more anxiety (as measured by the STAI-S) than Canadian males.

7. There is a remarkable similarity between Swedish and Canadian college students with respect to anxiety reactions in different kinds of situations.

Problems for Further Research

The results of the present study suggest a number of further problems that warrant additional research. Foremost among these is an examination of the conditions (or situations) under which A-Trait and A-State may be two separate entities. That is, the nature of the relationship between A-Trait and A-State warrants further exploration. The exact nature of the multidimensionality of both trait and state anxiety needs further exploration, both with respect to the nature and number of factors and with respect to the role of method variance (compare Fiske, 1957).

The low correlations between the two state measures, in spite of the fact that nearly half of the items were common, indicate a low stability for state reaction data under normal or neutral conditions. It is necessary to systematically investigate the reliability and stability of state anxiety under different conditions.

The factor analyses of the items that were common to the BRQ and STAI-S did not yield content factors, as was the case when the scales were analyzed separately. Instead, the items were distributed on factors in terms of method. It is necessary to systematically investigate the effects of method on the measurement of state and trait anxiety data. With respect to trait anxiety, what are the differential effects of using *frequencies* (as in STAI-T) or *intensities* of reactions (as in GTA)? What is the role of acquiescence?

Finally, further and more systematic cross-cultural studies are warranted. Why were there cultural differences on some anxiety scales and not on others? Do the present cross-cultural anxiety results. hold for populations other than college students? Are there cross-cultural developmental differences in anxiety?

SUMMARY

This study involved a cross-cultural comparison and investigation of the empirical relationship and dimensionality of state anxiety (A-State) and trait anxiety (A-Trait). Two measures of A-Trait (S-R GTA and STAI-T) and two measures of A-State (BRQ and STAI-S) were administered to samples of Swedish university students (54 males, 105 females) and Canadian university students (48 males, 71 females). For both Canadian and Swedish samples, subjects reported greatest anxiety on the GTA for the physical danger situation, followed by the ambiguous situation, then the interpersonal situation, and, finally, the daily routines situation. For the physical danger

GTA and STAI-T, females reported higher anxiety than males. However, for innocuous GTA, males reported higher anxiety than females. For the physical danger and ambiguous GTA, the Swedish sample reported higher anxiety than the Canadian sample, but for the STAI-T, the Canadian sample was more anxious.

Factor analyses of GTA situation scales yielded basically the same results for Canadian and Swedish samples with an interpersonal ego threat and a physical danger factor. Factor analyses of the GTA reaction scales and STAI-T reaction scales yielded two and three factors, respectively, for both Canadian and Swedish students providing evidence for the multidimensionality of A-Trait. For the A-State measures, the only sex and culture differences occurred with respect to the STAI-S measure. Canadian females reported higher A-State than Canadian males. Factor analysis of the BRQ and STAI-S measures yielded two or three factors for Canadian and Swedish samples indicating the multidimensionality of A-State. Factor analysis of nine pairs of common BRQ and STAI-S items yielded two factors, reflecting method rather than content variance. Results of correlations between the trait and state measures were similar for Canadian and Swedish samples.

In general, the correlations between the state and trait scales are higher than the correlations between the two state measures, and a factor analysis of the trait and state scales failed to yield separate state and trait factors, but rather an interpersonal ego threat factor and a physical danger factor. These results, as well as the intercorrelations of the trait and state scales, question the proposition that A-Trait and A-State are distinct entities.

REFERENCES

Basowitz, H., Persky, H., Korchin, S. J., & Grinker, R. R. *Anxiety and stress.* New York: McGraw-Hill, 1955.

Cattell, R. B., & Scheier, I. H. The nature of anxiety: A review of 13 multivariate analyses comparing 814 variables. *Psychological Reports*, Monograph Supplement, 1958, *5*, 351–388.

Cattell, R. B., & Scheier, I. H. *The meaning and measurement of neuroticism and anxiety.* New York: Ronald Press, 1961.

Cronbach, L. J. Coefficient alpha and the internal structure of tests. *Psychometrika*, 1951, *16*, 297–334.

Day, H. I., & Berlyne, D. E. Intrinsic motivation. In G. S. Lesser (Ed.), *Psychology and educational practice.* London: Scott, Foresman, 1971.

Ekehammar, B., & Magnusson, D. A method to study stressful situations. *Journal of Personality and Social Psychology*, 1973, *27*, 176–179.

Ekehammar, B., Magnusson, D., & Ricklander, L. An interactionist approach to the study of anxiety: An analysis of an S-R inventory applied to an adolescent sample. *Scandinavian Journal of Psychology*, 1974, *15*, 4–14.

Endler, N. S. A person-situation interaction model for anxiety. In C. D. Spielberger and I. G. Sarason (Eds.), *Stress and anxiety* (Vol. 1). Washington, D.C.: Hemisphere/Wiley, 1975. (a)

Endler, N. S. The case for person-situation interactions. *Canadian Psychological Review*, 1975, *16*, 12–22. (b)

Endler, N. S., & Hunt, J. McV. Sources of behavioral variance as measured by the S-R Inventory of Anxiousness. *Psychological Bulletin*, 1966, *65*, 336–346.

Endler, N. S., & Hunt, J. McV. S-R Inventories of Hostility and components of the proportions of variance from persons, responses and situations for hostility and anxiousness. *Journal of Personality*, 1968, *9*, 309–315.

Endler, N. S., & Hunt, J. McV. Generalizability of contributions from sources of variance in the S-R Inventories of Anxiousness. *Journal of Personality*, 1969, *37*, 1–24.

Endler, N. S., Hunt, J. McV., & Rosenstein, A. J. An S-R Inventory of Anxiousness. *Psychological Monographs*, 1962, *76*, No. 17 (Whole No. 536), 1–33.

Endler, N. S., & Magnusson, D. Interactionism, trait psychology, psychodynamics and situationism. *Reports from the Psychological Laboratories*, University of Stockholm, 1974, No. 418.

Endler, N. S., Magnusson, D., Ekehammar, B., & Okada, M. The multidimensionality of state and trait anxiety. *Scandinavian Journal of Psychology*, 1976, *17*, 81–93.

Endler, N. S., & Okada, M. An S-R Inventory of General Trait Anxiousness. *Department of Psychology Reports*, York University, Toronto, 1974, No. 1.

Endler, N. S., & Okada, M. A multidimensional measure of trait anxiety: The S-R Inventory of General Trait Anxiousness. *Journal of Consulting and Clinical Psychology*, 1975, *43*, 319–329.

Endler, N. S., & Shedletsky, R. Trait versus state, authoritarianism and ego threat versus physical threat. *Canadian Journal of Behavioural Science*, 1973, *5*, 347–361.

Fiske, D. W. An intensive study of variability scores. *Educational and Psychological Measurement*, 1957, *17*, 453–465.

Hebb, D. O. Drives and the C.N.S. (Conceptual Nervous System). *Psychological Review*, 1955, *62*, 243–254.

Hoy, E. A., & Endler, N. S. Reported anxiousness and two types of stimulus incongruity. *Canadian Journal of Behavioural Sciences*, 1969, *1*, 207–211.

Levitt, E. E. *The psychology of anxiety.* New York: Bobbs-Merrill, 1967.

Lewis, A. The ambiguous word "anxiety." *International Journal of Psychiatry*, 1970, *9*, 62–79.

Magnusson, D. An analysis of situational dimensions. *Perceptual and Motor Skills*, 1971, *32*, 851–867.

Magnusson, D. The individual in the situation: Some studies on individual's perception of situations. *Studia Psychologica*, 1974, *16*, 124–132.

Magnusson, D., Gerzén, M., & Nyman, B. The generality of behavioral data: 1. Generalization from observation on one occasion. *Multivariate Behavioral Research*, 1968, *3*, 295–320.

Newmark, C. S. Stability of state and trait anxiety. *Psychological Reports*, 1972, *30*, 196–198.

Oetzel, R. M. Annotated bibliography. In E. E. Maccoby (Ed.), *The development of sex differences.* Stanford: Stanford University Press, 1966.

Schalling, D., Cronholm, B., & Asberg, M. Components of state and trait anxiety as related to personality and arousal. In L. Levi (Ed.), *Parameters of emotion.* New York: Raven Press, 1974.

Shedletsky, R., & Endler, N. S. Anxiety: The state-trait model and the interaction model. *Journal of Personality*, 1974, *42*, 511–527.

Spielberger, C. D. The effects of anxiety on complex learning and academic achievement. In C. D. Spielberger (Ed.), *Anxiety and behavior.* New York: Academic Press, 1966.

Spielberger, C. D. Anxiety as an emotional state. In C. D. Spielberger (Ed.), *Anxiety: Current trends in theory and research* (Vol. 1). New York: Academic Press, 1972.

Spielberger, C. D., Gorsuch, R. L., & Lushene, R. E. *Manual for the State-Trait Anxiety Inventory.* Palo Alto, Calif.: Consulting Psychologist Press, 1970.

Taylor, J. A. A personality scale of manifest anxiety. *Journal of Abnormal and Social Psychology*, 1953, *48*, 285–290.

EPILOGUE
A Critical Review of
Contributions to
This Volume

12

Critique of Research on Anxiety Across Cultures

Wayne H. Holtzman
The University of Texas at Austin

Underlying any measurement of anxiety must be a theory, implicit or explicit, as to what anxiety is and how it can be recognized. In his brief review on the nature and measurement of anxiety, Spielberger clarifies the terminology used in anxiety research and provides a historical background for the cross-cultural work presented in detail throughout the rest of this book. As Bitterman and I noted 25 years ago in a review of theory and research dealing with anxiety and reactions to stress (Holtzman & Bitterman, 1952), the term *stress* has been used in so many different ways that its meaning has become quite confused. By carefully limiting a definition of stress to the objective stimulus properties of a situation and using the term *threat* for the individual's subjective perception and interpretation of the situation, Spielberger has cleared the way for a theory of anxiety and its measurement.

State or transitory anxiety arises when a situation or thought is perceived as threatening, regardless of whether or not others view the objective stimulus properties of the situation as stressful. Augmented by a labile reaction of the autonomic nervous system, the subjective feeling of tension and uneasiness accompanying such perception of danger or threat is defined as *state anxiety*. When an individual is strongly disposed to experience such anxiety with high frequency and in situations that do not appear that stressful to external observers, it can be inferred that he has a high amount of *trait anxiety*, that he is more anxiety prone than others.

The concept of anxiety as process refers to a sequence of cognitive, affective, physiological, and behavioral events that must be considered together if one is to gain insight into the deeper meaning of anxiety. The relationships among these different levels and kinds of activity are so complex as to defy simple description and generalization. Large-scale, multivariate studies of anxiety and reactions to stress have generally revealed only a very low order of intercorrelation among sociometric, self-report, perceptual, physiological, and biochemical measures purported to deal with anxiety (Holtzman & Bitterman, 1956).

It is important to note that such low intercorrelations across different levels of functioning occur when attempts are made to study enduring traits rather than to focus on the more situationally determined state characteristics of the individual. When an individual is placed under high stress, the relationships among these different internal systems become clearer. The organism is responding in a more or less coordinated fashion to stress and perceived threat with its accompanying state anxiety. Now the behavioral observations of the objective situation, verbal self-reports of state anxiety, content of fantasy and perception revealed by projective techniques, physiological indices of muscle tension and autonomic nervous system lability, and biochemical indicators of stress reaction will tend to reflect this total response of the threatened organism. The systems that appear isolated in a resting state become synergistic and more closely patterned under stress.

For Spielberger and his colleagues, the cognitive-perceptual system is of primary importance in the measurement of anxiety. The self-report inventory is the key method used for obtaining information about the individual's perception of his or her own life situation, inner feelings, bodily sensations, and reactions to stress. Spielberger has carefully built upon earlier inventories, refining items to distinguish between enduring trait anxiety and transitory state anxiety. The result is two short, 20-item inventories, one with a 4-point frequency scale for responding to each statement, yielding a total score for trait anxiety, and the other with a 4-point intensity scale that yields an objective score for state anxiety. Deceptively, the STAI looks simple. In reality, it is based on years of research during which countless items were discarded while the remainder were revised in order to produce highly homogeneous scales with significant reliability and validity.

Focusing on self-report of anxiety has both advantages and disadvantages. With literate individuals, scores can be obtained rapidly and with little effort or special training. The objective nature of the forced-choice response easily lends itself to a high level of quantitative, psychometric treatment. And the conscious, phenomenological aspects of anxiety can be readily captured by a cognitive approach where individuals report their feelings. The ease with which measurement can be accomplished by short, self-report inventories can be a mixed blessing, however. All too easily one is tempted to shift one's position from a comprehensive, multifaceted view of anxiety to an oversimplified, narrow conception in which anxiety becomes operationally defined as simply what the inventory measures.

What a subject may be willing to reveal about himself is an important factor determining the subject's score on the inventory. The score of an individual who denies or represses the threatening, anxiety-producing events or thoughts will be falsely lowered. Self-report inventories are always subject to serious distortion due to faking. For these reasons, as well as those cited earlier, a lack of correlation between scores on the STAI and other signs of anxiety from different approaches to personality assessment cannot be taken as evidence that these other approaches are necessarily invalid. Significant correlations, especially when the individual is under stress, are important to note, but lack of a relationship tells us little about either approach.

It is to Spielberger's credit that he fully recognizes the limitations of the STAI as well as its advantages for certain kinds of research and individual assessment. With these caveats in mind, let's turn to the main substance of these investigations, cross-cultural measurement of anxiety using the STAI and related research.

As Spielberger and Sharma (Chap. 2) note, translation of a self-report inventory from one language to another is a far more complicated task than it appears to be at first glance. When dealing with highly sensitive, subjective, inner feelings as assessed by the STAI, the difficulties are compounded still further. The development of the Spanish and Hindi forms of the STAI is presented in considerable detail by Spielberger and Sharma to illustrate the steps that must be taken if one wants truly equivalent techniques for cross-cultural studies. Few indeed are the verbally based psychological techniques that have been handled as rigorously in cross-cultural, cross-language research.

Initial translation of the original English STAI into other Western languages, such as Portuguese, Spanish, French, or Italian, is a relatively easy matter because of the common cultural heritage of these languages. Such obvious similarities frequently tempt investigators to take the easy route of merely translating the item content from one language to the other, doctoring it up a bit here and there so that it seems to fit more plausibly into the new cultural context. In developing the Portuguese STAI, Biaggio, Natalicio, and Spielberger (see Chap. 3) followed a much more difficult procedure, one that was more likely to assure the semantic equivalence of the STAI in the new language rather than merely the superficial literal equivalence. The main steps in their procedure were as follows:

1. Translation of item content from English to Portuguese by experienced bilingual psychologists.
2. Review of the adequacy of the translation by 11 bilingual Brazilian psychologists and psychiatrists who rated each item.
3. Development of alternative Portuguese translations with the help of a professional translator-interpeter.

4. Administration of the preliminary form of the test to selected samples of bilingual Brazilian subjects who also completed the English version of the same test. One-half of the subjects were randomly given the English version, followed by the Portuguese, while the other half received the two forms in the opposite order.
5. Computation of cross-language and item-remainder correlations, and selection of the items with the highest correlations for inclusion in the revised version of the test.
6. Computation of means, standard deviations, and reliability coefficients, as well as cross-language correlations for the total scores on the two scales.
7. Determination of the construct validity for the revised test as administered under various experimental conditions to determine sensitivity to stress versus nonstress conditions to see if similar results are obtained in the new language as were found originally in English.

The results reported by Biaggio and her colleagues are generally satisfactory—high internal consistency as measured by Alpha and significant differentiation between the A-State form and the A-Trait form as predicted with respect to sensitivity to situational stress factors. With additional time and resources at their disposal, the authors could have improved their design somewhat by increasing greatly the number of item alternatives in order to strengthen the validity of the final version by a more selective weeding out of mediocre items. Blind back-translation from Portuguese to English might also reveal minor weaknesses although the other precautions taken are probably sufficient since English and Portuguese are not radically different languages. Giving the preliminary version to a much larger number of bilingual subjects (they used only 84 cases in four different samples) would have yielded more stable item statistics on which to base final decisions concerning the instrument. And finally, a more complete research design would require test-retest administration in four experimental groups of bilinguals rather than just two. The additional two groups would be given the English version on two different occasions or the Portuguese version on two different occasions, providing a complete design for determining the extent to which the Portuguese and English versions measured the same characteristics with the same degree of precision. Of course, this more complete design would also be much more difficult to implement because good, truly bilingual-bicultural subjects would be difficult to find in large numbers. It is doubtful, however, that the final outcome would have changed substantially if such additional refinements had been undertaken.

The French version of the STAI was developed by Bergeron, Landry, and Belanger (see Chap. 4) to provide brief self-report ratings of anxiety for laboratory experiments and for research on French-English bilinguals. The translation was perfected by a series of repeated studies with hundreds of university students. Internal consistency reliability of the final A-State scale was .86 for boys and .90 for girls while the A-Trait scale was .88 and .89, respectively. It is interesting to note that the internal consistency actually rose when the A-State scale was given in a stress situation, suggesting that stress increases the consistency of responses and confirming Spielberger's earlier finding on this issue. Unlike the A-State scale, the A-Trait scale showed no variation in internal consistency under stress and nonstress conditions. Stress in these studies typically consisted of administering the self-report inventory immediately prior to a specific academic examination that meant a lot to the students participating.

The A-Trait scale shows higher test-retest reliability than the A-State scale with an interval of 18 days between the testing periods, a finding consistent with the definition of transitory state versus enduring trait. It is interesting to note that results are identical whether given under neutral or stressful conditions. Other findings led the authors to speculate that there is a gradual increase in state anxiety among women as the moment of the physics examination draws nearer, but not for men. An interesting question is raised concerning the extent to which the A-State scale, when given first, would influence the A-Trait scores. Under stress conditions, an order effect appears. The presence of defensive attitudes could account for this interaction. When placed in a stress situation, some people may have a tendency to minimize their trait anxiety. All these results on the French STAI confirm the earlier work by Spielberger and others concerning the distinction between state and trait anxiety as measured by the STAI.

The Turkish version of the STAI by LeCompte and Oner (see Chap. 5) went through four stages of development:

1. Translation from English to Turkish.
2. Demonstration of cross-cultural equivalence in meaning.
3. Collection of data bearing on reliability and validity.
4. Development of statistical norms for Turkish students.

The last two stages are by no means complete.

Back-translation from Turkish to English was used as a check on the adequacy of the English to Turkish translation. Agreement among experts as to the similarity of meaning was achieved. In addition, bilingual students took the test twice, once in English and once in Turkish, to see if equivalence could be defined in terms of similar scores by the same people. An interesting variation on the usual theme consisted of having four versions of each scale, two containing 40 items in either English or Turkish while the other two had one half the items in one language and the other half in the other language. Estimates of cross-language equivalence were provided by reliability coefficients across these four different forms.

The pure and mixed language forms of the STAI, when analyzed, show a tendency for the bilingual Turks to get higher scores when taking either scale in English than in Turkish. Upon retest two weeks later, however, these differences tend to disappear and the English and Turkish forms give almost identical means regardless of the mixture of the two languages in the form.

Assuming close equivalence of the Turkish and English scale, the authors go on to make cross-cultural comparisons where both the culture and language differences are confounded. By assuming equivalence of score regardless of language, however, it is possible to interpret the results purely in terms of culture. In this way they analyze Spanish, American Hindi, and Turkish samples, showing Turkish to have the highest A-Trait and Spanish the lowest. This kind of cross-cultural comparison is rather weak because of the questionable equivalence of the samples and of the STAI scores, where minor differences can yield significant results on a large number of subjects. Cultural differences in response set and willingness to admit anxiety are also confounded here, making interpretation of the results rather dubious.

One interesting bit of new data is the comparison of five samples of university students with 10-, 15-, 30-, 120-, and 365-day intervals between testing. A-Trait holds up nicely for at least 30 days, dropping only slightly thereafter. A-State jumps around somewhat erratically as one would expect of a measure of transitory emotional state. The Turkish edition appears to be well developed and to have psychometric characteristics similar to those of the original English version.

The State-Trait Anxiety Inventory for Children (STAIC) is a downward extension of the STAI in simpler form for 9- to 12-year-old elementary school children. The items are similar in number and kind, resulting in very similar A-Trait and A-State scales. A Spanish version of the STAIC was developed and validated in Puerto Rico by Bauermeister, Forastieri, and Spielberger (see Chap. 6). A somewhat different approach for translation was employed in this case. Several professors of Spanish at the University of Puerto Rico compiled word lists that implied either the presence or the absence of feelings of anxiety. Then these two lists of words were given to bilingual translators, who used the words from the lists in translating the STAIC into Spanish. And finally, two bilingual psychologists familiar with Puerto Rican children consulted with bilingual elementary teachers in order to use appropriate language for young children. Agreement had to be achieved between translators and evaluators with regard to the equivalence of Spanish and English items before the items were accepted.

The preliminary IDAREN (Spanish children's version) was given to bilingual fourth, fifth, and sixth graders with mixed results concerning the degree of correlation between the English and Spanish versions and relatively low internal consistency reliability, especially for the girls. The next time the preliminary scales were administered to young children, the children were interviewed afterward to find out how they had interpreted the items. Emphasis was placed upon subtleties of translation that would distinguish the transitory state from the more enduring trait. Both the IDAREN and the

IDARE (an adult Spanish version) were given to the tenth graders to determine concurrent validity. Construct validity was examined by having children take the IDAREN two times, once under standard instructions and once under simulated test instructions. The final product had a somewhat improved Alpha coefficient, higher stability over time for A-Trait than for A-State, higher scores under test than norm conditions, and satisfactory correlation between Spanish and English children's forms as well as between adult and child forms for the Spanish only. A behavior modification study using young children with the handling of rats also resulted in findings consistent with purported validity of state and trait scales in the Spanish version.

The Spanish children's version of the STAI appears to have been very carefully developed and provides an interesting downward extension of the technique so that cross-cultural or bilingual studies could be done with either children or adults or both in Spanish and English.

These five different research programs involving translation and adaptation of the STAI or the STAIC into Spanish, Portuguese, Hindi, Turkish, and French followed a common theme and stages of development that have insured the success of the final product. The languages and cultures are sufficiently varied to demonstrate the extent to which a specialized self-report inventory can be adapted to many different cultures if one is careful to follow all the recommended steps. More radically different languages and cultures may still present a serious problem, particularly where illiteracy may prevail. Obtaining semantic equivalence between Western versions and the tonal languages of Southeast Asia or the nonliterate tribal languages of Africa may prove impossible. At the same time, it is interesting to note that preliminary translations are already underway in such different languages as Japanese, Malay, Russian, Vietnamese, Lugandan, and Swahili as well as Danish, German, Greek, Hebrew, Hungarian, Norwegian, Polish, and Slavic. Until further work is done, one will simply not know the outer boundaries of cultural adaptation. In the meantime, it is already clear that sufficiently well standardized versions of the STAI exist in different languages to permit a great deal of genuinely cross-cultural research on the self-reporting of anxiety.

Parts III and IV of the book deal with five unrelated investigations in different cultures using the Spanish, Greek, Italian, English, and Swedish languages. In some cases, only the STAI was employed to measure anxiety while in others, different self-report inventories were used. These contributions vary considerably in their level of sophistication and the quality of the research design employed, depending on the resources available to the investigator and the conditions under which the study was made. Together, they serve a useful purpose in illustrating the variety of research under way in different cultures.

In the study by Gonzalez-Reigosa (Chap. 7), some evidence exists to suggest that bilingual individuals express their more primitive emotional world more readily in the mother tongue, making bilinguals particularly interesting for studies of the relationship between reactions to taboo words in either language and the A-State, A-Trait scores on the STAI. The case studies of bilinguals in therapy are particularly dramatic illustrations of this idea. The whole notion of using taboo words for bilinguals is based on Ferenczi's observation that arousal of anxiety caused by obscene words decreases when the words are pronounced in a foreign language even when the words are understood as to meaning.

Bilingual men were separated into high and low level on A-Trait and presented with taboo words in two languages to see what effect that had upon their A-State scores and reaction times. Subjects were also divided into high and low on English proficiency. Discomfort indices for the taboo English words and their Spanish translations showed no difference in the valence of each word.

The primary main effect across subjects occurred for A-Trait scores in comparing neutral with taboo Spanish words and in comparing taboo Spanish with taboo English words. None of the interactions was significant. Degree of proficiency in English made no difference. The high A-Trait subjects showed greater increase in A—State scores for taboo words than did the low A-Trait subjects. Interestingly enough, none of the main factors other than English proficiency proved important for reaction time as a dependent variable. In other words, the STAI was much more sensitive to the differences between taboo and neutral words than to the differences between the English and Spanish taboo words. Age of the person at the time that the language was learned, rather than proficiency, appears to be the critical variable influencing language-mediated emotional responses.

Using Kelly's personal construct theory and a Repertory Grid as a method for sorting concepts, Liakos, Papacostas, and Stefanis (Chap. 8) developed an anxiety grid with common elements; 13 neurotic patients and 12 control individuals each specified 10 situations or conditions that made them anxious. A great diversity of wording and content was noted, with no single pair of identical elements occurring among the 250 that were produced. Judges were able to boil these down into 44 categories, and 187 elements could be reliably sorted into these categories.

Ten of these categories were selected as standard elements for eliciting constructs by the triad method in a new sample of 26 neurotics and 17 controls. The Greek STAI was also given to them, although apparently this Greek version was not highly developed ans standardized. Correlations between A-State, A-Trait, and Grid intensity scores were computed for the neurotics and controls. Of particular interest are the significant differences in the expected direction between the neurotics and controls on both the state and trait anxiety scales. This study appears to be a preliminary one. The idea of a content analysis of an anxiety grid for each individual is interesting but not sufficiently well developed to be particularly significant at this point.

Development of an Italian form of the STAI is described by Pancheri, Bernabei, Ballaterra, and Tartaglione (Chap. 9). This instrument was given to 370 normals, 282 skin patients, and 78 heart patients. The women were undergraduates and most of the men were military draftees. The women obtained higher scores than the men; but this difference cannot be interpreted since it may be due to poor sampling. The heart patients did not differ significantly in A-State from normals although their A-Trait scores were higher. Just the opposite was true of the skin patients, who had higher A-State scores than normals. Most of the interpretative speculations are weak and post hoc in character. No cross-cultural implications are apparent.

An unusual cross-cultural, longitudinal study is reported by Diaz-Guerrero (Chap. 10). Sarason's Test Anxiety Scale for Children (TASC) was standardized in Spanish and then given repeatedly for five years in a row to 196 Mexican (Spanish) and 196 American (English) school children who were in the second, fifth, or eighth grade when the TASC was first given. (The TASC wasn't given until the second year of the six years of repeated testing that started when the children were in the first, fourth, and seventh grades.) The children from Mexico City and Austin were matched cross-culturally on age, sex, and socioeconomic status of the family. In the third year and thereafter, Sarason's Lie Scale (L) and Defensiveness Scale (D) were added to the self-inventory, providing a check on response sets. Among a large battery of other tests given each year to these same children was the Holtzman Inkblot Technique, which yields an Anxiety (Ax) score that measures the amount of symbolic anxious content in the individual's fantasies.

In both cultures, girls obtained significantly higher test anxiety scores than boys although the difference is not large. Some of this difference may be due to greater defensiveness and a tendency to fake good by the boys, as indicated by their higher scores on the L and D scales. The most striking differences occurred cross-culturally, the Mexican children obtaining much higher scores on the TASC than the American. While subtle irregularities in translation from English to Spanish could account for a slight dissimilarity in responses, a difference this large points to a rather fundamental divergence in the conscious way in which school experiences (and resulting test anxiety) are viewed in the two cultures. Just the opposite occurred for the Anxiety score in the Holtzman Inkblot Technique; the American children obtained much higher scores than the Mexican. Correlations between Ax from the inkblot test and TASC were consistently zero, confirming the finding of others that the presence of anxious content in fantasies is unrelated to self-report of anxiety when the subject is not under actual stress.

The last of the cross-cultural studies involved Canadian and Swedish college students who were given two different state and trait scales, permitting the analysis of method variance as well as content. Endler and Magnusson (Chap. 11) provide a wealth of empirical data as well as a series of tentative conclusions concerning the nature of state and trait anxiety and how they can be measured. Endler's revised S-R Inventory of General Trait Anxiety (GTA) is particularly interesting since 15 different reaction items ("I feel like crying," "I am happy," etc.) are responded to by a five-point intensity scale (from "not at all" to "very much") for each of four different situations (interaction with other people, physical danger, strange situations, and daily routines). In this manner, a systematic attempt is made to capture the interactions of situation and reaction (S-R) in a multifaceted approach. Another way of looking at the GTA is to think of it as a short anxiety scale administered four times under four different response sets (situations).

Endler's Behavioural Reactions Questionnaire (BRQ) is a similar attempt to measure state anxiety. A five-point intensity scale ("none" to "very much") is used to rate 21 anxiety items for the situation, "How do you feel at this particular moment." Giving the BRQ, GTA, STAI-S and STAI-T to the same subjects in a counterbalanced design makes it possible to compare the two methods of measuring trait and state anxiety, as well as to study the cross-cultural differences between Canadian and Swedish students. Nine items that are nearly identical in the STAI-S and the BRQ provide a common element of special interest. From analyses of variance, intercorrelations and factor analyses, internal consistency or reliability studies, and related observations from previous studies, Endler and Magnusson challenge Spielberger's distinction between trait and state anxiety as well as his assumption that trait anxiety is unidimensional. The specific conclusions drawn by the authors merit critical scrutiny one at a time.

Do the data really fail to support the conceptual distinction between trait and state anxiety? Endler and Magnusson argue that the moderately high correlation between State and Trait on the STAI (ranging from .44 to .69, depending upon the sample) and the pattern of intercorrelations involving the GTA and BRQ indicate that state and trait anxiety cannot be empirically separated, at least when measured under neutral, nonthreatening conditions. While it is true that these results fail to support this conceptual distinction, at the same time they do not refute it. A conceptual distinction may be correct while yielding only an imperfect empirical separation, just as conceptual identity may fail to show empirical similarity. When considered alone, the State-Trait correlation for the STAI can arise from a combination of partial content overlap in the items, common method variance in the two parts of the STAI, and true commonality of the two concepts. Spielberger has never claimed that there is complete independence of state and trait anxiety, conceptually speaking. Most of the empirical evidence from other studies using the STAI as reviewed in the earlier chapters of this book indicate that the conceptual distinction between State and Trait is indeed warranted.

Does the evidence support the conclusion that the state and trait anxiety scales are multidimensional? Factor analyses of the GTA Situation Scales and the GTA Reaction Scales form the basis for the conclusion that trait anxiety is multidimensional. The principal-components method of factoring with unity in the diagonals of the R-matrix and use of a sudden drop in eigenvalues as a basis for stopping the extraction of additional factors is well-accepted procedure. It should be noted though, that use of unity in the diagonals, rather than a more realistic lower estimate of commonality as in Guttman's image analysis, tends to produce more minor factors than may be justified. A close examination of the specific loadings on the two or three factors generally obtained is revealing. Note, for example, the two factors labeled "Distress tension" and "Absence of curiosity" from the analysis of GTA reaction item-intercorrelations in Table 6 in Chapter 11. Distress tension is clearly the major factor, accounting for about 70% of the common variance. High positive loadings for items like "feel anxious" and high negative loadings for items like "feel secure" indicate that this factor is the general trait anxiety scale. Four positively stated items contribute all the variance present in the second factor. The high similarity of content in these four items clearly shows that they are merely precision alternatives of the same thing. Reversing the polarity of Factor II so that all the signs in front of the loadings are reversed makes it easier to interpret. Rather than "Absence of Curiosity," Factor II is a minor factor defined entirely by the common thread running through "seeking out, look forward to, feeling comfortable, and enjoyment." Factor II is a combination of methods variance (all four are positively stated items) and variation in how much individuals seek out (enjoy) or avoid (dislike), *on the average*, the four situations in the GTA.

Factor-analytic results for intercorrelations among the 20 STAI-T items in Tables 7 and 8 are more germane to the dimensionality of Spielberger's inventory. Again, the first principal component explains most of the common variance; the first unrotated eigenvalue is larger than all the others combined, indicating that a *primary* factor is present with only one or two minor additional factors. Factor I after rotation consists almost entirely of positively stated items, while only negatively stated items define the second and third factors. Response set or method variance is probably the main reason for the two factors, rather than any genuine, conceptually important distinction.

The STAI-T Scale, as well as the GTA Reaction Scale, may indeed have more than one dimension, but it doesn't necessarily follow that the dimensions beyond the primary one have important conceptual significance. As noted in their third conclusion, Endler and Magnusson recognize methods variance as an alternative explanation of their results, although they do not give it the importance it deserves.

Are the stability coefficients for the state anxiety measures unsatisfactory? Test-retest correlations for STAI-S with a one-week interval run about .70 while the comparable correlation between the BRQ and STAI-S measures of state anxiety is .53. The slightly lower value for this latter correlation can be explained entirely by the method variation between the BRQ and the STAI. This variation is minimized when only the nine common items are considered in the correlation between the BRQ and the STAI. In this case, the correlation of .57 is not significantly different from the .70 obtained by Newmark for the STAI alone. State measures are supposed to be sensitive to change. If anything, stability coefficients of .60–.70 are too high rather than too low. In any event, one can hardly argue that correlations of such a magnitude are unsatisfactory when dealing with the stability of a *state* measure. The important consideration here is how sensitive the measure is to change in situational stress, a question that cannot be addressed by the present data.

The remaining three conclusions deal with mean differences attributable to sex and culture. While the sex differences are interesting and consistent with previous findings, the differences between the Canadian and Swedish college students cannot be attributed to culture alone. The Canadians are part-time, older evening students while the Swedes are younger daytime students. The conditions of administration in the two countries differed in some notable aspects. And a disturbingly large number of the Canadians failed to complete their questionnaires, · calling into question the meaning of the results for the remainder who cooperated fully.

Regardless of how one interprets these controversial issues, one can only applaud the thoughtful, realistic set of recommendations made by Endler and Magnusson concerning future research. Until much more is known about the situational and methodological factors that influence reactions to items in a self-report inventory of anxiety, it is impossible to draw strong conclusions regarding the meaning of obtained scores. The question of how many dimensions are present and how important they are in the measurement of anxiety still remains unanswered. It is not enough merely to assert that a single dimension is present in a particular inventory, since the inventory may have been developed in the first place by eliminating all items that are not homogeneous and unidimensional. Whether or not one uses frequencies (as in STAI-T) or intensities (as in STAI-S and in GTA) as a response scale for the subject to use in rating the items, the general importance of response sets such as acquiescence remains an unresolved issue that calls for further study. Until these fundamental issues are properly resolved, cross-cultural comparisons of anxiety cannot reach the high order of scientific rigor and definition that must eventually be achieved if this interesting field of work is to make a truly significant contribution to our understanding of human behavior.

It is indeed impressive that only five years after publication, more than 500 studies on the English form of the STAI have been completed. The studies reported in the preceding chapters go a long way toward demonstrating the potentialities for using self-report, paper-and-pencil questionnaires to measure anxiety in different languages and cultures. Whether this promising start can lead to significant cross-cultural studies of anxiety (rather than merely approximate replications in different languages and cultures) remains to be seen.

REFERENCES

Holtzman, W. H., & Bitterman, M. E. *Anxiety and reactions to stress* (Rep. No. 6, Project No. 21-37-002). Randolph Field, Texas: USAF School of Aviation Medicine, December 1952.

Holtzman, W. H., & Bitterman, M. E. A factorial study of adjustment to stress. *Journal of Abnormal and Social Psychology*, 1956, *52*, 179-185.

Author Index

Allen, G. J., 47, 49
Allport, F. H., 90, 105
Allport, G. W., 55, 66
Arellano, L., 92, 103, 105
Asberg, M., 167, 171
Auerbach, S. M., 8, 10, 53, 66, 67, 126, 132
Averill, E. M., 107, 121
Azpeitia, E., 71, 84

Bale, R. M., 48, 50
Bandura, A., 78, 79, 84
Banister, D., 108, 110, 111, 120, 121
Banks, R. K., 90, 105
Basowitz, H., 165, 170
Bauermeister, J. J., 22, 25, 71, 77, 84
Beck, A. T., 107, 121
Beck, S. J., 8, 10
Berlingeri, N. C., 22, 25
Berlyne, D. E., 166, 170
Bitterman, M. E., 90, 105, 175, 176, 187
Blanchard, E. B., 78, 79, 84
Bonis, M. De, 49, 50
Brislin, R. W., 55, 66
Bronson, W. C., 90, 105
Bruner, J. S., 90, 104
Bucky, S. F., 48, 49

Castaneda, A., 8, 10
Cattell, R. B., 4, 6, 7, 8, 10, 23, 25, 42, 43, 50, 52, 66, 135, 142, 144, 170
Chapman, R. C., 53, 66
Collado-Herrell, I., 71, 84
Colón, N., 71, 84

Cormier, D., 42, 50
Cox, G. B., 53, 66
Cronbach, L. J., 33, 40, 60, 66, 71, 74, 84, 139, 142
Cronholm, B., 167, 171

Darwin, C., 3, 10
Davidson, K. S., 8, 11
Day, H. I., 166, 170
Del Castillo, J. C., 92, 103, 105
De Long, R. D., 126, 132
Denny, J. P., 53, 67
Diaz-Guerrero, R., 14, 25, 135, 139, 140, 141, 142
Diesenhaus, H., 48, 50
Droppelman, L. F., 7, 11
Dunn, T. M., 53, 67, 126, 132

Edelman, R. I., 47, 50
Edwards, C. D., 70, 82, 85
Edwards, K. R., Jr., 126, 132
Ekehammar, B., 145, 167, 170, 171
Elizur, A., 139, 142
Endler, N. S., 8, 10, 107, 119, 121, 145, 146, 147, 161, 163, 164, 165, 166, 167, 168, 170, 171
Ervin, S., 91, 103, 105

Farias, M. E., 38, 40
Felling, J. P., 53, 67
Ferenczi, S., 90, 93, 103, 105
Ferguson, G. A., 43, 50

Fernandez, E., 39, 40
Fisher, J. W., 90, 105
Fiske, D. W., 169, 171
Flores, L., 92, 103, 105
Fogel, F. R., 22, 25
Francella, F., 111, 121
Freeman, M. J., 8, 10
Freud, S., 3, 10, 51, 67

Gilchrist, J. C., 90, 105
Goldfried, M. R., 8, 10
González, F., 70, 73, 77, 85
Gonzalez-Reigosa, F., 14, 15, 19, 22, 23,
    25, 30, 34, 40, 64, 67, 91, 94, 95, 103,
    105, 139, 142
Gorsuch, R. L., 4, 7, 8, 9, 11, 13, 15, 16,
    19, 20, 21, 23, 24, 25, 30, 33, 34, 38,
    40, 41, 43, 44, 48, 50, 52, 64, 67, 70,
    83, 85, 114, 122, 124, 128, 132, 135,
    140, 142, 144, 146, 147, 165, 170
Green, R. F., 7, 11
Grinker, R. R., 165, 170
Gropper, G. L., 90, 105

Hebb, D. O., 166, 171
Hernandez Cuesta, U., 140, 142
Herron, E. W., 8, 11, 136, 142
Hill, E. F., 139, 142
Hodges, W. F., 53, 67
Holtzman, W. H., 8, 10, 11, 135, 136, 139,
    142, 175, 176, 187
Howes, D. H., 90, 105
Hoy, E. A., 146, 147, 171
Hunt, J. McV., 8, 10, 119, 121, 165, 166,
    168, 171

Izard, C. E., 108, 121

Johnson, G. B., 95, 105
Jones, E., 93, 105

Kacelnik, E., 38, 40
Kelly, G. A., 108, 109, 121
Klopfer, B., 8, 11
Kniffen, C. W., 90, 105
Korchin, S. J., 165, 170
Krishnan, B., 23, 25

Lader, M., 7, 11, 119, 121
Lamb, D. H., 53, 67
Landry, M., 47, 50
Laosa, L., 135, 139, 140, 141, 142
Lara Tapia, L., 135, 139, 140, 141, 142
Lazarus, R. S., 5, 11, 107, 121
Levitt, E. E., 7, 11, 108, 121, 166, 171
Lewis, A., 144, 171
Liakos, A., 120, 121
Lighthall, F. F., 8, 11, 52, 67
López-Garriga, M. M., 71, 84
Lorr, M., 7, 11
Lowie, R., 91, 105
Lubin, B., 7, 12
Lushene, R. E., 4, 7, 8, 9, 11, 13, 15, 16,
    19, 20, 21, 23, 24, 25, 30, 33, 34, 38,
    40, 41, 43, 44, 48, 50, 52, 64, 67, 70,
    82, 83, 85, 114, 122, 124, 128, 132,
    135, 140, 142, 144, 146, 147, 165, 172

Magnusson, D., 145, 166, 167, 170, 171
Mair, J. M. M., 110, 121
Mandler, B., 8, 11
Mandler, G., 53, 67, 119, 121
Marks, I., 7, 11, 119, 121
Martin, B., 7, 11
Martínez, A., 70, 71, 73, 77, 84, 85
Martinez-Urrutia, A., 14, 15, 19, 21, 22,
    23, 25, 30, 34, 40, 53, 64, 67, 139, 142
McAdoo, W. C., 53, 67
McCandless, B. R., 8, 10
McGinnies, E., 90, 94, 105
McNair, D. M., 7, 11
McReynolds, P., 7, 8, 11
Mendenhall, W., 95, 105
Mischel, T., 108, 121
Montuori, J., 70, 82, 85
Morales, M. L., 135, 139, 140, 141, 142
Mote, T. A., 19, 20, 21, 25

Natalicio, D. C., 14, 15, 19, 22, 23, 25, 30,
    34, 40, 70, 73, 77, 85, 139, 142
Natalicio, L. F., 14, 15, 19, 20, 21, 22, 23,
    25, 30, 34, 40, 70, 73, 77, 85, 139, 142
Nazario, E., 71, 84
Neuringer, C., 8, 11
Nothman, F. H., 90, 103, 105
Nowlis, V., 7, 11, 48, 50

Oetzel, R. M., 161, 171
Okada, M., 145, 146, 161, 163, 164, 165, 166, 167, 171
Oliveria, E. S., 38, 40
Oner, N. P., 53, 67
Opton, E. M., 107, 121

Palermo, D. S., 8, 10
Pancheri, P., 131, 132
Papacostas, J., 120, 121
Paschoal, C. R., 39, 40
Persky, H., 165, 170
Pettigrew, T. F., 55, 66
Piotrowski, Z. A., 8, 11
Platzek, D., 70, 82, 85
Postman, L., 90, 104, 105

Reyes Lagunes, I., 135, 139, 140, 141, 142
Ricklander, L., 167, 170
Ritter, B., 78, 79, 84
Rivas, F., 19, 20, 21, 25
Rivera-Santiago, J. A., 21, 25, 71, 85
Rosenstein, A. J., 8, 10, 119, 121, 165, 171
Ruebush, B. K., 8, 11, 52, 67
Ryder, R. R., 90, 105

Sachs, D. A., 48, 50
Sarason, I. G., 53, 67, 107, 119, 121
Sarason, S. B., 8, 11, 52, 53, 67
Schalling, D., 167, 171
Scheier, I. H., 4, 6, 7, 8, 10, 23, 25, 42, 43, 50, 52, 66, 135, 142, 144, 170
Sechrest, L., 92, 103, 105, 108, 121
Sharma, S., 14, 15, 19, 23, 24, 25, 65, 67
Shedletsky, R., 164, 171
Singh, M., 14, 15, 19, 25, 65, 67
Sollee, N., 93, 103, 105

Solomon, R. L., 90, 105
Spielberger, C. D., 4, 5, 6, 7, 8, 9, 10, 11, 13, 14, 15, 16, 19, 20, 21, 22, 23, 24, 25, 30, 33, 34, 38, 40, 41, 43, 44, 48, 49, 50, 51, 52, 53, 64, 65, 67, 70, 71, 73, 77, 82, 83, 84, 85, 90, 103, 105, 107, 114, 121, 122, 123, 124, 125, 126, 128, 132, 135, 139, 140, 141, 142, 144, 145, 146, 147, 165, 171, 172
Stefanis, C., 120, 121
Swartz, J. D., 8, 11, 135, 136, 139, 140, 141, 142

Taruma, H., 39, 40
Taulbee, E. S., 53, 67, 126, 132
Taylor, J. A., 8, 12, 23, 25, 47, 50
Thorpe, J. S., 8, 11, 136, 142

Villamil, B., 71, 85

Wadsworth, A. P., 53, 67, 126, 132
Waite, R. R., 8, 11, 52, 67
Walters, R. H., 90, 105
Warren, N., 108, 121
Weinrich, U., 93, 103, 105
Welsh, G. S., 8, 12
Whittaker, E. M., 90, 105
Winer, B. J., 80, 85
Witzke, D. B., 135, 139, 140, 141, 142

Yospe, L., 90, 105

Zajonc, R. B., 90, 94, 105
Zigler, E., 90, 105
Zlotowicz, M., 49, 50
Zuckerman, M., 7, 8, 12, 52, 67

Subject Index

Affect Adjective Check List (AACL), 7, 52
Ambiguous (mood) situations, 161, 163,
    165
Analysis of variance (ANOVA), 97–99
Angor vs. *anxietas*, 144
Anxiety
    and Canadian students, 144–169, 183–
        184, 186
    and cardiac patients, 125, 128–132
    and creative self-expression, 3
    definition of, 5–6, 144
    and dermatology patients, 125, 128–132
    in fantasy (Ax), 135, 139–140, 183
    and fear, 3
    harm, 165
    and immorality, 3
    measurement of, 4
    in modern life, 51
    as process, 175–176
    and psychosomatic symptoms, 3
    self-report of, 176
    shame, 165
    and sin, 3
    as stable personality trait, 90–91
    study of, 107–108
    and Swedish students, 144–169
    and taboo words, 89–90, 93, 182
    as transitory state, 90–91
Anxiety constructs, classification of, 116,
    119–120
Anxiety elements, classification of, 113
Arousal level and performance, 166
Autonomic nervous system (ANS), 124–125,
    175

Behavioral Reactions Questionnaire (BRQ),
    146–149, 151, 158–162, 164–165,
    167, 184–185
Bilingualism, 18, 89, 114, 182
    and extramarital relationships, 92
    and fear of punishment, 93
    French-English, 115–119
    Greek-English, 115–119
    and psychoanalysis, 92–93
    and psychotic symptoms, 92
    Spanish-English, 92–104
    Tagalog-English, 92–94
    Turkish-English, 179–180

Canadian students and anxiety, 144–169,
    183–186
Cardiac patients and anxiety, 125, 128–132
Cardiopaths (*see* Cardiac patients and
    anxiety)
Cognitive preoccupations, 166
Constructs, definition of, 108–109
Creative self-expression and anxiety, 3
Cross-language equivalence of tests, 18–24
Curiosity factor, absence of, 185

Defensiveness scale, 183
Dermatology patients and anxiety, 125,
    128–132
Dermopaths (*see* Dermatology patients and
    anxiety)
Distress tension factor, 185

English STAI, 30–31, 37, 55, 59, 61, 63
Extramarital relationships and bilingualism, 92

Fantasy, anxiety in (Ax), 135, 139–140, 183
Fear
    and anxiety, 3
    definition of, 6
    (*See also* Punishment, fear of)
Fear of rats scale (FRS), 78–80
Forced-choice response, 176
French-English bilingualism, 91, 178
French STAI, 41–49
French STAI Test Manual, 44, 48

German, 91, 131
Greek STAI (STAI-GX), 114
Grid method, 109–110

Harm anxiety, 165
"Has to Do with Guilt" construct, 115, 119
Holtzmann Inkblot Technique (HIT), 135–140, 183

Immorality and anxiety, 3
Insomnia, 3
Intensity of relationship score, 110–111
Interpersonal ego threat, 165
Inventario de Ansiedad Rasgo-Estado para Niños (*see* Spanish STAI)
IPAT Anxiety Scale, 23, 42
Italian STAI, 126–129

Kuder-Richardson formula 20, 33, 43–44, 60, 74

Language Skills Rating Scale, 96
Lie Scale (Sarason), 183

Manifest Anxiety Scale (MAS), 8–9, 47, 52, 145
    Indian adaptation of, 33
Mean discomfort index, 95
Mexican vs. American children on anxiety tests, 135–142

Minnesota Multiphasic Personality Inventory (MMPI), 131
Multidimensional constructs, 166

Neuroticism grid, 111–115, 120

Obscene words, 89–90, 93
    and anxiety arousal, 182
    (*See also* Taboo words)

Participant-coping modeling (PCM), 79–80
Participant-mastery modeling (PMM), 79–80
Pearson product-moment coefficient, 44
Perceptual defense, 90
Performance and arousal level, 166
Personal construct theory (Kelly), 108–110, 182
Personality states vs. traits, 123
Physical danger situations, 161–165, 168–170
Portuguese STAI, 19, 29–40, 70
Profile of Mood States (POMS), 7
Psychoanalysis and bilingualism, 92–93
Psychosomatic research, 125, 128
Psychosomatic symptoms and anxiety, 3
Psychotic symptoms and bilingualism, 92
Punishment, fear of
    and bilingualism, 93
    and taboo words, 91

Questionnaire of How-I-Am (A-Trait), 72
Questionnaire of How-I-Am-Now (A-State), 72

Rat attitude scale (RAS), 78
Rat repugnance scale (RRS), 78, 80
Reaction Time Test of Bilingualism, 96
Relationship score, 110
Repertory Grid, 182
Response suppression hypothesis, 90
Rorschach Test, 7–8, 139

Self-description scale (SDS), 78, 80
Self-report of anxiety, 176
Shame anxiety, 165
Sharma scale, 23
Sin and anxiety, 3

Situations, classification of, 166
Spanish-English bilingualism, 92–104
Spanish STAI, 19–21, 25, 64, 71, 95, 180–181
S-R Inventory of General Trait Anxiousness (GTA), 145–148, 151–153, 161, 164–166, 168–169
State-Trait Anxiety Inventory (STAI), 4, 7, 8, 9, 13, 15–17, 24, 29–30, 54, 66, 70, 99, 117, 124, 129, 176–177, 181–184
    English, 30–31, 37, 55, 59–61, 63, 177–179
    French, 41–49
    Greek, 182
    Hindi, 22–25, 64–65
    Italian, 126–129, 177, 183
    Portuguese, 19, 29–40, 177–178
    Spanish, 19–21, 25, 64, 71, 95, 177, 180
    Turkish, 51, 179
State-Trait Anxiety Inventory for Children (STAIC), 14, 70, 82, 180
    Spanish, 69, 71–84, 139
State-Trait Anxiety Inventory Test Manual, 124, 128

Stress, definition of, 4–5, 175–176
Surgery, reactions to, 53
Swedish students and anxiety, 144–169

Taboo words, 182
    and anxiety, 89–92, 103
    and fear of punishment, 91
    reaction times for, 101
    saying vs. writing, 90–91, 97
    (*See also* Obscene words)
Tagalog-English, 92–94
TAT stories, 91
Test Anxiety Scale for Children (TASC), 135–141, 183
Test Anxiety Questionnaire (TAQ), 8
Threats
    definition of, 5, 175
    in testing, 139
Transitory vs. enduring trait, 179
Triad method, 110
Turkish-English bilingualism, 179–180
Turkish STAI, 51, 54–66